Intersections of Race, Gender, and Precarity

Intersections of Race, Gender, and Precarity

Navigating Insecurities in an American City

Stephanie M. Baran

LEXINGTON BOOKS
Lanham • Boulder • New York • London

Published by Lexington Books
An imprint of The Rowman & Littlefield Publishing Group, Inc.
4501 Forbes Boulevard, Suite 200, Lanham, Maryland 20706
www.rowman.com

86-90 Paul Street, London EC2A 4NE

British Library Cataloguing in Publication Information Available

Library of Congress Cataloging-in-Publication Data

Names: Baran, Stephanie M., 1985- author.
Title: Intersections of race, gender, and precarity : navigating
    insecurities in an American city / Stephanie M. Baran.
Description: Lanham : Lexington Books, [2022] | Includes bibliographical
    references and index.
Identifiers: LCCN 2021051701 (print) | LCCN 2021051702 (ebook) |
    ISBN 9781793608536 (cloth) | ISBN 9781793608550 (pbk.) |
    ISBN 9781793608543 (epub)
Subjects: LCSH: Poor—Social conditions—Wisconsin—Milwaukee—21st century. |
    Welfare recipients—Wisconsin—Milwaukee—History—21st century. | Poverty—
    Wisconsin—Milwaukee—History—21st century. | Milwaukee (Wis.)—Economic
    conditions—21st century.
Classification: LCC HV4046.M55 B37 2022 (print) | LCC HV4046.M55 (ebook) |
    DDC 305.5/690977595—dc23/eng/20211021
LC record available at https://lccn.loc.gov/2021051701
LC ebook record available at https://lccn.loc.gov/2021051702

Contents

List of Figures

List of Abbreviations

ADC	Aid to Dependent Children
AFDC	Aid to Families with Dependent Children
BPP	Black Panther Party
CARES	Coronavirus Aid, Relief and Economic Security
CBPP	Center for Budget and Policy Priorities
CCCSBP	Citizens for Central City School Breakfast Program
EBT	Electronic Benefit Transfer
FHA	Federal Housing Association
FSET	Foodshare Employment and Training
GPLC	Gathering People's Lutheran Church
GSS	General Social Survey
HOLC	Home Owners Loan Corporation
HTF	Hunger Task Force
HUD	Housing and Urban Development
IRB	Institutional Review Board
PWORA	Personal Responsibility and Work Opportunity Act
SNAP	Supplemental Nutrition Assistance Program
TANF	Temporary Assistance for Needy Families
TEFAP	USDA's Emergency Food Assistance Program
TSA	Transportation Security Administration
USDA	United States Department of Agriculture
WIC	Women, Infant and Children

Preface

While I was writing this book there were important moments that occurred which highlighted the lack of a safety net in the United States: first, there was the Shutdown of 2018–2019; second, the 2020 Great Pandemic which resulted in over 20 million unemployment claims in a month and a half span of time. Prior to this, I found myself unemployed, as a temporary visiting professorship ended. However, the experiences that I had during unemployment highlight a key problem within the system we have set up—there is no safety net. Illuminating my situation hopefully helps broaden the understanding for all individuals who experience rapid and unexpected changes in their lives. We find ourselves in a reality where typically "rational" systems become wholeheartedly irrational. I recently graduated and received my PhD in sociology and my dissertation, which is the inspiration for this book, focused on cash and food assistance (SNAP) recipients, so my work was becoming my own reality.

But before I experienced all this in the last year, as a PhD student, my work revolved around race and racism but I was stuck on this idea of perceptions, which aren't always what they seem. The case in point was that I was a graduate student teetering on the edge of poverty, but no one saw the poverty. My work began almost seemingly by sheer luck, by examining how welfare benefit recipients similarly navigated these in and out roads of poverty.

In the United States, approximately 40% or almost half of Americans are one to two paychecks from poverty.[1] Said another way, if something unexpected happens, most Americans have no financial recourse if they find themselves unexpectedly unemployed. I became part of this statistic and my ethnographic research became my lived experience. The university so kindly provided me with additional paychecks and insurance through the month of January 2020 and I waited to apply for unemployment because of these severance checks (which can be seen as a privilege). However, this was simultaneously a blessing and a curse. The experiences from here ramp up in excitement, also known as terrifying.

During my PhD, in the winding reel of red tape, qualifying for benefits as a student in Wisconsin can be quite difficult, to say the least. I recall trying to qualify for benefits and the case manager on the other line told me to "go ask my parents" and as a thirty-year-old woman at the time, it seemed rather patronizing. Fast forward to January 2020, I applied for unemployment under the assumption that December 2019 would be my last and final paycheck (this part is important). Along with unemployment, I applied for Oregon Health Insurance. After paying all my bills for the month, I was left with $500 to my name and at this point began driving for Postmates to try and make up the difference in income. (Unless you want to run your car into the ground, this is a terrible option.) It was approaching the last few weeks of January and I still had not started to receive unemployment, because the state of Wisconsin employment office had not confirmed my wages. Regardless of that, I sent Oregon my paystubs for a whole year's worth of work—they still needed to confirm with Wisconsin that this was correct. In addition, I sent my W-2 income tax to Oregon from Wisconsin, but still they were not able to begin the unemployment status change. A week later, I received a letter from the Wisconsin unemployment office that I needed to send all paystubs (the paystubs that Oregon needed to get Wisconsin to confirm my wages) to their unemployment office. If you are also confused and needed to read this again, it was a confusing time for me too. I was living in a Weberian irrationality of rationality. I was on the brink of financial disaster, with no employment in sight.

Therefore, I was entered into a state of precarity because I was not receiving unemployment nor was there any income coming through, and I simply broke down. You might say "just get a job," as if there's a job tree where job offers hang. However, for unemployed, able-bodied individuals who have no children, there is no safety net. I told one worker, "I have no children, do you see where I am coming from?" and her response was "I'm sorry." Temporary Assistance for Needy Families (TANF) is a government program for people with children and provides a safety net for those individuals who qualify. However, a single woman with a cat is not considered "family" and therefore would not qualify for assistance. Similarly, the "earned income tax credit" has such limited income restrictions that most people fail to qualify for this assistance as well. "Just be patient," the caseworker at the Oregon unemployment agency told me when I described the fact that my money was running low, had bills to pay, and three weeks of unemployment had not been approved yet. However, even with all these, I still have some good fortune that others do not—I live with a roommate and do not have a rent payment.

Therefore, my situation does not mirror how most people find themselves. What is clear is that often what happened to me can be a typical gateway toward homelessness, and issues that could have been avoided become additional barriers.

To highlight this, at the end of January 2020, I was paid an unexpected final paycheck from the university I was first employed. Unclear if this was a mistake or not, I confirmed. Some might read this as a great thing—but it was a blessing and a curse. I had just qualified for health and food benefits, and I was experiencing dental work issues that needed to be completed. I was on the verge of losing everything because of this one-time payment. Thankfully, because of some surprising reporting rules, I was able to keep my health care and get the care I needed for my dental work. This exact situation is how people often become confused or disillusioned by social benefits. This one paycheck, yes was money, but it would not have improved my life for a long period of time. This situation mirrored an earlier encounter I had with social services in Illinois. I had similarly lost my job and was unemployed. This time, however, I had my own apartment. I applied for rent assistance, but the income restrictions were that you had to have *more than* $1,200 in your bank account. To qualify for food assistance, you needed to have *less than* $1,200. At that moment, I was in the crux of the two, neither "poor" enough for food assistance nor wealthy enough for rent assistance.

Most social programs operate on the notion of "income thresholds" or a ceiling amount that, if crossed, automatically disqualifies you from receiving a benefit. Therefore, if you are unemployed and single, you only have unemployment, health care, and food stamps to get you by. If one of those is unavailable, there are no avenues for recourse. Therefore, millions of Americans, like me, are placed in this precarious position. It also details that poverty is not a choice but something that happens to just anyone—and is not dependent on a class or an education level. Poverty is a spectrum that affects different people in different ways and lacks a one size fits all response.

Often, the response toward people who receive assistance is often from individuals who lack the experience of needing benefits and include retorts to "get a job." The issue is that with most social assistance programs, there are very clear work requirements and income ceilings. So, if you go over the income ceiling by $1, you no longer qualify and you lose your benefit access. However, just because you make over the threshold does not indicate that you are no longer in poverty. Often, once benefits like food, health, cash, rent assistance, and so on are unavailable, people are placed in even more precarious situations than they were before.

Income thresholds are seemingly rational systems that place people in precarious situations because of their rigidity and cause irrational outcomes. I know that I am not alone, but my situation is not always what people experience. These created and constructed barriers place millions of people in positions and situations that are not actively sought out by the people experiencing them. This book seeks to explore how living on the edge is more common than we might expect and how experiences of poverty can affect an individual's navigation through different systems. It affects those with no diploma, a General Educational Development, bachelors, masters, and doctoral degrees. My hope is that this insight helps us unpack how people find themselves in poverty.

"I feel like I'm robbing Peter to pay Paul" is a statement my mother says often. By visual standards, my parents would not be considered people who might be experiencing issues of poverty adjacency. They have a nice house, live in a small, Midwestern town in Illinois, and my father has a regular nine-to-five job that he worked for my whole life existence. In many cases, I was very fortunate and had what Lareau[2] describes as a middle-class childhood. However, like many families and children, unbeknownst to me as a child, my family also experienced financial struggle. I had a very stereotypical upbringing for a white, "seemingly" middle-class Midwestern child. Like Lareau[3] writes, middle-class parents put their child in every activity under the sun—dance, softball, soccer, basketball, theater. However, when we went shopping for clothes, my mom always taught me to start at the back of the store and then work forward because the sale items were always in the back; perhaps this is relatable to readers who have so kindly picked up this book. We also frequented discount stores, commonly referred to as thrift stores, such as Goodwill, Savers, and St. Vincent DePaul. For some, these stores are novelties with "vintage" finds, but for most individuals, they are as important as food. As a child and through my present years, I continued this habit and it helped me, but I never really thought about the origination. As my parents aged and I decided to enter my postsecondary education, my parents fell on harder times. While yes, my father had a job and provided for the house, much of their life was spent "robbing Peter to pay Paul," or in some cases, having to choose between one bill or diabetic medicine, and so on. My mother had an associate degree in child education and worked a myriad of part-time jobs. I feel it is relatively important to say that within one year after many in pain, she had both her hip and knees replaced, which I feel is a testament to her Midwestern you-can-do-it attitude and a critique to doctors who allowed her to be in such a state that she was almost immobile. However, back to the original point, the commonality of discount shopping is probably more broadly shared than we know, but the perceptions that we have about "other" people in poverty hide that connectedness in experiences. Most Americans are closer to poverty than they are to being millionaires, but because of our poverty perception, we create an illusory disconnection. When people make the usual notions of wealth and poverty as an "us versus them" nature or other more colorful descriptions of their fellow friends, neighbors, and enemies, they continue harmful commonly held narratives. While my parents are not considered visibly poor, because of how class status is viewed with racialized lenses, they experience the "positive" perception of attained middle-class status which hides what is behind the veil.

What brought this issue into the light and out from the veil was the pandemic of 2020. It opened the understanding that middle- and working-class people were far closer to situations of poverty—upon losing access to jobs and income and needing to rely on unemployment, social safety nets like SNAP and Foodshare, and, for many Americans, food banks and pantries. People are far more connected to each other in economic and social terms than they think—the ties that bind us together have familiar knots.

Representations of poverty tend to guide one's attitude toward the poor. If we think about social issues, like poverty, we can use the Collins theory of controlling images, which are specific images that appear in our minds when instigated by a word. Maybe we have several images that appear which configure someone in poverty—they often emerge from what we see on the news or in general media, such as movies and television shows. We also have ideas about how we think they got to that place. Yet, many of the images that appear in our minds are contrived because controlling images do not necessarily convey what poverty means for people. One may have ideas about people in poverty, but it would be a difficult one to have without first-hand knowledge or experience. This book examines how people navigate poverty and the benefit recipient system. Additionally, these following pages provide an understanding of people hidden or erased via inaccurate representations—often along racial and gender lines—about recipients and the ways they spend their assistance.

NOTES

1. https://www.cbsnews.com/news/40-of-americans-one-step-from-poverty-if-they-miss-a-paycheck/.
2. Annette Lareau, *Unequal.*
3. Ibid.

Acknowledgments

I would like to take this opportunity to formally thank and appreciate the support and guidance from my chair Dr. Aneesh Aneesh and the support from my committee Dr. Cary Costello, Dr. Timothy O'Brien, and Dr. Anne Bonds who were collectively named "The Awesome Squad," because at the beginning of this adventure that became this book, dissertation committee seemed all too daunting.

There are not enough ways I can say thank you.

In addition, without the assistance and contributions of those who participated in this research, none of this would be possible, nor would there be any words on these following pages. The work that is done at these pantries and in these organizations is nothing short of amazing and it is because of their hard work that people in Milwaukee find help and community.

Furthermore, without the ongoing encouragement I received from my friends and family, who always gave me the continual boosts of energy, support, and inspiration that I needed, this book would have been much harder to complete. While there are many people, and y'll know who you are, special mention goes out to my parents Dennis and Patricia Baran, and my friends Bridget Carsten, Kaylin Taylor, DaJuan Ferrell, Daniel Bartholomay, Michael Biggio, and Pasha Kopelyan.

A special thank you and appreciation go to my aunt, Noreen Raphel who supported my academic adventures and is a strong woman role model in during her Science, Technology, Engineering, Mathematics (STEM) career.

And to my New Orleans family, without your unending support and cheerleading, this book would not be possible. It has only been a short time that I have lived in New Orleans, however, you all accepted me and I am beyond grateful. Therefore, I extend a giant thank you to Jason Paulin, Patrick Brown, Joey Laura, Stephen Joseph, Amanda Toth, and Eric Fuller and the lovable characters at 504 Craft Beer Reserve. I am forever in your collective gratitude.

I want to give special mention to Jessie Senini, Demi Varuso, and Sarah Virginia Yongue. While we are new friends, it's like I've known them for ages, and I am grateful for their beautiful friendship.

To my Nicholls State Family, Dr. Whitney, Dr. Jefferson, Tina Granger, and Rebecca Picou are instrumental in getting me acclimated to southern life and without them I would be pronouncing everything wrong. They are the best faculty a colleague can ask for in an institution.

This book is also in loving memory of my uncle, Julio Raphel, with his stories of Cuba and who was always supportive of my endeavors and always asked what we were doing next.

In memory of Harley von Fufflepants, and her fluffy feline support.

In memory of Frank Ballero, Jr., who always listened even when he didn't understand.

As I completed the final edits of the book, my mother, Patricia T. Baran passed away unexpectedly. She is the reason I am a strong woman and where I learned empathy, care, understanding and how to be confident in my convictions. She is the reason I have a deep love for education and helping others. Her memory lives on.

Note on Methodology

The purpose of this book is to introduce the research methodology used for this study regarding how welfare benefits participants, how case managers and poverty organizations see themselves and others, and how they believe others see them. In this research project, I used a qualitative method to analyze the different experiences encountered during the research process. A reflexive approach to in-depth interviewing and participant observation are discussed at length in this throughout the book. The research plans, including methodology, participants, procedures, analysis method, and ethical concerns, are the primary components of this throughout the book.

RESEARCH QUESTIONS

At its base, the research that follows is a study of perceptions: how welfare recipients of diverse racial identities perceive themselves and their welfare benefit status; how they think others perceive them; how they view other people in related situations; lastly, how case managers perceive benefit recipients receiving assistance. Relatedly, how do structural and social inequalities manifest themselves in the daily lives of these individuals and how do they navigate these barriers?

Whiteness in the Field

Qualitative ethnography takes time and dedication because as an outsider, both as a white woman and someone from Chicago, I needed to build rapport and comfort with my presence there. In May of 2018, after Pastor Patricia asked the patrons for their approval for me to come to the pantry, she recommended I keep coming back each week so the patrons would see me as a familiar face. Over time, I was able to start interviews; each interview took between 30 to 45 minutes in the office area of the church. Each time I attended, I left contact sheets with the purpose of the study and how they could reach me. In the fall of 2018, I was able to start giving gift cards to local grocery stores as an appreciation of their time. Each Wednesday morning and afternoon was spent at the pantry for a year and a half. In addition, I spent time at their respective houses or helping with other tasks and errands. I wanted to involve participants in the process and asked them to clarify any details to avoid confusion or errors in my interpretations. Study participants were asked clarifying questions in order to mitigate any error in interpretation and to avoid unclear statements.

Qualitative Research

To analyze perceptions, the study uses a qualitative methodology that allows me to capture people's self-perceptions and perceptions of others while also recording welfare processes through micro-interactions. Conducting in-depth interviews allowed for the collection of rich data. While modest sample size means qualitative data may not be generalizable beyond the case at hand, it does allow for insight into a particular population, particularly as I employed a semi-structured interview process, which includes some direction but allows for the participant to add information to the conversation. While I had a list of questions, I also wanted interviews to function more like conversations. This method uses questions to contextualize experiences and obtain rich descriptions of events. The interviews helped to obtain data about how recipients live their daily lives, that is, how recipients spend the money received, what is important in their lives, and encountered struggles. The questions asked were about their daily life, how they cope and make decisions with issues they may encounter, the type of assistance they receive, support networks, views on other recipients, and general demographics. To capture different voice inflections or verbal cues, a recorder was utilized. The participant was given the option if they wanted to be recorded or not; however, no one declined the recording. By helping make the interviewee feel comfortable and build a connection which often took several interviews, it helped uncover how the structures of inequality manifest through the experience of interacting with the welfare system and its impact on a group of individuals in a city. Also, some participants did not feel comfortable coming to campus or speaking in a public place, nor were able to access campus. Therefore, the interview location was their choice. I interviewed 26 recipients, 15 social and state workers, 3 employees at Hunger Task Force, and 2 community members about their experiences and perceptions of poverty in addition to working at the pantry.

Participant Observation

I worked at a food pantry and soup kitchen for a year and a half, providing food insecure people access to food and community. In order to obtain data for the research process, I developed rapport to eventually become entrusted by the community that I was studying and became friends with my respondents which led to the type of data that I was able to collect. This study is connected to my work on understanding racism and white supremacy. To accomplish a study on welfare recipients, I examined the ways in which poor people and people of color manage in the city of Milwaukee under such conditions, how those conditions affect them, and how they feel about people with shared life circumstances.[1] Therefore, my purpose as a sociologist and emerging scholar is to ensure that I am not continuing practices of oppression or trying to "fix" marginalized people but helping to fix conditions that marginalize people. Also, I recognize that as a poor white, cisgender woman, who is ineligible for assistance due to my student status but experiencing some of the structures of poverty, I may be able to find common experiences with the respondents of the study. I experience oppression and sexism differently than women of color or transgender women. I disclosed that I was in the process of receiving my PhD at an urban university, while being poor but having the privilege to live in a middle- to upper-middle-class suburb of Milwaukee, though within walking distance from a neighborhood that has a fraction of the resources as Shorewood. Prior to the conception of this project, I began attending a church located in the Harambee neighborhood as was recommended to me because of its strong foundation in social justice. My reasoning was that establishing these connections early on would assist in identifying study participants and earning their trust.

Sociology has a fraught but important history with communities of color and a history of not appropriately amplifying those voices. Being a sociologist requires that my practice be intentional and inclusive, always remembering the voice I am seeking to amplify. It also requires me to acknowledge when I may be wrong and be comfortable addressing my privilege. To use my privilege appropriately, my academic work focuses on identifying color-blind racism within left-wing political parties, racism and its effects on mental health, intersectional feminism more broadly, and the ways in which white feminism often hides or erases work and thought from feminists of color more directly.

Participants

While not singular to Milwaukee, institutional, structural, and systemic racism and inequality established the city as one of the nation's most segregated metropolitan areas despite its population size. I solicited subjects by placing advertisements in local coffee shops, grocery stores, community centers, and local churches located throughout the city of Milwaukee, accounting for the segregated nature of the city. I met with local poverty advocacy groups that work with those in poverty, such as Hunger Task Force (HTF), an organization that advocates for individuals experiencing food insecurity. Interviewing organizations, HTF, assisted in understanding how dominant discourses shape the point of view and institutional culture for those who work with people receiving benefit assistance. These advertisements included basic study information, like the purpose of the study and how to become a participant. While perhaps problematic in some settings, convenience sampling also helped me find participants—both recipients and case managers. Sometimes, convenience sampling can be problematic because the researcher has access to specific networks or relationships and there is the possibility for issues of power and coercion. However, convenience sampling and snowball sampling proved necessary to obtain sufficient interviewees. This was completed through personal connections, advertisements on social media, and through word of mouth through colleagues and locally connected friends, but not through cold-calling people to participate in the research.

What I originally perceived as more difficult was the recruitment of welfare case managers that often decide whether others are eligible for welfare. Interviewing case managers in Milwaukee is a delicate dance. Asking case managers directly about their thoughts about race, racism, and gender led to a calculated answer, or as one supervisor retorted, "I know how to creatively answer *those* questions," to avoid potentially exhibiting racist or sexist thoughts.

To deal with this tension, it was beneficial to approach welfare case managers as experts in their respective fields because approaching them in this way relieved some of the tension. Helping frame the interview as an inquiry about their professional opinion elicited coded language regarding Milwaukee, their feelings about how recipients use assistance, views on poverty, work ethic, and so on, more often than I expected.

For recipients to feel at ease, case managers were not connected to the recipients. This disconnect was important for recipients to feel comfortable about being honest regarding their experience and to avoid the risk that the case manager could resent or retaliate against the recipient. To ensure this, the interview pools were separate from each other. In the interviews, questions were not asked about *specific* recipients, but rather their broader ideas and the way that they conceptualize a welfare beneficiary. For example, how do caseworkers find themselves in this work? What motivates them to help others? The case managers were sourced through interpersonal connections by speaking to locally connected people who work as social workers or are connected to organizations or advocacy groups that handle benefit assistance cases in Milwaukee.

Feed the Need

I first started coming to the pantry right before people started to eat, and I distributed my materials about the study. I met with the worker at the church, who put me in touch with the day pastor, who I met with shortly thereafter. Essentially, she acted as the gatekeeper for the pantry and gave me permission to speak with people at the pantry. I went every Wednesday at 11:00 a.m., placed my materials on the tables, and gave a short synopsis of my purpose. At first, my goals were simply to have the patrons see me as a returning face. Often during my short introductions, people would interrupt with questions, mostly revolving around whether I could help them with services, whether I was a social worker, whether I was working for the state, and whether or not I would report them if they told me any incriminating information. All these questions were responded with a no (however, it is a subtle caveat that technically I do work for the state, since my university is a public institution, but I do not report to any social service organization for this work, so I felt comfortable informing them no, I would not). Currently, I was unable to provide any incentive for their interviews, which obviously impeded patron involvement. For approximately a month, beginning in May of 2018, I would simply go in, leave my information, make my speech, and then leave, and return each Wednesday. Since many of the patrons are Black/African American/people of color more generally, I wanted to be cautious about taking up space in this particular manner.

My whiteness in this space was always front and center in my mind. Previously, students from the University of Wisconsin-Milwaukee (UWM) descended on the neighborhood only to take information for their research and then leave once their research concluded, and I wanted to try my best to stay away from doing just that. I also did not want to come into the Feed the Need community and assume they needed my help. Just as much as my whiteness was on my mind, there was a general distrust (based on the history of students from the university) toward me. This distrust was based on a combination of several factors: the fact that I was a UWM student doing research in the area and the assumption of wealth due to my whiteness. In my initial recruitment, many of the pantry patrons asked me, rightfully so, "what are you going to give me?" While some may interpret this as greed, it is important to understand the significance of this statement. People in poverty, especially in Milwaukee, are prodded for information about their lives, but often they receive no benefits or compensation after telling people about their lives. It was important to me to be a constant presence at Feed the Need. Therefore, building rapport, even though it is often a necessarily slow process, was incredibly important to me. However, after my initial limited involvement, over time my duties at the pantry expanded.

Encoding the Data

The codes that developed from my qualitative portion emerged from the interviews and data collected from the participant observation. I made sure that the respondents had access to my informed consent form, and they were able to exit the interview; however, there was no time during data collection that it happened. To protect the confidentiality, I created new "characters and scenes" that were a representation and collection of many interviewee experiences but did not represent one specific person—in the event a person or scenario was *too identifiable*.[2] Exceptions to the rule included some well-known geography and intersections that were important to set and locate a particular change over time.

Many researchers recommend the assigning of a pseudonym as a collaborative process between the participant and researcher, so that participants feel a sense of connection to their contribution to the work, to create rapport with the research process, and promote a better and deeper conversation and data.[3] For example, Allen and Wiles[4] suggest asking to check the spelling of their name, asking if they want to select a "pretend name," for the purposes of research. Previous research shows that participants choosing their own pseudonyms as a meaningful process—sometimes reflecting on a close family member, friend, word, or meaningful attachment.[5] If the participant could think of a "pretend name," an effort was made to choose a pseudonym that reflected the self-identified culture and ethnic background for the participant unless specifically requested that I use their real name. While the participants in the study advocated that they wanted their real names, for their personal protection all names were changed to fully follow a feminist ethnographic ethic. The participants were given the opportunity to come up with their own names because allowing the participants to first choose their pseudonym acknowledges the power of the researcher and brings the participant into the research.

For a proper analysis, figuring out this research puzzle and connecting it to newly collected information are crucial. This intimate, working knowledge of my interviewees' lives and situations was present in my mind when I was writing and reviewing the interviews.[6] This intimate knowledge informed my ability to generate more informative case studies and create an interesting and informative web of lives and experiences to tell the story of recipients in Milwaukee. Preliminary codes were identified by the comment analysis project, but interviews illuminated others—such as stress, juggling bills, families, the police and incarceration, stigma, racism, and others through the interpretation of the data uncovered through the interview process.

Each day after the pantry, I reviewed my notes and recorded my own feelings. I gave the participants my consent form and I gave each participant time to read it. Over time, the regular pantry patrons would ask about how the writing was going and if they could help or get another interview if I needed more information. I never wanted the patrons to feel like they were being watched, so while at the pantry, I would quickly enter the instance/encounter into the note feature on my phone (many people would text, so it was not out of the ordinary). After my day at the pantry ended and people were driven home, I would voice record the events of the day. Upon reviewing the conversations that took place over the course of my observation, I found that they could be corroborated by past research on how people in poverty discuss themselves and others. However, how individuals talk about themselves is not the same manner as that of people outside of poverty. The individuals described in the following pages were aware and consented to my writing about them at the same time.

Qualitative data are not just about noting what interviewees or participants say but understanding what they mean. To avoid transcribing errors of respondent interview responses, I made available my notes and asked for clarification. Doing this, I found that rapport and confidence were created, but I did not require the respondents to spend any additional emotional labor for this research. While this research is about poverty, it was also about telling my participants' stories and amplifying their lived experiences.

Qualitative

Over time, as I listened to my interviewees, I noticed thematic patterns in how they were talking about themselves, others, and how they thought others perceived them. To analyze the qualitative data, I organized my recordings with code names. While listening to the recordings, I would note any stops, pauses, or reiterations. I also documented laughter—nervous tendencies included. The following themes emerged from each interview I was fortunate to encounter, and each of these themes is highlighted in the chapters that follow.

Theme	Instance that met this theme
Anxiety	Shopping, card balance, rush, waiting at the office/on phone/mail, inability to assist, health, self-care
Stress	Card balance, budgeting, knowing exact amounts, not being able to buy needed items, high caseload, personal development, time management
Self-perception	Guilt, demoralization, sadness, happiness, family
Perception of others	Getting by, positionality, greediness of others
Dignity	Being able to shop, EBT card versus stamp book, being seen, wanting to be heard
Perceptions of them by others	As a "taker," not trying, lazy, distant, unhelpful, working *for* the system
Joy/emotion	Having extra to buy something special, guilty pleasure, assisting a client, sharing, being open, expressing notions of sadness
Stigma	Rudeness, disbelief, not hospitable, internalized
Precarity	Food access, food deserts, high-priced food, veggies/fruit often rare, space (built environment)
Racism/implicit bias	Coworkers, whiteness conferences, coded language, workplace practices, geographical connotations, "those people," recipient check use patterns
Whiteness	"Getting it," nicknames given, acknowledgment
White savior complex	Helping people who can't help themselves, we'll do it for them

These themes helped to organize the data in a meaningful way and potentially analyze the theme, its expression, and what it meant to the data. Each of my respondents—recipient, social worker, and poverty organizations—found themselves interconnected via these mutual experiences.

Geographical Methodology

Understanding the geographical nature of Milwaukee's nutritional redlining was similarly integral to data collection. Using Social Explorer, a website interface that uses census level data to analyze population demographic change over time helped created the maps in a later chapter. The census tracts do extend farther than the neighborhood boundaries, but the neighborhoods of Harambee and Riverwest are denoted by pink and blue boundaries. In addition to the census tracts, archival research informs how the neighborhood that became known as Harambee at one point had grocery stores throughout the neighborhood. Just like the white flight that created a vacuum, so did the movement of grocery stores. While not all the corner stores are noted in the maps, the focal neighborhood, which is Harambee and is compared to the large land area that surrounds it, is noted in the map. The city boundaries that surround Harambee show how far full-stock grocery stores are from Harambee. Similarly important, the maps detailing the location of grocery stores are not an exclusive city list but show that in a small area like the upper and lower east side, there are more grocery stores than in the neighborhood of Harambee.

Limitations

By virtue of being a qualitatively focused study, it lacks the ability for me to truly generalize these experiences for a whole population. What is important about this research is that while my participant pool was small, I found that many of the respondents would detail similar experiences about how they navigated poverty. Another limitation is quite simply the interpretation. It would be foolish to think every white, ciswoman researcher will have the same analysis as what follows in these pages—because the idea and understanding of whiteness and racial knowledge are not shared in the same way by every person.

Much of the interactions throughout the project were built over time and a level of trust was necessary before I was ever able to interview people at the pantry. Building rapport takes time, effort, consistency, patience, and understanding—and many of those things are learned over the course of data collection. For example, a white researcher *may be knowledgeable* in their field, but upon entering the doors of the location that will be observed, the researcher is no longer the "expert." Knowing how whiteness functions and manifests is important because one's whiteness necessarily needs to be acknowledged and understood. Until that moment happens, communities of color are understandably wary and mistrustful of white people and, in this instance, white researchers that collect data in marginalized communities. That acknowledgment and historical awareness of how whiteness takes up space inform my analytical framework which might differ from another white scholar.

It is perhaps important to note that approval from the Institutional Review Board (IRB) was obtained from the UWM as well as completion of Collaborative Institutional Training Initiative (CITI) training for interviewing human subjects. Once the approval was given, I started dispersing my interview flyers around the city.

NOTES

1. Collins 2003; Collins and Bilge 2016; Gilens 1999; Quadagno 1994.
2. Hopkins 1993; Kaiser 2009.
3. Allen and Wiles 2016.
4. Ibid.
5. Ibid 2016: 155.
6. Marshall and Rossman 2011.

Introduction

'No one wants to work, they just want to be on the government dime,' 'My family never received assistance and we pulled our own self up' or 'They have that car AND they are on welfare, they should sell it and take the money to help themselves out.' You may have heard some of these statements, or something like them from the news, politicians, family members, or maybe even yourself. Tropes of welfare recipients as shiftless, undeserving, and irresponsible people not just looking for a handout, but also portrayed as living high on the hog, are common partly due to their negative portrayal in the media. In view of these specious representations, this book examines (1) how welfare recipients of diverse racial identities perceive themselves and their welfare[1] benefit status; (2) how they think others perceive them; (3) how they view other people in related situations; (4) how case managers perceive recipients who are receiving benefits; and (5) how do structural and social inequalities manifest themselves in the daily lives of these individuals? (6) how do individuals experience and deal with different social and structural barriers? (7) how are these barriers manifested through social and political policy actions?

Think about walking into your kitchen as a child and lacking basic access to quality food. For some readers, this may be an experience that is completely unfamiliar. I know as a child, I could walk into the kitchen and have access to fresh fruits, vegetables, and meat. My mother often prescribed the protein, vegetable, and starch plate. I recall as a child, I had access to several food items, and I never went to bed hungry. However, as I aged and experienced life, I began to realize that my childhood was not shared by every child or family.

Food insecurity is a real problem within a country that believes it to be the richest nation on earth, yet millions of families and children go hungry

1

and must use food pantries and community meals to find sustenance. In Milwaukee, Wisconsin, 1 out of 11 households are food insecure—meaning that they lack access to quality foods in their kitchens. In Milwaukee alone, almost 30% of families live under the poverty line and in that 30%, almost 40% of children are unable to access food.[2] Milwaukee is a city of almost 600,000 people and in this metropolitan area, there are clashing cultures that border each other that have very divergent histories.

Milwaukee, Wisconsin, is the place where residents of German, Italian, Polish, Black Hmong, and Latinx heritages bask in the free-flowing nature of its beer and other malty beverages and call it home. Milwaukee, in relation to its population size, is named the nation's most segregated city.[3] While the history of segregation goes back to long before the Great Migration (1910–1970), particularly during the post–World War II second wave when many African Americans from the southern United States migrated to Milwaukee, its continuance can be partly explained through the decades of "urban renewal" displacing families and creating new neighborhoods of concentrated poverty.[4] The modern Milwaukee, due to its high rates of inequality and the legacy of racial segregation between its white and Black residents, cannot be understood without the understanding that its history is characterized by segregation, poverty, food and economic insecurity, including the lack of access to stores selling nutritious foods.[5] Work by Matthew Desmond highlighted Milwaukee's high rate of eviction and its effects on poor white and Black residents.[6] Not only is experiencing an eviction a demoralizing experience, but it also hampers an individual from finding future accommodation for themselves or their families. Therefore, housing and eviction are unquestionably connected to issues of poverty and inequality. Other works examined Milwaukee's high percentage of poverty and racial segregation.[7]

Locally known as the "Selma of the North," Milwaukee's racial history makes it an interesting case because of its position in the northern part of the nation, and its perception to be out of the range of common racial geographies.[8] Much of the racism discourse during the decades of the 1940s through the 1970s focus on the Southeastern United States with their explicit "Jim Crow" Laws and *dejure segregation*—or segregation by law. However, just because the northern states were not governed by these laws does not make them innocent. Northern states used what some scholars might argue as a more insidious form of segregation—which is de facto *segregation*—or segregation commonly led by emotions, attitudes, and feelings, which is significantly harder to "prove."[9] During this time, much of Milwaukee's northside was shaped by the construction of new highways such as I-43, which bifurcated parts of the southside and Milwaukee's Bronzeville and Black neighborhoods. Businesses were closed and this forced people to migrate to the north.[10]

However, the people of Wisconsin existed long before its current demographic makeup. Starting at 1848 or even present day, erases the history of the Miami tribes that called "Meskonsing[11]" as the "river running through a red place" and if you've lived in Wisconsin for any amount of time, this "red place" takes on a double meaning. For Miami, it referenced the red sandstone bluffs that are currently known as the "Dells." Presently, "red place" might indicate its infamous conservative and swaths of red voting districts that advocate for stricter antiwelfare legislation that many families statewide rely on to meet their needs.[12] While discussing contemporary Milwaukee, it makes sense to honor its indigenous heritage, which accounts for its name, thanks to its original inhabitants—the Potawatomi, Ojibwe, and Algonquian tribes, among others.[13] Different indigenous tribes attribute the etymology of Milwaukee as the "Good Land" or the "Gathering Place" and as someone who is not affiliated with these tribes, it seems important to name this indigeneity.[14]

THE RESEARCH AREA

Milwaukee, however, is not alone in issues of racism, segregation, and inequality. The following unpacks this long, historical legacy of racism and geographical segregation to find that all these concepts are inextricably linked. Since spatiality is not naturally occurring but a phenomenon socially constructed through migrations, restrictive covenants, government and industrial policies, and societal attitudes in different cities, the effects of these issues can be seen in subsets of society, that is, disparate racialized impacts.[15] It's hard to "prove" that infrastructure intentionally created barriers in particularly non-white communities, because there are ways to use coded discourse and talk *around* that.[16]

Similarly, how cities come to terms with the reality of segregation related to racist and classist policies can be examined by analyzing the geographical location and spatiality of grocery stores. Therefore, connected to the segregation, the geographical location, and spatiality of where grocery stores are located is also related to how people perceive themselves and others. In segregated Milwaukee, we can explore more than just *residential redlining*, or the historical denial of mortgage lending in Black and brown areas, and consider *nutritional redlining*, where grocery stores are spatially located near interstitial areas (where white and Black neighborhoods blur), and access to healthy, nutritious food is placed at a distance for Black and brown families.[17]

The city of Milwaukee lost a 2016 residency requirement court case[18] that mandated all city employees to live within the city limits. A state court ruled against this mandate, and now caseworkers and other workers can live outside Milwaukee in places with a different socioeconomic and racial makeup, affecting how caseworkers understand, perceive, and encounter the people they serve. This study hopes to add to the rich and growing literature in this field. The overall purpose is to shed light on how Milwaukee residents conceptualize social and structural inequalities in their lives, how they deal with those daily struggles, and how they understand themselves and others in the process.

I interviewed 44 people as case managers, recipients, and organizations about their experiences with poverty. Along with those interviews, I conducted a participant observation that accounts for about 350 hours at a local community lunch and food pantry. These experiences and observations highlight the ways in which perceptions emerge in many ways. For example, none of the participants expressed a lack of desire to work nor wanted to be on assistance for a long duration. Many people wanted to finally overcome this barrier and be self-sufficient. This work also examines how people in poverty navigate and negotiate systems of poverty—relying on friends, families, and social networks. It also lends an examination of constant feelings of anxiety, food insecurity, precarity, and a social safety net that is more confusing and fraught with misinformation than actual assistance. Respondents and case managers alike expressed frustration and hopelessness when trying to work with federal systems like Supplemental Nutrition Assistance Program (SNAP)/Foodshare and cash assistance, because they feel people making the laws and requirements lack a basic understanding regarding the lived experience of poverty in America.

How a Researcher Can Appropriately Research

While there are amazing works on poverty, one book cannot capsulate the entire experience of poverty, so this book hopes to be an addition to that literature collection. However, these definitions of poverty arise from how people are continually changing and are connecting to different power structures which can and should be disrupted through learning and engaging with others.[19] Elwood et al.[20] note that geographical conceptions of geography are constituted in three distinct ways: socio-spatial, epistemological, and politics of possibility. Other researchers explore this engagement through sites of encounter or contact.[21] Allport's contact hypothesis can similarly be used to understand how when observing the researcher can be more mindful of the shared space between strangers collecting data from participants.[22] Therefore, not unlike workers that may live in different areas than the people that are their clients, researchers doing work in marginalized areas should consistently remain mindful of the role inequalities play in restructuring how race and gender often interact is vital.

Harambee

The neighborhood where much of the focus will be is located on the northside of deeply segregated Milwaukee. Harambee is home to a predominantly Black population that borders a predominantly white neighborhood, Riverwest. The name Harambee was adapted in the 1970s and signifies a Swahili word for "pulling together"—which is a theme that runs throughout the neighborhood. Over the years, community initiative projects and programs tried to revive the area since the rapid change in the 1960s. The spirit of community building is a thread that holds the fabric of Harambee together, and much of that is done through the work at Gathering People's Lutheran Church (GPLC), where much of the following occurs.

Theories behind the Research

Focused and Erased

The humanity of people often gets erased when thinking about government policy, which sounds rather farcical when thinking about how government impacts people. The effect on people usually is lost in budgets, legislation, and general talking points. However, government (in)action affects real people in different ways. For example, Black women, poor families, and non-white recipients are the usual targets against funding the social safety net. However, these last two years (2019–2021 and counting) showed us that poverty is much closer than many of us realize. Perhaps a way to understand the visibility of welfare recipients and the effect of poverty is through symbolic annihilation. The main idea of symbolic annihilation is not put into use in discussing the regulation of others through these policies, even though the lens of symbolic annihilation might potentially add to their analysis.[23] For example, if the media primarily presents Black women as poor and as single mothers who are struggling, then that controlling image is associated with a Black woman/man and is integral to how symbolic annihilation occurs, but it is not described as such.[24]

Symbolic annihilation is defined as the media presence[25] or absence based on gender, race, and socioeconomic status of a particular group.[26] First, as "welfare queens," Black women are presented as a monolithic group without much consideration of the total population of Black women, making Black women who do not fit the stereotype invisible in the discourse. To understand symbolic annihilation, one can observe how stereotypes present all Black women as loud, dominating, and demanding. Another way to examine the symbolic annihilation is through absence, and often men are absent or excluded as recipients, perhaps due to the gendered construction of W-2 programs. Most of the research about the lives of benefit recipients is centered around women.[27] However, at the same time, Black women are the controlling focus as "welfare queens," poor whites, or white-passing individuals experience the absence in terms of "positive" symbolic annihilation because they can fade to the back and access levels of class privilege.

What happened during the Shutdown of 2019 and the pandemic of 2020+ showed or should have shown how the government (in)action can directly affect people's rights in their pocketbooks and, in many cases, these experiences were clearly present, but the impact was seen as unimportant to people in power. While many would like to make this a deserving/not deserving binary choice, the problem is that both groups are deserving and have real needs. And many people are experiencing the issue of being present and absent, sometimes at the same time.

Symbolic annihilation research examines issues of welfare policies, and how their punitive sanctions specifically affect various women.[28] Kingfisher[29] compares the United States and New Zealand and how both nations demonize a collective "other" in relation to welfare "reform." Here, Kingfisher concludes that, in both nations, indigenous and Black women, as groups, are seen in the media as savage and uncivilized, thus supposedly requiring more punitive measures because these women need reformation. These notions map onto how Black women are prominently featured as "welfare queens" or how Black men are depicted as bad fathers—images of old tropes reformulated with Reagan-era welfare "reform" and maintained through repetitive use of racialized and gendered media tropes for a new audience. The presence of these perceptions allowed for the continued transformation of welfare rhetoric in US anti-poverty policies, as these became racialized and further stigmatized in the "post-civil rights" era.

A large proportion of recipients are poor, white Americans. While they can benefit from many of the privileges that are attached to whiteness, they are also marginalized in the sense that they are poor.[30] White welfare recipients are simultaneously annihilated in the sense that they are absent from view; their situations are not taken seriously; they're often seen as inferior to other white people; and they often participate in their own annihilation due to attachments to how they understand deservingness. For example, Bobo[31] notes that even if white folks benefit from policies aimed at lifting others, white voters will sabotage themselves, vote outside of their class interests, and harm themselves if they believe that others will receive more benefits. They can (un)consciously participate in perpetuating racism depending on how they understand political ideology.[32] This exact scenario was enacted time and again throughout 2019 and 2020 (and ongoing) regarding how people felt about giving payments to people affected by the pandemic—which was a large, expansive group of people.

Like the ways that symbolic annihilation affects women and women of color, men are often left out of the benefit recipient narrative. While men receive welfare, Kost[33] notes that many men interviewed felt varying levels of shame and stigma associated with benefit assistance. Kost[34] noted that many men would use benefit applications as a last resort, or if they did receive benefits, they would never use them or have friends who were women purchase items for them. Much of the welfare/benefits-assistance discourse revolves around women and children, but fewer studies examine how men experience issues with welfare structures as well. Another reason why men may be reluctant to receive benefit assistance could be connected to notions of patriarchy, masculinities, and the perceptions of men as breadwinners.[35] Some researchers may argue that the reason there is less data on men as recipients is because they account for fewer of those recipients. Examining men of varied demographic sectors as recipients may highlight how patriarchy annihilates the ability for men to feel comfortable in reaching out for assistance. If patriarchal structures establish men receiving benefits as "less masculine" then assessments of hegemonic masculinity and masculinities in general might be overlooked or erased.[36]

Other researchers examined symbolic annihilation in relation to cities and gentrification.[37] Mitchell[38] focuses on the symbolic annihilation of the homeless through anti-homelessness laws in several large US cities. Additionally, the welfare state governs where people can exist. For example, welfare structures the residential lives of people, such as where they can shop for goods, what they can buy, and what they can do with their funds. More directly, due to welfare reform in 1996, welfare structures are more able to intrude on the lives of the poor, making them more vulnerable due to meeting the requirements to receive benefits. Researchers also tackled important work of examining how people exist within a city and navigate situations of poverty.[39] Lipsitz[40] notes that

> poverty by itself is an impediment to securing adequate shelter; race and gender discrimination adds new obstacles for women of color. . . . Impoverished women of color have fewer housing options than white women or men of all colors and rarely thus subject to severe housing insecurity.[41]

These laws work in a way to demonize those that are deemed less worthy of interacting in normative society.

Marginalized groups experience annihilation of their personhood on a frequent, if not daily, basis. The repetition of racialized stereotypes in media becomes seen as facts of life—because the issues that are portrayed in the media affect people's assumptions and policymakers' beliefs—thus becoming internalized perceptions of others. For example, news outlets that often show images of Black women as welfare recipients and Black men as criminals are transferred to real-life dialogue wherein Black and African Americans are only seen in this one-dimensional way and other populations are configured in a completely different light.[42]

This same one-dimensionality in media is mirrored in the ways that poverty organizations feature or hide connections to people of color. In Milwaukee, HTF, a free and local food bank, owes its existence to a group of Black Panthers meeting with a local pastor of Cross Lutheran Church. This rich history is symbolically annihilated from their media campaigns to protect the influx of donations from white people in Milwaukee's suburbs. The vague origins of HTF are purposely curated to shield white fragility due to white perceptions of the Black Panther Party (BPP).

Web of Systems

As I was describing my research, it became evident that there are many governmental and nongovernmental bodies involved in benefits provision and if not properly described, one might get lost. Therefore, the "systems map" attempts to simplify the links between all these actors and how they work together. At the top, there is the figure of the president and of Congress where significant back-and-forth legislation occurs—in this case, spending bills (or the lack of a spending bill, which initiate shutdowns, like the one in December 2019). The web of systems is often impacted by congressional action—depending on who has power—and what that power focuses on at the time. Funding is distributed to departments under the president that in turn goes to state governments and local agencies. The United States Department of Agriculture (USDA) works with local farmers and buys what is unable to be sold (in this case, due to tariffs imposed), then distributes that food to organizations like HTF at a discounted price. The SNAP is run through the USDA and rent and housing assistance is distributed to Housing and Urban Development, but aid is disbursed through individual state and local agencies (i.e., Wisconsin Department of Health and Human Services). Eventually, the recipient finally receives the benefits from these agencies.

Individual Recipients

Impacted by governmental (dis)organization, the individuals had the fortune of meeting while understanding poverty helped understand its impact. The stories of Harold, Wynette, Brenna, and all the wonderful people I met help shed light on how poverty or closeness to poverty is shared across communities more than we might realize. Through their unending generosity, I was able to have a window into a new perspective and hopefully understand

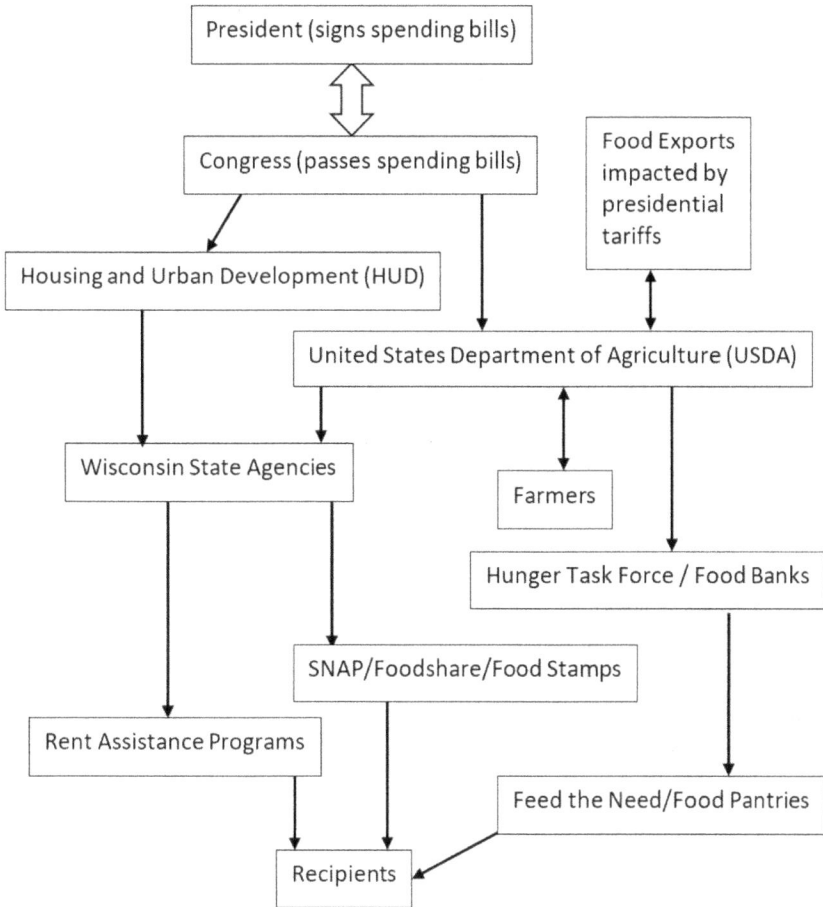

Figure 0.1   Web of Systems Map.

how poverty and food insecurity that are impacted by social service agencies are managed.

Chapter Organization

The following chapters work together to show how interconnected these experiences are—it's not just one group and one group alone that is familiar with poverty, but that they transgress various boundaries, areas, and ideas about socioeconomic status and how government action impacts that experience. Hopefully, by exploring these connections, we can find more realistic and helpful ways to discuss elements of poverty. They are attempts to weave together multiple experiences of poverty navigation. Through the experiences of the recipients at Feed the Need and my study participants, we have a better understanding of how people who are experiencing wealth inequality may exist outside the city of Milwaukee.

Chapter 1 focuses on the recipients at a pantry that I refer to as Feed the Need to protect their identity. Here, we learn a little more about the main cast of characters that create the ability for the pantry to function. It describes the interactions between members, the purpose and layout of the pantry, and how people use it to survive. The chapter also introduces the HTF which is a free and local food bank that provides food to pantries in the Milwaukee area.

Chapter 2 details the national perspective of how to benefit recipients who are perceived in the anonymous comments that followed articles about welfare policies. Often, comment boards are discredited place via the prowling rhetoric of internet trolls who only seek to inflame situations versus improve them. However, while some might devalue anonymous comments, they also say a great deal about how random individuals understand issues like poverty, welfare, class, and privilege.

Chapter 3 explores the historical timeline of welfare policy. Then the chapter connects it to Milwaukee for a more grounded approach. This chapter is also far more theoretical than others to help guide the reader through the rest of the chapters. It also explores and builds upon how race and racism often factor into how welfare and those that benefit from assistance are racially situated. The chapter ends with connecting these issues to how they appear in Milwaukee, one of the most segregated metropolitan areas *and* an area with one of the highest poverty rates in the nation.

Chapter 4 describes the social geography of Milwaukee—how it became the most segregated city in the entire United States. Exploring segregation as a deliberate and constructed social fact allows the reader to look at how neighborhoods were formed over time—not as natural occurrences—due to actions by institutions. Not only does this geographical component display visual segregation maps, but it also points to nutritional redlining. With the high concentration of Black and brown Milwaukeeans that lack access to healthy food options, these maps illustrate the context in which the recipients experience and navigate precarity in terms of food insecurity.

Chapter 5 explores life outside the pantry with the participants that I met through working at Feed the Need. This chapter explores the ways in which a white researcher can engage with and learn from others. While the experiences shared might not map onto everyone's experience, we all might find common ground in the ways in which community can be created.

Chapter 6 is a snapshot of one of the more recent government shutdowns that affected approximately 800,000 federal workers and 30–40 million benefit recipients and their children. In addition to all the above, I was able to examine how the effects of the longest US government shutdown in history

(December 22, 2018, until January 25, 2019) reached far beyond the 800,000 federal workers who were furloughed or went unpaid. Much of the media focused on federal workers; however, many people in the welfare sector were affected by similar issues—lack of access to pay, rent, cash, and food assistance. The tension of benefit expansion weaves a new layer through which we can understand the diverse experiences at Feed the Need through my ethnographic observations as well as interviews with participants and case managers. Media outlets solely reported on the 800,000 workers who are important, but the total impact was invisible. Many benefit recipients often are blamed for things that go wrong or are completely erased and forgotten. This chapter also introduced a third actor in the study—the social worker.

Chapter 7 connects recipients and social workers in more detail than chapter 6. The purpose is to show how the lives of recipients and social workers are interconnected. This chapter more explicitly features how recipients see themselves, others, and how they think others see them. These same questions are posed to the social workers because the workers can be seen in sometimes negative ways and configured as "ineligibility agents," as one former social worker described the personality of state workers.

And finally, chapter 8 finishes the analysis with the HTF, an organization mentioned in previous chapters, wherein proper attention is given to how it tries to advocate and end hunger in the greater Milwaukee area through various programs. Putting symbolic annihilation into practice, the organization has foundations in breakfast programs founded by the BPP in Milwaukee. This organization is another piece of the web of how recipients access food during times of precarity. HTF also engages in symbolic annihilation and violence through how it implements its service programs.

The collection of these chapters allows us to reframe how we think about poverty and how we might be able to relate to the individuals profiled, especially considering the Shutdown of 2018–2019 and the COVID Pandemic of 2020+. When actually "doing" the research, you never really know where it is going to take you or what is going to happen, but the fascinating part about qualitative research is the unknowns or the rabbit holes you might find along the way. When this process began, I had no idea that 10 months later there would be a government shutdown affecting millions of people and even larger, a year later that an "invisible enemy" also known as COVID-19 or Coronavirus would shut down whole countries, place millions out of work, and create strain on food pantries, social workers, and unemployment agencies. Much of the writing and editing for this was during the pandemic, so it might also act as a diary of the experiences of those unexpectedly shifted into being furloughed in a way that seems unfamiliar. During the shutdown, those affected were benefit recipients and some government workers deemed "nonessential." For the pandemic, 20 million people in a month's time applied for and were waiting for unemployment. The entire nation waited as Congress stalled on "stimulus packages" and then when it was clear $1,200 for 10 weeks would not be enough, they had to create a second bill to help families and workers hurt by this virus. During the time of the pandemic, it was hard to figure out how to write these chapters because every day there was a new level of avoidable precarity. Much of this precarity was understood by other nations but within the United States, lawmakers were worried that people would not want to work if they were helped. During this time, it became clear that Congress has no real clue how most of the nation lives in situations that are poverty adjacent. In many ways, we are all in this together. These chapters capture the ways in which recipients are conceptualized or erased in media, in dialogue and in their everyday lived experience. This combination provides a new way to conceptualize how people understand their lived experiences through points of contention. During the pandemic, many of the areas included in the following chapters were also those with the highest rates of infection, highlighting that there is a connection with segregation, redlining, nutritional redlining, health care access, and simply how others feel which bodies matter and do not, who is "following the rules" and who is not. While white people and their population representation account for a higher number of recipients, their experiences differ from Black people in comparable situations due to racialized understandings of welfare. More broadly, we need to examine how racial and gender privilege in the United States—specifically in Milwaukee—manifests through specific narratives about race and gender that have real material consequences for welfare recipients' lived experiences.

Throughout the conversations with recipients and the large-scale issues like shutdowns and pandemics, there are real solutions to these problems that are faced by people in poverty and adjacent to poverty. These solutions are probably considered radical to the average person—even though most would benefit—because most families in the United States are far closer to needing assistance than they realize.[43] Even within the United States and throughout other nations around the globe have instituted programs like basic minimum income, where people no longer worry about providing the basic needs for their families or themselves. Critics often proclaim that these programs disincentivize work; however, this result was not explicitly evident from the governmental institutions that have provided them. You might be asking yourself, well, this system map is already making things confusing, and government (in)action placed people in precarity. However, from the pandemic, it became evidently clear that US residents could be easily reached and supported *as soon as* the government acted. If there is anything, the pandemic and shutdown showed us that people are far closer to precarity than perhaps they might admit. The recent shutdowns and global pandemic made this clear.

NOTES

1. https://www.hungertaskforce.org/about-hunger/hunger-in-milwaukee/.
2. https://www.hungertaskforce.org/about-hunger/hunger-in-milwaukee/.
3. Loyd and Bonds, "Where Do Black Lives Matter?"; Rosenblatt and Cossyleon, "Pushing the Boundaries."
4. Massey and Denton, *American Apartheid.*; Niemuth, "Urban Renewal."
5. Bonds, "Racing Economic Geography"; Glauber and Crowe, "Milwaukee Poverty"; Halpern-Meekin et al., *It's Not like I'm Poor*; Heynen, "Back to Revolutionary Theory"; Loyd and Bonds, "Where Do Black Lives Matter?"; Moynihan, "The Negro Family"; Sims and Rainge, "Urban Poverty"; Squires and O'Connor, *Closing the Racial Gap*; Trotter, "The Great Migration"; Wacquant, *Punishing the poor.*
6. Desmond, "Disposable Ties"; "Disposable Ties"; *Evicted*; Desmond and Valdez, "Unpolicing the Urban Poor."
7. Bonds, "Racing Economic Geography"; Halpern-Meekin et al., *It's Not like I'm Poor*; Heynen, "Back to Revolutionary Theory"; Sims and Rainge, "Urban Poverty"; Squires and O'Connor, *Closing the Racial Gap.*
8. Golightly, "De Facto Segregation"; Jones, *The Selma of the North.*
9. Bell, *Silent Covenants*; Crenshaw, *Critical Race Theory*; Wilson, "On Geography and Encounter."
10. Niemuth, "Urban Renewal."
11. https://madison.com/wsj/news/local/ask/just-ask-us/just-ask-us-how-did-wisconsin-get-its-name/article_942ec3a6-041a-52c9-a432-cd8c16707a79.html.
12. Desmond, *Evicted.*
13. Prigge, "What Does."
14. Ibid.
15. Elwood, Lawson, and Sheppard, "Geographical Relational."
16. Bell, "Serving Two Masters"; "Brown v. Board"; *Silent Covenant*; Pulido, "Rethinking Environmental Racism."
17. Blauner, "Internal Colonialism"; Cho and Clark, "Disparities"; Eisenhauer, "In Poor Health"; Kwate et al., "Retail Redlining"; McBride, "Nutrition"; Schram, "*Supermarket.*"
18. https://www.staffordlaw.com/blog/municipal-law/wisconsin-supreme-court-holds-that-milwaukee-cannot-enforce-city-employee-r/.
19. Elwood, Lawson, and Sheppard, "Geographical Relational."
20. Ibid 2016:746.
21. Allport, *The Nature.*
22. Valentine, "Living with Difference"; Valentine, Sporton, and Bang Nielsen, "Language Use"; Wilson, "On Geography."
23. Collins, *Black Feminist Thought*; Mills, "White Supremacy"; Roberts, *Killing the Black Body*; "Shattered Bonds"; *Fatal Invention.*
24. Collins, "Toward a New Vision"; *Black Feminist Thought*; *Black Sexual Politics*; "New Commodities."
25. It can also be defined as the absence, such as white welfare recipients being the largest group of welfare beneficiaries. Or, only seeing Black people as athletes and not chemists or scientists, and so on.

26. Ducille, "Dyes and Dolls"; Gerbner, "Comparative," "The Dynamics"; Kane, "The Media's Role"; Klein and Shiffman, "Underrepresentation"; Knight and Giuliano, "He's a Laker"; Lind and Salo, "Feminists"; Merskin, "Sending up Signals"; Milkie, "Social Comparisons"; Tuchman, "Symbolic Annihilation," "Mass Media."

27. Lareau, *Unequal Childhoods*; Roberts, *Killing the Black Body*; "Shattered Bonds"; "Prison"; Seccombe, *Cadillac*.

28. Diamond, "Psychoanalytic Speculations"; Kingfisher, "Welfare Reform."

29. Kingfisher, "Welfare Reform."

30. Harris, "Whiteness as Property"; Harrison, "Persistent Power."

31. Bobo, "Affirmative Action."

32. Bobo, "Symbolic Racism"; "Affirmative Action"; "Prejudice as Group Position"; Bobo, Kluegel, and Smith, "Laissez-Faire Racism"; Bobo and Smith, "Jim Crow Racism."

33. Kost, "Meaning of Work."

34. Ibid 1997:15.

35. Collins, "Toward a New Vision"; Connell and Messerschmidt, "Hegemonic Masculinity"; Hochschild and Machung, *The Second Shift*; Popay, Hearn, and Edwards, *Gender Divisions*.

36. Connell and Connell, *Masculinities*.

37. Mitchell, "Annihilation"; Wilson and Grammenos, "Gentrification."

38. Mitchell, "Annihilation."

39. Bourgois, *Righteous Dopefiend*; Gans, *Urban Villagers*, *War against the Poor*; Newman, *No shame in my game*; Small, *Villa victoria*.

40. Lipsitz, *Possessive Investment*.

41. Crenshaw, "Intersectionality," 1446; Lipsitz *Possessive Investment*.

42. Dowler, "Consumption"; Emerson, "Womanhood"; Quillian and Pager, "Black Neighbors."

43. https://www.vox.com/future-perfect/2020/2/19/21112570/universal-basic-income-ubi-map.

Chapter 1

"Let's go eat in the office"
Life at a Milwaukee Food Pantry

Often when we visualize benefit recipients, we lack the understanding of how policies can affect real people, which are detailed in these following pages. For some readers, perhaps experiences at a community lunch and food pantry are unknown. However, there is also a possibility that the recent events in the last two years—shutdowns and a global pandemic—shifted more people into economic precarity. People were more likely to use a food bank or pantry—and lines were significantly longer—harking back to images of people in long bread lines during the Great Depression. If there is inaction on the part of those in power—a government, for example—people are unable to satisfy their daily needs and are left in positions that are extremely dangerous, which will be discussed more in a later chapter. Not only does this inaction affect food access but also rent and housing protections and job security for every person in the United States.

FEED THE NEED

"Line up! Who didn't put their name on the list?" pantry volunteers would ask the crowd awaiting food pantry access. The following chapters explore the day-to-day interaction experienced at a food pantry in Milwaukee and introduce a cast of characters that hopefully through their experience shed a different light on the experiences of those receiving assistance. In addition to all of these, the following chapters discuss how government (in)action can harm average Americans. Situating a pantry within Harambee allows the reader to not just read about the neighborhood and its development over time, but to experience the realities of people that live and work nearby in a real way. Following the experiences of Idgie, Jenny, Harold, Wynette, and others inside and out of the pantry, the dimensions of poverty are shown in a real way—that people are just trying to get by and provide for themselves and their families. It also functions as a collection of stories and experiences of individuals that I met through volunteering at the pantry. It not only explains an average day at the pantry but reveals relevant themes, such as work ethic, conceptions of good/bad whites, what "real" Blackness is, implicit bias, dignity, and self-preservation that emerged over time as well.

Feed the Need operates completely via the work of important volunteers who make their way to the church every Wednesday. Without these important people, there would be nothing to serve the patrons, and a good part of a community would be without important services. Harold and Wynette, two of the people that I became the closest to throughout my obervations have their stories interwoven throughout this chapter. While at first, they were co-volunteers, they eventually became close friends and through that rapport that was developed over some time, it became an avenue for frank and honest discussions of race, poverty, and class.

The Feed the Need pantry and community lunch are located in the basement of Gathering People's Lutheran Church situated in the Harambee neighborhood, known as a place, where local community members can come every Wednesday, enjoy a meal in the company of others, and shop in the connected pantry that can add to their monthly food allotment. Since Feed the Need is related to a church, it derives its name from the verse where the hungry are fed and the thirsty are satisfied. Noting this is important because even though this is how the pantry represents itself, it does not mean that the people who operate and work at the pantry are outside the normative discourse of how we talk about people in poverty.

The community lunch serves approximately 30 people a day, sometimes more depending on if people bring their children. The meals are cooked in large batches and served in large aluminum pans. The meals would change every Wednesday, with solid meat, starch, and vegetable offering—and always delicious. The pantry itself can accommodate 28 families—more if the families are smaller. It was typical to have a pantry almost emptied after each Wednesday pantry visit. However, during the Shutdown of 2019, the cupboards were often left bare. The community lunch/pantry mostly feeds people from the surrounding neighborhood, but many attendees also rode the bus to attend the lunch, lecture, and pantry (see figure 1.1).

Figure 1.1 Food Pantry at Gathering Place.

How This Adventure Began

Ava, the administrative assistant for the church, was one of the first people I interviewed. Ava was a middle-aged white woman, married to a tall, skinny Black man named Fred. She was the mother of three children. I had been a member of the church where Feed the Need operates from the basement each Wednesday. Ava encouraged me to speak to Pastor Patricia about recruiting participants. Pastor Patricia worked as the day pastor and coordinated the day-to-day activities of the community lunch. When I was being introduced to her, she was in the process of ending her call at Feed the Need, the community lunch that is served every Wednesday, and was preparing to train the new pantry director, Pastor Donte. Pastor Patricia was a sweet, middle-aged white woman with short sandy blonde hair who understood some of the barriers and issues experienced by the pantry patrons. She understandably was cautious in allowing me to speak at the pantry, but after I spoke with her about the project, she let me come into the lunch and gave me about 5 minutes for a short presentation and the recipients would be the ones who would secure my continued return each week. While I waited to do my 5-minute announcement in front of the nine tables in the basement of Gathering People's, we talked about how many of the patrons were (understandably) wary of outsiders, and in particular representatives from the university. We discussed the importance of visibility and how repeated attempts to discuss my purpose for being at the pantry could build rapport over time and how the respondents could potentially get used to my presence at the lunch and pantry. For the first month, I would simply come in, give my 5-minute speech about what I was doing and how they could be a part of it and leave my leaflets with my information. The patrons would ask me questions about social services and inquired whether I could help them get more services, access to additional benefits, or if I was there as a state representative.

At the beginning of the project, I was financially unable to offer incentives. However, by the start of the school year, I was able to afford gift cards to the local grocery store where the respondents could buy whatever they wanted— this often included items prohibited by their food assistance or items that they considered "luxuries or guilty pleasures" that they normally would not or could not purchase at the store with their benefits. After being able to offer these incentives, my participation rates increased dramatically, and people offered more information at their leisure than before when I could not offer them the gift card.

Pastor Patricia was beloved by the pantry and lunch patrons. You could feel a warm and welcoming personality and presence. She has always greeted the patrons entering the pantry with a greeting or warm embrace. The volunteers enjoyed her hands-off approach to the pantry—as she let the volunteers organize and run the pantry by themselves. She saw the volunteers as experts and respected them as such. She was married and was the foster mother of a few multiracial children and discussed with me the troubles of child welfare services. In her mind, these services were disorganized and unhelpful and were oblivious to the needs and desires of the children that were in her care. At the time that I met her, she was in the process of fostering a child and negotiating with their birth parent and was growing frustrated at the process.

There are three pastors who spend their time at GPLC. The day pastor is different from the main pastor who gives the Sunday services and provides general oversight of the church. The duties of the day pastor include overseeing the weekly community gatherings, while the main pastor oversees preaching to the church on Sundays. Typically, at the weekly gatherings, the patrons first gather for a community lunch (where they can sign up for the pantry), then attend a Bible study, and then the patrons can use the pantry. While pantry patrons are not required to sit through Bible study, if they leave and miss their name being called, they are pushed to the end or if there are no more food items, they are unable to participate and get the full shopping experience. For patrons to gain access to the pantry, there's a CCTV camera and buzzer by the back door that functions as an alert for people coming into the pantry. After the community lunch, the patrons distribute well-worn Bibles which are kept on the shelf nearby to the other patrons. The Bible study usually centers on some level of community, sharing, removing negative thoughts or ill will toward others, or overcoming the issues experienced in poverty.

Pastor Patricia and the incoming Pastor Donte oversee the orders from HTF, an organization discussed in the introduction, that functions to help supply people and organizations with food. Every month, from the wish list created by the pantry, she would go on to the HTF website and order the items. Often, the wish list items are not available, so substitutions are made, and even then, you might not get exactly what you order. In some sense, the pictures and items acted as stand-ins for similar items. For example, one time, Pastor Patricia ordered soft drinks for the pantry and the selection on the website was 12-ounce bottles, which hypothetically could be given away on the pantry table (which will be explained momentarily), but what came were larger bottles of soda, which were not enough for the individual patrons but enough for the community lunch.

While there was a general collegial relationship between volunteers and Pastor Patricia, the same could not be said of Pastor Donte. Pastor Donte is a six-feet-tall Black man from the Milwaukee area, who often wore collared shirts and jeans with patterned dress shoes, he always looked, put together, with a groomed beard and mustache. Aside from his attire, he also had a different perspective on his Bible study presentation. While often being unable to capture the attention of the patrons, he would sometimes pull out a portable microphone to amplify his sermons over the rolling and impatient noise of the pantry patrons. There are some volunteers who have health issues, lift restrictions, and so on, and he often admonished some of the other volunteers for not helping, regardless of if they may have duties in the kitchen or actual pantry. In one instance, the food delivery for the pantry was late and Pastor Donte felt as though the volunteers were not "working hard enough" even though the work at the pantry for most is unpaid. That said, when Pastor Donte would get "hyped up" as many of the volunteers referred to his actions, however, never talked back but would roll their eyes, and say things like, "he's doin' it again," and so on. For example, one day during the summer, Pastor Donte thought the volunteers lacked speed and weren't working hard enough. Tensions rose, with Harold saying, "I don't get paid for this, so I could just leave" and with the volunteers echoing similar statements, but no one ever raised the issue directly with Pastor Donte.

While the change of pastors was routine, many of the pantry volunteers were less welcoming to Pastor Donte. Upon his arrival, he required all pantry volunteers (except for me) to sign a pantry volunteer agreement: which stipulated how volunteers were to use the pantry and if they failed to abide by these policies, they would be removed from their duties. I found it curious that I was never provided this sheet nor had to view it or sign it. When I asked for a copy, I never received it. That said, many of the volunteers refused to sign it because they felt it was restrictive and too punitive for volunteer work. More deeply, many of the recipients thought about the pantry not as volunteer time or work, but as a moment to commune and eat with others and spread the good news. In some ways, the pantry began to model some of the red tape that the volunteers experienced with the various social service offices.

The Pantry Layout

While some may feel the following details are unimportant, visualizing the pantry might be helpful to understand the layout. There are two parts to the pantry: the actual pantry, which is approximately 20′ × 10′, and which includes two walls of cabinets, a desk, and a freezer where the pantry meat is stored and distributed, and a large open space with eight round tables where diners sit. Along the wall were the table items and bread shelves. The pantry is in the basement of the church and looks very much like a schoolroom with light blue walls and the drab beige cinderblock color. The back wall had a children's reading area that led out to some stairs that would take you to the sanctuary after you pass the washrooms. On the opposite side of the room was a small stage with an extra moveable pulpit and sacrament table both pushed up against the wall. This small stage is also where the delivery boxes are broken down and taken to recycling. There is a small delivery door up a small set of narrow stairs where the deliveries and donations are made. Circular folding tables and stackable chairs are placed in the middle of the room and two rectangular tables line the south wall, along with a large shelving unit that holds the bread items. Perpendicular to those tables and shelves are the food line tables that consist of one long rectangular table and one round table that usually holds the desserts. On the other side of these tables are another set of old and creaky stairs that lead to the exit and upstairs and sanctuary.

Connected to the pantry are the storage room and a larger kitchen, which has a typical industrial kitchen look and feel. There are two stainless steel refrigerators, two sinks with one being directly connected to the dishwasher, four ovens, and a large eight-burner stovetop. To the right and left of the refrigerator, there are large shelving units and an island with metal countertops in the middle.

Families and patrons can only use the pantry once a month. The pantry itself is stocked in two ways: via HTF and personal donations. The volunteers of the pantry usually consist of approximately six people, including myself. The main volunteers besides myself were Harold, Wynette, and T oya. Idgie and Leticia were main volunteers until there was a change led by Pastor Donte. However, sometimes there are volunteers who come and go each week so the number of people at the pantry varies each week. The people who purchase the items to stock the pantry are an older white couple and another white woman who comes in every so often with items that are necessary for the pantry—rice, beans, boxed potatoes, canned goods, and so on. The delivery usually comes with approximately 15–16 boxes of items from Aldi, an affordable food market.

The pantry itself has basic foods: tomato sauce/paste, mushrooms, rice, mashed potatoes, pasta and pasta sauce, Mac n' cheese, cereal, pancakes/syrup, and sometimes there are granola bars. There's always luncheon meat (generic spam), tuna, canned ravioli, chili, and soup. Then there are the beans and vegetable cabinet, peanut butter/jelly, and Jiffy muffin mix. The last area contains meat, sweets, and personal hygiene products. An older white couple, Tom and Mary, bring in all the items for the pantry. These items are often delivered right before the community lunch opens; therefore, there is often a little rush and a sense of organized chaos to put everything away and get everything out; however, somehow everything is done in time. Sometimes the deliveries included more than just food—like school supplies for the back-to-school rush and winter coats and boots in preparation for winter. These items are given out in a lottery system, with note cards given to patrons indicating they are to receive a coat.

Also, often the pantry volunteers try to give extras to people that are their friends or do extra work around the pantry. While I was volunteering, patrons discovered that if you help unload the car you might get in the good graces with the volunteers—like Idgie. For example, for a family of three, there are a certain number of items listed above allotted per family. While in the pantry, the shopping assistant is the only one who is "allowed" to touch the items, the shopper can only say or point to the item. Whatever items the shoppers grab first is what they must take. There are no exchanges or switches. Shoppers must make very quick snap decisions in a very short manner. The usual time it takes shoppers from the entrance to exit is approximately 5–7 minutes. Whenever I was in the pantry, I tried to make the experience feel as real to a solo shopping experience as possible, sometimes allowing the patrons to touch the food and allow them time to avoid making rash decisions on what went in their bags.

Shoppers are also never sure about what is available in the pantry. Meat varied from hot ham, chicken feet, ground beef, ribs, various sausages, and more. While people ate in the community area, the freezer in the actual pantry was loaded with prepackaged goods to be distributed. Often the food would be from the local grocery stores that would be deemed unsellable. For example, if a frozen product is pulled from a shelf at the store but not purchased, that item cannot go back into the freezer. The pantry was also stocked with frozen but expired meats that were distributed to the patrons. In some sense, the pantry freezer almost worked like the basket from the show *Chopped*. The pantry patrons never knew what they would find and would have to think of recipes that they might be able to make with the allotted items on the table. The pantry functions as an assembly line of sorts, and there is one assistant per shopper, with three assistants in total, plus the assistant that checks identification and addresses. As one shopper exits, another entered the room.

Pantry Rules, Regulations, and Perceptions of the Pantry Patrons

When I first started volunteering at the pantry, Leticia—Idgie's daughter— oversaw signing up people coming in, checking if the patrons already visited the pantry that month, and organizing the received materials that day but because this was not always enforced, the patrons would not remember to bring their documents every time. Leticia was a Black woman of average height, who had a gruff but sweet exterior. She is a strong woman, who is usually seen as angry by the dominant culture, and she often said that she used to volunteering at the pantry to build empathy because she said she struggled with patience. Just like there are rules and regulations for public assistance, the pantry operates in a similar punitive manner. As such, it operates in a very particular and deliberate manner with a system and structure, which mimics the state operation. Each person that comes in to sign up for the pantry sees Leticia, who checks their identification (ID and piece of mail that corroborates the ID address), and then their information is recorded on the sheet. While the community lunch is being served, she checks the list with previous Wednesdays in the month to make sure no person goes twice in one month. If someone, as she says, "forgets" and signs up twice, they are only able to pull from the table, but for those who can use the pantry, they can take from the table and pantry.

The table setup and pantry meat section create a bit of competition and are usually vigilantly policed. Outside the pantry, there are the two tables "free for all items." People often come in and scoop out the food available on the table. However, the table selections function as follows. No one is allowed to take from the table until after Bible study and only when announced. The patrons line up, and during the first pass-through, the patrons can only take one item from each table but can take unlimited amounts of bread items. The second pass-through allows for the patrons to take as many items as they would like. The table items usually include basic staples, a combination of fresh items, and almost-expired items. Sometimes the pantry will place items they cannot use on the tables as well. There was only one time during my volunteering where meat was placed on these tables, and that created an extra amount of chaos between some of the patrons. Other than that anomaly with the meat selections, depending on what was available, there is a bit more action surrounding the table, as Leticia would phrase it, "people tryna be slick" and grab the "good items" before the table opens. During my stay, I've only seen a few limited arguments over the tables and people standing too close to it, which usually results in someone yelling, "step away from the table," in some fashion. The pantry volunteers never tried to collect these items and bag them up because they wanted the patrons to be able to freely take what they wanted versus simply being given things that perhaps they did not want.

While the point of Feed the Need is to feed the hungry, I also found that there was some variation in how the volunteers spoke about the pantry patrons. Most of the people who attend the pantry are of the same class status—poor and working class. When thinking about needs, having access to food, and being fed, an outsider might look at how the pantry patrons operate as "I'm going to get mine," and in some sense, that is true, but not for the common reason most people perceive. It is the sense of control that people get to pick what they want and have access to "good" food. People clamor to be first on the list so that they can have access to what they perceive is better food, meat, and so on. Pastor Donte pulls out the meat to be distributed from the refrigerator, and it all depends on what he picks first. For example, one day at the pantry, we were quite low on items because after a holiday we received less food, a man stated, "no worries, I came late" but he still fared well because he was able to take a large package of chicken drumsticks. That said, if the patrons do not express an appropriate level of gratitude, the patron is rebuked as "pushy," "ungrateful," or that they "take, take, take." This is not unlike the perceptions held by members of society writ large. However, the volunteers themselves often take more than necessary at the pantry but this is often described as "I'm a volunteer," so they rationalize this food as payment for their time at the pantry. While the pantry patrons and volunteers often say that others are "taking," race is not what the volunteers comment on because the collective is by and large identifying in the same way (many of the patrons presented as Black or African American), but what they *do* comment on is their demeanor. Thinking about this more deeply, this might at some level *be* coded language that runs rampant in white racist/classist discourse, in terms of how poor Black and people of color "take" from the system. If we look at the way race is not explicitly mentioned, but some coded wording takes its place, there might be an implicit bias that runs through the discourse of the pantry in terms of social norms, class status, and race.

Idgie helped grow the Feed the Need community lunch and was the cook for the past 26 years. Idgie was the lifeline of the Feed the Need pantry. After moving with her family from the south, she found GPLC church. Originally, she attended other churches in the Milwaukee area, but fell in love with the church that became GPLC. She has the kindest heart and simply desires to make food for people. She started the community lunch with her friend Caroline, and she has been able to maintain the kitchen on donations and the food from HTF. I encountered Idgie first when I started coming in to do my short demonstrations.

During my time volunteering, I likened her to the hype woman before a show. She would often emerge from the kitchen, and with her positive, boisterous voice would ask the patrons how they were feeling that day. She always talked about being neighborly, bringing food, checking up on friends, family, and neighbors. She also would ask if anyone would like to bless the food or if there were any prayers to lift up for people in need. Shortly after, Idgie asked me if I wanted to eat, before that I had never stayed particularly long because I felt that at this moment, I didn't want to necessarily intrude, but I did want people getting used to my face and presence.

One day, she asked if I would stay and help serve the food. Understanding how white people can often occupy space, I wanted to be aware of the space that I was taking up. I wanted to make sure that I was invited into the pantry/community lunch versus just assuming that I could be helpful. Idgie showed me where the supplies were and I grabbed an apron, set of gloves, and hairnet. While I wish I could say I was a stellar volunteer my first day, that would be a gross mischaracterization. My first day helping at the pantry, I was pretty terrible; I worked on the line with Harold, Wynette, and Toya and I didn't necessarily know how much food to give people nor was I particularly fast. However, like anything else, volunteering necessitated a learning curve. I kept returning each Wednesday and over time was given more and more responsibility. Gradually, I got better at the line and was tasked with other directions.

My duties at the pantry increased significantly, mainly because it is very hard to turn down the way Idgie asks questions—that is, "Can I count on you to help out at the Thanksgiving Dinner on Sunday?" It is very hard to tell someone that no, they cannot count on you. My sense of duty toward the pantry was always on my mind. Because gaining access to this community was so important to my work, I worried that if I had another engagement or travel plans, that I would not be seen as being helpful. Understanding the perceptions of how the previous students, in particular white women, doing work in the area carried out their work and how they left without giving proper credit was something I wanted to avoid, given my identity as a white woman researcher in a predominately Black space.

Change of Staff

Much of the disagreement with Pastor Donte and the volunteer staff occurred with the more veteran members and most often with Idgie, the founder, lifeline, and spirit of Feed the Need. However, there was some change up in the pantry regarding staff and volunteers. Earlier in the summer, I interviewed the caretaker of the community garden and one of the day pastors at GPLC, Karen, about the work that she does there and how the garden helps the community. She discussed that sometimes people might "steal" from the garden, but that is okay because it just might mean that they need the food but are not particularly sure who to ask for assistance. The garden itself, which is just the size of a city lot, can produce over 800 pounds minimum of produce. There are beds for cabbage, corn, root vegetables, and so on, and the garden upkeep relies on the help and good stewardship of volunteers. At three areas within the garden, there are receptacles for water which help make the garden a zero-waste. During the interview, Karen spoke to me with care and compassion—especially at how the garden provided for community members in need. At this point, I could not detect a sense of anger or frustration about how passersby or community members might take what they need, only that she kept repeating that the purpose of this garden is for people in need.

However, this same compassion was not extended to Idgie and her family. Idgie was never one to explicitly talk about race; however, one day she pulled me aside and asked about some suspicious interactions she had noticed with the white women that worked at the church. She said that while she had been working at the pantry for about 27 years as the cook, she still lacked access to keys to the church and kitchen refrigerator. She asked me if that sounded shady, and then noted that she felt like she was not given these items because she was a Black woman and people did not trust her. She counted all the white women who had access to keys and noted that Pastor Donte, who is a lighter-skinned Black man, had access to the keys as well. I could tell during this conversation that she was rather hurt. She expressed that Feed the Need was her life, she enjoyed cooking for the people that came to eat, and she always remarked about the reputation that she had to uphold in the community. People who attended the pantry and meal, by and large respected her. However, one day at the pantry, she was asked to come upstairs, and she was fired for allegedly stealing from the pantry. I found that there was a bit of dissonance with this particular response. In a prior interview, the manager of the community garden discussed "stealing" quite differently. Denise noted that if someone was going to take from the community garden, it must mean that they need it; therefore, it does not seem right to call it stealing.

In very real ways, the pantry treated Idgie with the same irrelevance that most people treat people experiencing poverty. Without evidence, they simply cast her aside for "stealing" from a pantry, instead of reaching to her and asking her if she was okay—or what could they do to help her. Her situation was invalidated to bring in this new cook, Jenny—who was friends with a variety of individuals at the pantry. In many ways, the pantry annihilated her experience—instead of reaching out, they cast her aside and failed to care for her well-being, while being a place of love and fellowship.

Leticia, who was formerly in charge of the pantry, would let people who worked at the pantry shop before everyone else could come in. This often resulted in Harold and Wynette receiving more than the typical food allotment. Leticia expressed frustration with Harold and Wynette because of how they did many of the same activities that Idgie was accused of doing. After the split between the volunteers, Leticia was angry at the whole situation and asked me to be her eyes and ears at the pantry. As an observer, it is a bit of a weird position to be in, seeing as though I'm supposed to be objective and just record data. To maintain my qualitative and researcher integrity, I chose not to report because everyone was conspicuously quiet about it around me, probably given my close relationship that developed over time with Idgie and Leticia. A few months later, Jenny commented to Harold, when he clearly had an overallotment of items in a box, that maybe Pastor Donte was watching him too.

An outside viewer might view this as "take, take, take," however, many of the volunteers dedicated their time to the pantry and felt that with the extra work they do, they were able to extend their allotted benefit amount for each month. Also, there were moments when new items would come to the pantry that may be a one-time donation, so they approached it as a moment of opportunity. For example, an online comedian wore a suit that had one-dollar bills pinned to it, with a sign that said, take what you need. He videoed the social experiment and it showed people with access to money, seemingly well-dressed, walking down the same NYC street and taking the money off the man. When the person took the money, he would ask what they were using it for, asking if the money was for wants—nail appointments, extra cash, and so on—and not needs: food, shelter, and so on. He approached a homeless man, who only took a small amount off the man's suit, and said he was going to use it for lunch. Therefore, we often fault the poor or people in poverty with being the sole "takers," but the spectrum exists here as well. Rich people "take" as much if not more, but because their perception is different, their loopholes are seen as positive, thus illustrating that the proximity to power allows some behaviors to be hidden, while homeless and poor people are left holding the blame for trying to scrape by each month.

The Main Volunteers

Volunteers at the pantry often ebbed and flowed, but the following individuals remained consistent in their return to the pantry each Wednesday. They all expressed that the pantry offered them something that they were missing in some place in their lives and the community and fellowship felt here in that space were important to them. While sometimes they would reference the pantry as "work," they never saw it as a job that they would necessarily ever ask to be paid for because they all saw it in connection to service in the eyes of the church.

Jenny

While the relationship between Idgie and Pastor Donte began to sour, Jenny, a young Black woman in her early 40s with three teenagers started volunteering at the pantry. She had long hair, lashes, and a small stud nose ring; she had a few tattoos on her arms and worked in health care at a hospice clinic with patients diagnosed with failing mental health issues and Alzheimer's in a far suburb of Pewaukee—at least 30 minutes away in good Wisconsin traffic. She often struggled with the long commute between her home on 39th and Burleigh, one of the rougher Northside neighborhoods. That trip would be easy if one had access to a vehicle, but the city of Milwaukee lacks a transportation system that could transport people out to the suburbs, and cars are especially needed once you leave the metro area of Milwaukee. Recall that at one point, Milwaukee did have rail transit to the suburbs but as the demographics changed, so did that access to the outlying whiter suburbs.

Instead of alleviating this headache, Governor Walker turned down high-speed rail transportation funding from the Obama administration and instead spent it on controversial road projects (Harding 2004; Mulvany 2014). Wisconsin, unlike its southern neighbor, Illinois, does not have a regional train line like the Metra to carry people from metro Milwaukee to the outer suburban areas, and vice versa. Because her gross income puts her over the maximum needed to qualify for benefits, she consistently uses Feed the Need to meet her food and nutrition needs because of her inability to find an affordable car or available public transportation. The notion of precarity emerges again because while Jenny does have a job and is gaining income, she is unable to meet her daily needs for her and her child. Jenny once detailed to me the weekly expenses just to transport herself to work, which in each week could be between $80 and $360 because, at the time, she lacked a personal vehicle and took ride-sharing services—like Uber and Lyft.

After Idgie was fired from the pantry, her schedule afforded Jenny to become the new cook and pantry manager. While Jenny was a great person and cook, her meals were not always as thought out as Idgie. One might argue you could taste the love in a meal cooked by Idgie. This doesn't cast any indifference to Jenny, as she was a wonderful cook, but the meals were not as thought out as before. Perhaps the difference in the cooking could be explained by age. Idgie was much older than Jenny and retired, so time constraints were not the same as they were for Jenny. Jenny worked a few jobs in food service, which might explain the desire to get the food out quickly to the pantry patrons. For Idgie, there was a sense of giving people a home-cooked meal, because this could be their first and only meal of the day. She would arrive at the pantry at 8:00 a.m. to begin cooking that day's meal. For Jenny, many of the meals lacked that sense of care; they were often simple, easy to cook things that did not require the same time commitment.

Jenny, someone who was poverty adjacent by herself, would sometimes fall into this trap of blaming people—and often they were the Black patrons at the pantry—lending to some implicit bias or internalized racist discourse, wherein she harbored some white mainstream ideals about how specifically Black people use and apply for benefits—most often that they misuse them or are lazy. She would almost always comment on how the pantry might be below or at capacity that day, depending on the days when benefit checks were cut. At the same time, Jenny and I routinely chatted about how she found the SNAP application ridiculous and purposefully difficult.

Harold

The other volunteers were also church members as well as pantry patrons. Harold, a Black man in his late fifties, does much of the heavy lifting at the pantry, taking out the heavy pans from the oven and maintenance tasks around the church. Many considered Harold the flirt of the pantry. Harold and Wynette both live in the same low-income housing units on the East Side of Milwaukee, near one of the University of Milwaukee dorms. They were best friends and often relied on each other for mutual support and were coworkers at the church. He is one of the more direct or matter-of-fact volunteers, and often engages in some mild bantering with the patrons. He also enjoys getting through the line quickly and efficiently. Often, his job is managing the meats or hot foods and he usually takes on the organizing or facilitating the lunch line. While Harold would talk to me, he took some time to really feel comfortable in telling me personal information about himself. It was not until at least six months into my volunteer gig that he started telling people in the line about my study, usually with the lead-in that I was giving out $10 gift cards to the local grocery store. It was finally at that moment that I had built up enough rapport with the staff, volunteers, and patrons that I no longer had to leave my information on each of the tables.

Wynette

Wynette, a Black woman in her late forties, was the last woman to really come around and warm me up, like Harold, which was understandable. Since many students from surrounding universities used Harambee and similar areas as their field studies, there is a history of just going in, taking information, and quickly exiting. Often, many of the pantry volunteers, like Wynette and Harold, would ask me when I was leaving, and I would tell them, whenever I was hired by another school. Only after my continued appearances at the pantry, and willingness to help with different activities, did Wynette express any interest in talking with me. Trust was built with Wynette over time, as she was a strong Black woman, who was quite guarded with how she extended welcomes. I was working at the pantry for almost three months before Wynette invited me over to her home for a cookout.

Like many of the other patrons that I interviewed, her family also migrated from the south, but all her eight children live in the Midwest area. Most of them have working-class, blue-collar jobs. As a divorced woman, she expressed little interest to marry again, but was open to dating. She had escaped several abusive relationships, which led to her marriage aversion. She, like many of the other patrons and volunteers, found GPLC because of its welcoming atmosphere and attachment to the community. One day, as I was taking Wynette to see Toya, another volunteer who recently had knee surgery, she confided in me that one of her children was in jail, but she had not seen him in some years. After being interviewed by police, all his friends who committed the low-level crime all took plea deals, but stuck DJ with the crime and he was incarcerated for 18 months. However, while I was volunteering, he was in the process of being released and I was invited to his homecoming party, which I thought was special. Many of the items for the party were from the pantry, snuck out under the nose of Pastor Donte.

The Regulars

The pantry and community lunch serve at least 10–12 regulars that come in weekly. Alfie, an older Black man in his early 50s, is the resident grump who often causes the volunteers additional headaches, and many describe him as having an "attitude." He is a usual source of patron discontent because of his attitude and his frequent tries to cut the line to get on the pantry list first. Typically, the patrons that sign up first have the best selection of items in the pantry. Therefore, some patrons are very particular about pantry order call and are vigilant about who is in line, where and when they signed up, and if the order becomes jumbled. However, no one is particularly angry, nor does anyone harbor any real feelings of anger or ill will, but they do express notions of annoyance or feelings of unfairness.

While most of the volunteers tolerated Alfie, the curmudgeon, they had less love for Wilhemina, a Black woman, who lived in the neighborhood who usually came at the end of the month when benefits were running low. There is probably no actual way to detail the character of Wilhemina that does her justice. She often came in, smelling of some type of liquor and cigarettes, wig askew, and pants almost falling. For the outside observer, she probably was the perfect poster woman for what a welfare recipient would look like, however, that would be inaccurate. She and Alfie had many of the same characteristics that annoyed fellow patrons, but Alfie never received the same level of scrutiny (which is a gendered lens); they also operated under different social conventions. Alfie was a contentious figure, but he was not rude to people, never called people by names, and usually addressed people with respect. He sometimes tried to cut in line but when he was called out, he'd go back to where he needed to be. When he was reprimanded, he'd follow it with "sorry, Miss Leticia or Idgie" and all would be forgiven.

Wilhemina, on the other hand, often came into the pantry with a beer can in hand (which was not allowed), swore at people, and often tried to take more than what she was allotted. Often, she lacked access to a vehicle but would demand help from people. As I look back at my interactions with Wilhemina, perhaps what people missed is she was, as a woman, probably faced many barriers and never felt heard. I always tried to give her extra food, in hopes that whatever liquid she had consumed previously would be counteracted and because it was important for her to eat. Many of the volunteers and patrons ignored her antics, but it showed another angle of people who live in poverty—access to services—specifically, health and mental health services. Wilhemina might not have acted out, used alcohol as a coping mechanism had she had access to proper services. Self-care should not be a luxury, but often it is in American life.

Jane, Idgie's sister, often came in early and helped by double bagging the plastic bags that are used in the pantry. Like many of the volunteers, she also was slow to be interviewed by me, but over time started asking me questions about what I was doing, what I was doing it for, and how was I going to write about them. She, like many of the respondents, recalled the travels that her family made to finally stop in Milwaukee. Annette is an older Black woman in her late 50s, who often is early to the pantry. Before the pantry opened, if you were friends with or a relative to someone who volunteered, some regulars who are "nice" got extra food or first pick before people came in for lunch. I would sit at different tables each week and one day when I asked to sit at one, the gentleman that was there started asking me about what I was doing, where I went to school, where I was from, basic small talk.

Martel was a tall, well-statured Black man, who talked about getting a job. He was on his way after the pantry to go talk with a social worker who was specialized in job placements. He said he just needed to do a drug test, which would be no problem, but he expressed significant worry because the house he was staying in had residents that frequently smoked marijuana. He told me, "I don't smoke, but they do." He then continued, "do you think just breathing in the house will come up?" I told him no, it doesn't really work that way. This interaction really demonstrated something I felt was kind of special. Number one, he was being made to get a drug test, and number two, I was this white woman college student whom he had never met being asked how weed works. He also went on to say that he was trying to get out of his living situation, so getting this job was extremely important. There have been a lot of housing developments in the city of Milwaukee, the typical city "affordable housing" that gets peddled to people, usually with restrictions in small writing, and at the time, many of these were being built to "revitalize" a strip of Water Street, which is the main thoroughfare to get to the East Side of Milwaukee. These buildings are the usual modern loft styles with bourgeois writing on the side, no more than five to six stories tall. He said to me, "it would be nice to live in one of those nice apartments, even for just one month." It was this notion or feeling that those apartments were still somehow out of his reach; he also knew or maybe thought that those apartments were not meant for him. In his own city, he could still feel the weight of division, even invisible ones—like home attainment. He hadn't been to the pantry for a few months, but one day, he was in the lunch line. He got the job and was finally able to move out of his living situation, but still not living in an apartment on Water Street.

Gender at the Pantry

While the different interactions in the pantry between Alfie and Wilhelmina highlighted the difference, gender, femininity, and masculinity all played a role in how people are often seen as caregivers, breadwinners, or not. At the pantry, there were very traditional identifications of gender. To explain more thoroughly, the men did what could be considered the dirty work—like taking out the garbage or the heavy lifting of unloading the deliveries. The women oversaw the cooking, cleaning, general care work. The women would often help unload the deliveries but were given the lighter boxes, and they never took out the garbage nor were asked to do so. In addition to those mentioned, these traditional roles were seen in the labor divisions within the pantry. While Martel soon found a job and stopped coming to the pantry, he was not the only person who identified as a man and used the pantry. Sometimes, when I would help in the shopping area of the pantry, I would have short discussions with each of the people that entered through the door. Since the pantry room had gendered jobs, women usually did the signing of people in, checking their address, and acting as shopping assistants. Meanwhile, Harold and David would complete heavy lifting tasks, like breaking down the boxes, mopping the floor, and taking out the trash.

Rodney, who towered over many of the patrons in the pantry at over 6 feet tall, was an older Latino man, with a sweet voice who I saw at least once a month at the pantry. He was one of the few men who applied for food assistance and was adamant about how he could provide for his family. Poverty research focuses on how women are the typical recipients of assistance and receive help through the WIC program, or Women, Infants and Children program, therefore biasing caregiving as a feminine or womanly attribute. Rodney, however, had children but did not identify as a woman but was adamant about using his benefits and getting what he needed. To be discussed at length in another chapter, some men would give their benefit cards to a woman they knew to spend their benefits for them or shop without understanding or thinking about their budgets. Rodney expressed that for him, "it wasn't even about that" and that "[he's] going to do whatever it takes to feed my family." For Rodney, it did not matter how he was able to provide, so long as whoever stepped in this home would have a warm meal to eat.

In terms of gender binaries, the people who attended the pantry were cisgender, heterosexual presenting individuals. During one encounter, Alfie, the resident grump mentioned above, discussed with me that anything not heterosexual was a sin against the church and God. Knowing this, I always viewed the pantry as a place that was strictly gendered and explicitly heterosexual. Even trying to reason with Alfie, based on my commitment to marginalized communities, was not enough to convince him of his own biases against others. Alfie also had some of the most implicit bias against other Black people and their "overuse" and "greedy" attitude toward food stamps. Alfie, however, was his own hypocrite. On many occasions, he would be caught trying to jump the line to get food or the pantry first and chided the volunteer that exposed his movements.

When they would enter the pantry or food line, I asked them how they were and followed it with "sir" or "miss." One distinct encounter involved a frequent pantry patron who had too many plates from the line and had no extra hands for his drink cup. I told him, "don't worry, I got you, sir," and helped him with his drink to his seat. Gender and heterosexual relationships, meaning traditional binaries inside and outside the pantry, were vigilantly enforced. Once in the while, there would be personal hygiene products available for the patrons. Often, they were not full-sized but travel-sized and did not last very long. Previously, these products were available to anyone who needed them, unless they were products considered gendered, like "feminine hygiene products." However, after his arrival, Pastor Donte thought it would be better to split up the items between men and women. While the church writ large is welcoming to people, the idea of gender or sexuality outside the binary is not seen as something tenable, and common social constructions of these two categories are reinforced through these binaries in different ways, that is, women and children eat first, men second, men get more food per plate.

When I called him sir, his face softened and he gave me a sweet smile, "That's real nice of you" and when I got to his table, he continued to extend phrases of gratitude—which often is midwestern to a fault. And while it is just common courtesy to be helpful, it probably also matters to be addressed in a way that might indicate dignity, given the response from them to me each time I either addressed them as Mr., Mrs., Miss, or Sir. It seemed important for me to address them in this way, given that I was usually the youngest person in the pantry and as a white woman.

While most of these moments happened inside the pantry, only once was an LGBT matter discussed outside the pantry. Once while attending a party at Mikayla's, her daughter Aubrey and her brother Ben were discussing some-one who was thought to be gay—in a variety of unkind names but refrained from using slurs. Aubrey turned to me and asked, "what do you think Steph?" Placed in a situation where saying something might lose me my participants but knowing that I was uncomfortable with the dialogue but knowing that the people I was around attended church quite frequently, I went with the classic, "Everyone is made in the image of God and I think that's beautiful." It seems pertinent here to discuss cross-marginalization in terms of long-standing historical oppression of Black people and the connected histories of LGBTQ oppression and how those often intersect. Recently, the General Social Survey (GSS) found that Black women are more likely than before to be identified as bisexual.[1] However, sexualities, race, and class can and do intersect in complex ways.

Whiteness at the Pantry

As I volunteered and became a fixture inside and outside the pantry, my whiteness and being a woman were always visible. Often, because I am the only white person in the pantry or space, there have been times where my whiteness was present in interesting ways. For example, early in my volunteering, when I first started taking on more duties at the pantry, I began doing the dishwashing and Harold was going to teach me how to use the dishwasher, because it was one of those large industrial machines. However, previous grunt work at a local restaurant, when I was an under-graduate, taught me all I needed to know about these machines, so I knew how the levers and trays worked. He responded with some surprise because he said I was white, so why did I need to work? This, therefore, brings up some interesting notes about perceptions; it's not that "unbelievable" that I might have access to money, due to long-standing wealth disparities that exist in the United States between white and Black families. However, when my whiteness equals wealth, it shows how powerful these messages are for day-to-day existences. Sometimes when Harold would ask me to borrow cash and I would not have any available, he responded with shock that I too lived paycheck to paycheck. This highlights something important about how we see poverty and its connection to whiteness, and it is that we *don't* see it.

When poor people of color are the focus, often we forget how economies impact people across the spectrum. If white people experiencing hardship never see anyone that is in their same position, we then edge closer to being able to maintain racialized perceptions about poor people of color, while maintaining harmful dialogues about ourselves. Therefore, the absence of white people in poverty cements this idea that poverty is not something that is experienced by white people and that if it does, it is their own fault and not how systems and structures are maintained. The difference is white people and families have systems and structures that function in ways to help them hide these issues due to potential access to privileges, "benefits" of racism, and so on. White people do not experience the same level of scrutiny in applications for personal or housing loans, with the police or when out in public anywhere, in anyway like how Black and brown people experience it when they are living their lives. That is, poor white people get class privilege despite poverty.

Interlacing Race and Gender in the Kitchen

In connection to my whiteness, I also identify as a woman and the perceptions of what I *can do* are based on this idea of my strength as a woman. For example, patriarchy in terms of lifting things or what is considered "women's/ men's work" is clear. I might be clear to do work in the kitchen, but Harold has never asked me to take out the garbage, even when I asked. Later in my time at the pantry, when I had a couple more days of experience, I began to have a system in place for expediting and streamlining this part of the pantry. At first, Harold would work with me in the kitchen, cleaning dishes, pans, and scrubbing what often is stuck on food from the oven.

However, if Harold was busy, I worked alone in the kitchen, and it offered time to "zone out" and I could think about my dissertation, the project, or more often, trying to remember the happenings in the pantry that day. Other times, David would join me in the pantry, an infrequent pantry patron who comes in every month to shop the pantry, and he will be in the kitchen helping with the mopping and other works. David was a well-dressed, tall Black man in his early 40s, with a short, flat hairstyle (think Danny Glover in *Lethal Weapon*), and he always sang songs to me, with his favorite being from Twenty One Pilots. David was originally from Milwaukee, but like many people I interviewed, his parents and grandparents also experienced the Great Migration, or when Black families left the south for the industrial and manu-facturing jobs in the north. David would often reminisce about Milwaukee, when it was thriving, and had good jobs. In the 1980s, like what Wilson[2] describes, David noted the rapid deindustrialization. He had a great job, but eventually lost it to the company closing and has trouble finding steady and solid work that gave him the same pay rate as before. David also talked about the prospect of finding a job and how difficult that was for him, namely because he lacked a vehicle and Milwaukee County Public Transportation was not always reliable—mapping on to the lack of access with transportation to large grocery stores in the previous chapter.

What people often don't realize about issues of poverty is that many of us are closer than we believe. It was also clear throughout my time volunteer-ing at the pantry that some of the main rhetoric espoused by regular people was used against other recipients. It speaks to the strength of how rhetoric can seep down to even those who rely on assistance programs. It shows how powerful the ideas of those in power can be used against people in similar positions—meaning poor people against other poor people. In some ways, the participants engaged in the same annihilation that the general government did upon them. However, these ideas aren't so different from how people who are not receiving SNAP or cash assistance discuss people receiving assistance, which will be discussed at length in the next chapter.

Working at the pantry allowed the collection of data that one would not be able to get otherwise. Finding out ways where researchers can simultane-ously be insiders and outsiders and build rapport over time was important in this project. Ensuring that when doing research, your participants (not subjects) trust you is nothing short of necessary. During the entirety of the observation, I was able to detail and explore how the volunteers and the patrons saw themselves, others, and what they thought their reflections were from others. These experiences helped me understand and detail that pov-erty is not a single issue or person experience, but that we might share these issues more broadly. From participants simply wanting to feed themselves and their families to harboring implicit bias about recipients, this chapter explored life at a Milwaukee food pantry and how it helps people who might not have any other options. It also highlights how people navigate their experiences of poverty and demonstrates the general function of a food pantry.

While this chapter explored a facet of poverty, it feels important to discuss how people view those in poverty. Perhaps, the people chronicled above are not *so* different than us because we all desire to find ways to meet our needs of food, clothing, shelter, and human connection. The following chapter explores the public perceptions of welfare and benefit recipients through online media communications. In this next chapter, the opinions of average people are examined and explored because this is how inaccurate rhetoric about recipients is most easily conveyed.

NOTES

1. Oppenheim, "Young Black Women."
2. Wilson, *Truly Disadvantaged.*

Chapter 2

Benefits

How Public Perceptions Hurt Recipient Access

Communication and rhetoric about welfare recipients do not just drop down from thin air, but from a variety of mediums. Given that much of our communication is completed through digital measures, it seems important to discuss how welfare issues are discussed among the average person (who may not have access or the willingness or desire to find out legitimate information about recipients but receive talking points from politicians or pundits who hold similar opinions). If we understand how the average person discusses welfare (anonymously) we might have a better understanding of how to combat these issues.

In online communications, when behind the comfort of a screen, there is an impulse that is collectively known as a "keyboard warrior." These "warriors" often express ideas and thoughts they may not outwardly express without the comfort of an anonymous screen name; however, given the legitimation of this rhetoric by important political figures, many people are saying the quiet part very, very loud. Moreover, they often do the work of existing power structures to uphold anti-welfare, immigrant, racist, and misogynistic narratives. During a conversation, Harold, a Black man in his early 60s with a quick wit and warm personality, who worked as a volunteer at Feed the Need, often expressed exasperated frustration at how people talk about people receiving assistance. When I asked him how he thought people who perhaps lacked experience with poverty thought about poverty, he said, "I wish people understood I'm no different than anybody else. I need to eat, want to have a good time and want to live. I'm 60 years old and I work here at the church, and I just wish people didn't talk about us like that." This sentiment was often shared by recipients across the board, fueled by inaccurate reporting and the relative ease of opinion dissemination on these chat boards and Facebook/ Twitter threads. The ideas and opinions expressed by the people that frustrate

Harold are very similar to ones I encountered when having conversations I had in the past with family members and other more general community members. The following unpacks how people incorrectly configure welfare recipients who are often lost in the sea of misinformation.

The path I took to begin this work was a winding road that started with a content analysis of online comments that accompanied news articles on the internet. Participating in online forums may be a common experience for some readers. It's a place where people can create pseudonyms that are anonymous (save for the computer engineer/hacker that can find IP address information) and express a variety of opinions, sentiments, and inaccuracies. The online comment/forum area is also met with a level of demonstrable disdain. While compiling the data for this chapter, I found myself having an extra glass of wine just to deal with the complex emotions that emerged from the posts that I was reading. Even when I would describe the project to people, they would shudder to think of doing the same and asked how I thought this project would be helpful. The internet forum—like chat rooms and Facebook threads contain copious amounts of public opinion data—regardless of it being true or not, it is people expressing thoughts they hold true and believe in and are often spurred by pundits or politicians who may potentially also hold those beliefs. Engaging with online anonymous internet fodder is utterly connected to how individuals do or don't comprehend complex issues.

Thinking about the way information is disseminated, online chat forums, regardless of their accuracy, are instrumental in understanding how people understand, consume, and repeat information. In connection with transmitting (mis)information, there can also be emotions tied to their post—either fervently for or against whatever it is the main original post was about. However, people who post on these boards are not individually coming up with these inaccuracies on their own. There is a mutual relationship between how the average person understands and thinks about people in poverty and what information source they are viewing for that information or what the general newsprints about poverty measures. Sometimes, it depends on what news source a person thinks is "accurate" as well as how they understand the information being discussed in the article. Much of the information that trickles down from mainstream media can lack contextual information of how people operate within the confines of benefit recipients. Welfare recipients who are eviscerated in the media via crafted language reinforce negative notions and result in the annihilation of their perceptions and lives.[1] One might wonder why the use and focus of regular people are posters and not politicians. The purpose of this chapter is to show how easy it is for this rhetoric to trickle down, what people are saying here *is* the dominant narrative from politicians because the comments are attached to articles with politicians saying this same rhetoric.

The Redditor/Facebook responder helps do the work as it was regarding maintaining the perception of the welfare recipient—and thus highlights and erases them simultaneously—by equating all recipients as only one thing—a lazy, bad parent, non-working monolith living high on the public dime. Online news article comment boards create space for remarks ranging between responses of avoidance, conversations akin to a pseudo-Reddit forum, ableist comments about the perceived intelligence of others, and that people have too much time on their hands.[2] Online communication is no different than the ways people communicate in person, other than the obvious in-person manner, but even online banter still exists within a social structure. These linguistic structures of power organize how others are viewed within specific socialized frames, such as racialized, sexualized, and gendered perceptions represented in media outlets. Power and representation in all its media forms can be useful when thinking about the anonymous online internet comments. While there is literature about how language and power relations impact the real lives of welfare recipients, there is a lack of literature that does not address the ways online communication allows for racialized and racist statements to be made openly (though being anonymous) about welfare recipients. The following pages detail how language and power function to create meaning and representations and connect that to how anonymous commenters use established social meanings and language to annihilate the lives of welfare and benefit recipients through online comment boards.

In language there is the power to name and indicate ideas, create discourse and cultural markers. It is constructed by systems and structures in power, which rely on a large group of people to keep supporting those in power. Language can be a foundation for creating divisions between and among people, even those in the same social situation. If recipients are configured as one monolith, it creates the opportunity for society to view them in negative ways. Placing poor people at the center of the debate reduces the ability to fight against the language configured about them. Regardless of the statistics detail that the white folks are making up a larger share of total recipients, the symbolic representation of welfare recipients is often Black women. To maintain this idea, symbolic power structures create language and construct the lives of welfare recipients as not just racialized but also either explicitly present through that racialization or erased.[3]

SYMBOLIC VIOLENCE AND POWER

Bourdieu[4] argues that society creates a legitimate language and then subjugates all other languages as less important or unimportant. Bourdieu[5] finds that language creates a kind of wealth and maintains a dominating social structure. Language becomes a political process and creates political unity.[6] If you have access to this formalized, political language, the state and its inhabitants can use that to construct difference.[7] Negative language describes welfare beneficiaries, but we are all beneficiaries of the system: white people, the middle class, wealthy and corporations, and so on, all benefit/have benefited from some level of welfare or assistance. However, to ignore all that (specifically the corporate welfare part), media representations assign the brunt of the descriptors on a particular group—poor people, people of color more generally, and Black women more specifically. Language functions in a way that facilitates the continuation of dominant structures and habitus.

Bourdieu associates this term with symbolic violence. The important piece with the establishment of a "legitimate" language requires access to power, as well as determining who that language configures in society. For example, the development and continuation of the phrase "welfare queen" are specifically targeted at Black women.[8] This phrase illustrates the power of language and symbolic violence. Beginning in 1976 with Reagan and continuing 42 years later, when someone says or alludes to poor women, a particular racialized image appears due to repetition over time. Presently, the nonexistent welfare queen image dances in the minds of society, with low-key racism, racial resentment, coded language, and images that are contradictory to the actual benefit recipient. While Bourdieu develops the concept of symbolic violence using language, the theory leaves out the real ways in which communities can experience violence from current online representations.

Symbolic Annihilation

As alluded to above, using the theory of symbolic annihilation, or the presence or absence of race, class, gender, sexuality, and so on, might be a better way to connect the lives of benefit recipients depicted in the media.[9] While symbolic violence elevates or privileges the customs or cultural attributes of a dominating group over another marginalized group, symbolic annihilation describes how other groups are erased or highlighted in relation to a dominant force. If people see Black women as predominately struggling, poor, single mothers in the media, then the controlling image of the recipient will emerge, which is integral to symbolic annihilation.[10] Black women can play many roles in society, but are often symbolically annihilated when singularly portrayed as one-dimensional characters on television or movies. Tuchman[11] noted that women often play secondary or one-dimensional characters to men by the women being assistants, shown doing paperwork/filing or as romantic storylines. Women are absent from strong roles by their presence in those positions being annihilated or erased.

Annihilation and Media Representations

Symbolic annihilation is manufactured through commodities or artistic expression. A range of scholars argues that this simple attachment erases much of what it means to be Black, Asian, Indigenous, and so on. Considering how race and racialized understandings and social messages are intertwined with language and habitus, examining the connections between media outlets, social space, and language is important. Researchers examine how media facilitates the messaging of welfare beneficiaries and alters the way people communicate.[12] Here there might be a moment to connect theory to experience, as Bourdieu notes the relationship of symbolic power to social space, and one might argue that the internet and media communication is an extension of that social space. Language, power, and social space all convene to construct and maintain socialized norms and, for this article, poverty. One might argue that the original intent of the internet was for information exchange versus trolling anonymous people on comment boards, but here we find ourselves. While the internet does not shape messaging or social constructions, it funnels information to a larger group of people and puts it out in public.

Meyrowitz[13] uses McLuhan's[14] idea of technology acceleration and examines the change in communication over time. One might argue that *how* people are communicating about welfare recipients is different, but what they are *saying* about recipients is the same. Socialized constructions of language create hegemonic identifications of a mythical welfare recipient. This perhaps configures the way people communicate "anonymously" which impacts "who-communicates-what-through-it-for-what-purpose."[15]

Racialized Media Perceptions of Welfare Receipt

The preceding pages specifically mention symbolic annihilation; the following literature does not but allows for the appearance of symbolic annihilation materialized through how the commenters discuss welfare recipients. Since the outcomes of civil rights legislation *hypothetically* made forms of discrimination illegal, scholars found that white people felt that there were no barriers to advancement for people of color and that the civil rights movement only inflamed racial tensions.[16] Roberts[17] found welfare programs at one time were reserved for white women were now open to Black families, but their image was not deemed worthy (as it was for white women) and deemed undeserving. As the percentage of Black families increased in social worker caseloads, racialization of policies and feelings about Black families' dependency and lack of work ethic increased.[18] Work requirements were added to qualify for benefits, which was the opposite of the former eligibility requirements when designed for deserving widowed, white women.[19] All these qualifications were developed by Congressional administrations over time. It is also that these pieces of literature point to the fact that Congress—or the legislative branch of government has a history—present day included large percentages of white men, policing the bodies and lives of marginalized individuals, especially after the perception of welfare recipients changed from a white face to a Black face.

Other research compared attitudes of welfare recipients and middle-class people. Bullock[20] found the voices of the poor are often overlooked or silenced in a study assessing both working- and middle-class Americans' attitudes on poverty and welfare programs.[21] The findings concluded that of the 236 (112 middle class, 124 working class) interviewees, most held anti-Black feelings toward recipients and many recipients had negative feelings toward other recipients and the race was a factor in expressing those feelings.[22]

Scholars argue those being assisted by the welfare institution are defined by those in power in racialized terms and this racialization invisiblizes most white welfare recipients that receive assistance.[23] Therefore, a reversal of roles occurs now—Black families at once written out of the welfare recipient debate become the focus. One example of this change is through child welfare and families receiving assistance. In some cases, social workers were more likely to describe Black and African American women with more scrutiny, use terms such as hostile and aggressive, and assume they had substance abuse addictions without making the same assumptions about white parents in similar situations without giving any context for these notes in their client's case files or making similar notes about white parents.[24]

However, this information is not particularly new and is built upon old literature regarding welfare recipients and marginalized people profiled in the media.[25] Representations of Black, African American, and Latino in welfare recipient reform contributed to the maintenance of problematic stereotypes on marginalized groups versus white recipients.[26] Coinciding with popular discourse, there's a connection between news stories that create an ebb and flow between immigration and welfare reform, most of which increased post-2015.[27] There are conflicting narratives around the trope "a nation of immigrants" or how most describe the United States, by finding that media constructs images of acceptable and unacceptable immigrants which directly affects perceptions of social service access (Perry, 2016). Given the current political climate, the constructed immigrant stokes fears and can contribute to hostile attitudes.[28]

Symbolic annihilation, however, is a two-way street—because while Black and brown people are the focus—being seen only in one distinct way; white folks are never seen as recipients or if they are recipients, their participation is explained using some sort of excuse or classed slight (redneck, white trash, etc.). It is important to discuss the ways in which white people are often free from criticism while also benefiting demonstrably more from welfare benefit receipt. However, the next few pages highlight how language matters and is disseminated through and down to the public and keep very clear class and race lines drawn—especially when it comes to the issue of poverty and assistance.

In the pages that follow, the flow explains the relationship between symbolic annihilation and controlling images of marginalized people in poverty, through anonymous comments. By having this anonymous mode of communication, it may give permission to individuals to state racialized and gendered claims. Coded language, or language that lacks outwardly identifiable racial or gendered slurs, allows people to make problematic statements without feeling bad about them—since they are seen as socially accepted (i.e., "I'm not racist, but . . . ," etc.).[29] However, often coded language can be connected to how people can potentially hide their intentions but have direct connections to racial and social identifiers.[30] Perhaps, through this communication method, popular and repeated rhetoric about the ideas of recipients filters down through the class structure and ultimately affects the viewpoints and perceptions of those outside the wealthier classes. It is probably the only time where to trickle down anything "works."

This project required a high level of patience and focus, since many comments were written with problematic language and what is often referred to as "textspeak" (e.g., "BRB," "IMO," etc.). Concerns might arise via collecting data from online comments because of "trolling"; however, the comments resemble rhetoric promoted by anti-welfare and fiscal conservatives.[31] The internet gives the ability to hide one's personal identifiers and allows people to express their beliefs with little to no repercussions.[32] Therefore, based on this knowledge, the data collected can be interpreted as valid, even though the comments cannot be attributed to a screen name.

I used online newspapers that were relatively known for their viewpoints, had well-written articles, and were respected publications. To provide a complete picture of the data, the analysis also includes an "objective" news source, which was harder to find than expected. This search used a variety of search terms (welfare, poor, poverty, assistance) for each news source and the comment sections were examined. *Reuters*, *AP*, and *BBC* did not have articles with comments and their news articles did not fit my question. To eliminate some level of bias, articles were not chosen from *PBS* or any public broadcasting due to how others might feel about their viewpoint (which has been politicized over the last few years).

In the same vein, news sources viewed as very left- or very right-wing were excluded from the study due to the chance that finding the exact comments needed for the study would be too easy. While it is important to be through with the types of news sources that are available to the public, this study is less about the content of the articles themselves and more about how the people are responding to the individuals that are either profiled in the articles or about welfare/benefit assistance recipients more generally.

However, to determine a political skew of a news source, a study was completed by the University of Missouri School of Journalism regarding media trust on how newsrooms and their employees engage with the public regarding how they report the news (Chang, 2017; Meyer, 2017). In the current political moment, support of news sources often falls squarely on political allegiance, with most right-wing or conservative readers trusting *Fox News* and most left-wing or liberal readers trusting more mainstream news, such as the *New York Times*, etc.[33] Given the political climate, the possibility that right-wing focused newspapers may have more likelihood of overtly racist comments and the lack thereof might be present for news outlets that report in an overtly left-wing fashion, which often present news in a color-blind or covert manner. This does make one worse or better than the other.

Since in recent years the news media has come under intense scrutiny, understanding and evaluating trustworthy sources are incredibly important. Therefore, this study examined news articles from the *Chicago Tribune*, *Washington Post*, and *Alternet*. I chose the *Chicago Tribune* because the periodical's editorial policy does have a conservative skew but also has a history of editorial work that transgresses conservative boundaries (*Chicago Tribune* Editorial Board, 2016). On the other hand, the *Washington Post* is another legacy periodical that has a more left-leaning or politically mixed editorial board. Both newspapers have won an extensive amount of Pulitzer Prizes for editorial excellence throughout the years and in the current political spectrum have taken measures to avoid incorrect or wrong media reporting by acknowledging the error and making staff changes. This is incredibly important when evaluating news sources and media streams. During my search for these news sources, *Alternet* was viewed as one of the more progressive news sources since much of their reporting uses trusted sources like *The Guardian* and *NPR*.[34]

When searching for articles, I only selected articles written in the recent past because I wanted to keep the sheer number of comments to a minimum. Often with content analysis, researchers can be accused of cherry-picking the worst data to prove their hypothesis. To avoid that accusation, articles that could be deemed positive were included in the analysis as well. These comments were termed "positive" cases because they discussed welfare and those that receive benefits without using aggressive or demeaning language. Most "positive" cases came from *Alternet*. Positive comments were included in the analysis and termed "positive" cases because they discussed welfare and beneficiaries without using aggressive or demeaning language; however, they were in the minority of comments. To select the websites, an initial search was completed to determine which sources were deemed trustworthy.

The articles selected were only those that had comments attached to them. The analysis does not include comments focused on specific policies, government reform, correcting grammar, or anything unrelated to the research questions, such as sarcasm about the Grand Old Party, causually referencing the Republican Party or trolling the organization or the supporters.

The analysis concluded with approximately 60 comments that were sourced from 518 comments found from 20 articles. The remaining comments were cataloged into eleven distinct themes via an Excel spreadsheet. The comments were examined two separate times. First, each comment was examined for content and second, if it met the criteria of the study. For example, if the comment in the article mentioned women, women of color, Black women, Black men, or used any racializing indicators, such as "welfare queen," "thug," "lazy," "breeder," and so on, these comments were placed in an Excel file. After all the articles in the study had their comment boards analyzed, the comments saved in the file were examined again to understand how the comment addresses and discusses welfare recipients.

The second review analyzed more thoroughly the word choice, tone, and specific references to groups or individual people. Another part of the criteria is that the comment had to include something about welfare recipients. It could not be a general comment about welfare programs—in the sense that the commenter thought that they were good or bad. The comments necessarily needed to connect welfare programs with a recipient. Since the main purpose of the study is to examine how online commenters anonymously discuss benefit recipients, the comments had to include something about recipients themselves, welfare programs, and the commenters own beliefs about what the people who receive this assistance do with it or if the recipient even should deserve these benefits.

Based on the criteria, the comments began to reveal different and important themes. These themes include work ethic, immorality, deservingness, enlightened racism, lack of reproductive autonomy/eugenics, white people, immigrants, superiority, heteropatriarchy, coded racist language, and willful forgetting. These themes were constructed based on what was coded and extracted from the comments. For example, if the comment mentioned Black women and reproductive choices, families, and relationships to fathers or the configuration of Black mothers as bad, it was included in the study. Comments were eliminated if they were not about recipients or if the comment was an opinion about a specific welfare policy, such as government level or a state-by-state basis, and did not address recipients specifically, or were just off-topic. Data collection stopped when themes were blending into one another.

What Is Going on Here?

The comments below reveal various themes of how the public views people receiving some type of assistance. These comments stem from an inaccurate understanding of welfare/safety net history. These content themes developed via the words used by individuals in the corresponding articles, that is, mentioning Black women and reproductive choices, families, and relationships to fathers or the configuration of Black mothers as bad in relationship to perceived welfare recipients.

However, the controlling image of a welfare recipient is often Black women, and white voters (who receive and *have received* the largest share of benefit assistance throughout history to the present) will often vote against social safety net assistance policies that would equally benefit them but are perceived to "give something extra" to marginalized populations.[35] White recipients may indirectly be affected by racism against non-whites by the way they perceive other welfare beneficiaries as worthy or unworthy.[36] To be clearer, in the words of DJ Khalid, "Congratulations, you played yourself," white people to exclude Black people and people of color writ large; they often impact their own access to social safety net benefits by voting against their own interests. Previous research from scholars helped inform the interpretation of these comments and how language facilitates socialized ideas from a top-down, trickle-down approach.[37] Doing so allowed for a more nuanced approach to the discourse analysis and gave a basis to understand potential coded language in these comments.

Work Ethic

Work ethic is a concept that reinforces much of the recipient and anti-welfare rhetoric that spans over a large time within the American context. Mostly the general commenting public are very concerned about taxpayer waste when considering poor individuals, but often do not expand on larger taxpayer-funded issues, such as corporate tax benefits (which could be considered corporate welfare) or military funding. To illuminate how work ethic played a role in how people understood welfare benefit recipients, *Iodides*, an anonymous commenter noted that,

> Not only should we know where our taxes are being spent, but we should also be privy to how they are wasted buying votes. Along with publishing where these, often career, recipients of "welfare" live, they should also be removed from the voter rolls until after at least three years of being self-sufficient.

There is a lot to unpack in this excerpt, and a key place to begin is the discussion on voting access. Historically through and to the present, voting has been a class-based privilege, beginning in the late 1700s as only allowing propertied white men the vote and thusly excluding unpropertied white men (as well as everyone else). Prior to the Voting Rights Act in 1965, Black men and women were the recipients of poll taxes, literacy tests, and the litany of other disenfranchising policies and procedures. If we fast forward to the present, we can see the influx of voter id laws disproportionately affect poor and marginalized groups across the board in gaining access to their own documentation. Voting history aside, it is unclear how welfare recipients impact voting access. Because they so happen to be receiving benefits, clearly, they cannot be trusted. Motive unknown in this posting, but because welfare recipients are almost exclusively seen as Black and Black voters are almost directly associated with democratic leaning voting records, the poster could be alluding to welfare recipients being connected to "buying" votes for democratic party support. This assumption leaves out the very large and important Black conservative vote, which is its own book entirely. While the comment does not specifically mention race, there is a desire to increase surveillance on recipients and absolve them of their autonomy. Perhaps this commenter does not know about the history of welfare which helped white families attain a substantial level of wealth over time. The 1935 Social Security Act specifically required white women to stay at home. It barred migrant, farm, and domestic workers from this benefit who, at the time, were mostly Black and brown people to secure Dixiecrat support.[38]

Deservingness, Enlightened Racism, Poverty Is So Simple

People are, by virtue of living, complex and intersectional beings that have all sorts of experiences with which they approach different situations that they come upon in their lives. Class and race are often intertwined when discussing issues of welfare recipientship. General notions of deservingness, enlightened classism, and very simplified (and often incomplete) understandings of how people end up in poverty are documented throughout the study of poverty. Poverty research is filled with general explanations of how people end up experiencing poverty—none of which broach the fact that a large majority of Americans themselves are either living paycheck to paycheck or are two paychecks from poverty. Often the easiest explanation used to analyze poverty predicaments are usually due to bad decisions making and whether these bad decisions necessitated receiving benefits.

Because of the stranglehold that the "American Dream" and the bootstraps myth has on the American psyche, individuals critical of welfare recipients feel that recipient's writ large should be grateful that they receive assistance at all. Another way to create an "us versus them" strategy is to minimize the entrance into poverty, not as the historical or continued barriers that bar certain groups from success, but that poverty results from school drop-outs, teen pregnancy, and drug addiction among others. However, losing a job, having a government shutdown, and a large-scale pandemic all placed millions of families into the realm of precarity because of how we as a people see assistance and welfare structures. As a reader, we might even figure in our minds a controlling image of people who we know have said, or perhaps we are those people that uttered these phrases about welfare recipients, not considering how easy it is for anyone to be in that group. The purpose of symbolic language is how easily repeated rhetoric can make "common sense" but do not challenge established power structures. Therefore, this places poverty as an individual problem versus a social or public issue. It reaffirms socialized notions that poverty is the cause of personal decisions and not because of systems and structures that create barriers for people to emerge from poverty. For example, *liberty4allus notes*:

> By global standards we have very few truly poor people in the United States. Unlike other countries the poor here still have opportunities to work their way out of poverty. billions across the globe don't have these opportunities. If we are honest most of the chronic poor who spend a lifetime on [welfare] are people who have made bad decisions in their lives such a dropping out of school, teen pregnancies and drug abuse or are the very unfortunate/helpless children of such bad decisions. Why should we continue to accept and pay for these bad decisions?

The problem is this assumption disregards how people fall into poverty. It should also be noted that there is no "suitable level of poverty" in a nation that touts itself as the best and most modern. Children and adults within the borders of the United States experience issues with poverty, food insecurity, and inability to access clean water—all dependent on city and state legislation. Often, the public just assumes that if one just would "get a job," "work at Taco Bell," an so on, then seems as though people just assume that job equals the ability to save; however, often people who are experiencing poverty are simply unable to save money. If a worker is not provided with the ability to earn enough to save, it creates the larger problem of exacerbating paycheck to paycheck issues.

Also, since most Americans are poverty-adjacent but may not see themselves as in poverty, there appears to be a disconnect or dichotomy with the experience of poverty. For example, people receiving assistance must meet specific work and income per family size requirements, which differ by state. Once you exceed that income and work threshold, all those benefits you had cease. The wages earned at Taco Bell, and other places, are not living wages, even for the savviest saver. Therefore, the situation of poverty is not remedied just because this person works at Taco Bell, in fact, they are placed in more harm.

Connectedly, the "Fight for $15" campaign for raising the minimum wage is fraught with general misunderstandings due to how the narrative is controlled. Stating that paying people $15 per hour would impact the consumer—admits the fatal flaw in capitalism—that it cannot pay people living wages. Also, telling people to get a minimum living wage (or the least amount a business owner can pay a worker) would arguably help people, but it may continue experiences of poverty because escaping poverty is a gradual process. Once you make over a minimum income, your benefits cease and the former recipient is still in a place of precarity, so the minimum wage would still not be adequate *unless* the established wage provided standards of living. The same people (probably) that demand recipients to get a job are similarly against increases in the minimum wage—because they are just "burger flippers" and their jobs are devalued. When the line is too long at McDonald's or other fast-food places, however, it becomes clear how important those workers are in the grand scheme. Levels of deservingness still operate on exclusions and value judgments are placed on service work occupations, that is, line cooks, nail technicians, bartenders, and so on. Poor people are expected to be visibly invisible. They should work for their benefits, but how dare they desire a living wage because they are only "simple workers." What is revealed from these notes of deservingness is that workers, no matter their job, are underpaid. The "divide and conquer" rhetoric—"if I can't have it, no one can"—is an example of rhetorical gymnastics that infiltrates many common tropes in society, like student loan erasure, for example.

But Poor People Shouldn't Have Lobster

One of my favorite authors, Dr. Dorothy Roberts, wrote in 1997 a book called *Killing the Black Body*, which was about how reproductive rights are always raced and that in the Clinton era, legislators tried to have welfare benefits tied to birth control. Now, it never passed, but the suggestion never went away. The reduction or removal of autonomy, bodily or otherwise, often appears regarding how welfare beneficiaries should live their lives. Often the rhetoric around welfare reform articles usually describes some lawmakers with some desired changes regarding what qualified purchases people can use with their cash assistance or how one qualifies in the first place. The changes included prohibiting items like candy bars, sweets, and alcohol, and expanding exclusions to include fish, crab, lobster, and some cuts of beef as "luxury food items" and if they were to have an IUD implanted.[39] These ideas are reaffirmed below:

> You obviously did not properly read the above. We want to help people, but we do not want our money wasted on items we cannot afford! Keeping candy, ice cream, sodas, and other assorted unhealthy items is a good thing. Buying lobster and steak, and other expensive items [as I've seen], and that [cannot]

be tolerated. They usually do not buy vegetables, [and buy] fruit and meat that
is top of the line, [and] insult us by eating [food] better than [other] families,
including ours, [who] cannot afford [it] because they are using our money to
flaunt and insult us!

What this really states is, how can middle and upper-class families
understand their class position, if people with Foodshare, SNAP, or other
cash-assistance programs are purchasing "luxury" items? The fact that non-
recipients are being "insulted" and are the deserving recipients of these food
items really homes in on how some food is seen as out of reach for the poor.
There is a socially constructed demarcation line that creates acceptable food
for poor people and food for non-recipients.

Unaddressed are systems and structures that regulate economic, costs of
living, or poverty lines which might be the problem. Therefore, if they cannot
afford these items, poor people should not either, in this "us versus them" narrative. This assumes that poor people should not have access to healthy foods
or quality meat. Instead of noting that there should be no food out of reach,
we find that this divide and conquer rhetoric used over and over is being used
again here to discern between the deserving and the food stamp recipient.
What this indicates is not that poor people are buying these items but that
there is a problem writ large about how people are paid across the board that
prohibits the purchase of these items. In fact, a century ago, lobster, crab, and
some shellfish were deemed poor man's lunches, until the wealthier classes
found out they might be delicious, the narrative changed.

Symbolic annihilation functions via how proponents of restrictive benefit
assistant policies feel recipients should have no right to privacy. People with
less power often receive harsher restrictions versus examining the even larger
cost of corporate welfare.[40] Corporate welfare ends up costing the public more,
with its large tax breaks or loopholes that often have the general taxpaying public picking up the rest of the tab.[41] Many of the individuals anonymously posting
about the large waste of money on people who are struggling are not thinking
about power or how power functions in relation to welfare or benefit assistance.

Color-blind Racism and Immigrants

Often implied in anti-welfare rhetoric is the color-blind racist language
woven through these comments about recipients. While scholars note color-
blind rhetoric is covert racist language, the people posting these items may
not read them as racist because they do not contain outright racial slurs, which
is really the "goal" of color-blind racism. In the era of "post-racial" rhetoric, we as readers should note the awareness that some words are stand-ins

for previously overt racial slurs or are highly racialized, such as the words, "thug," "welfare queen," or phrases like "those people."[42] To give these following comments, it comes attached to news articles about the struggles of Black women who receive benefit assistance and contained more explicit notions of race and relied heavily on coded language. For example,

> Irresponsible ignorant woman. Generational welfare at its finest. UGH. Stop ALL welfare and see what happens to these lazy breeders.

Reflecting annihilation, the advocation that recipients do not even deserve the basic subsistence to survive is clear. The racialized language contains rhetoric in reference to an article about a Black woman and her struggle with poverty. The use of "these lazy breeders" suggests that this commenter believes Black women are not even people but associated with terms often used for animals.[43] Whites and people with access to power long used and demeaned marginalized populations via associations with animals—much of this fueled the idea that Black and white people were separate "species"—thus continuing Black people's marginalization throughout US history. Much of racist rhetoric is under the discussion of human beings being different species is based on long-standing and continued anti-Blackness. This long-standing racialized and racist language marginalized and demeaned Black lives over a historical period beginning in slavery as white slave owners referred to enslaved Black women as their breeders.[44] This language strips Black people of their humanity. Echoing symbolic violence and annihilation by saying that poor, Black women are not to be seen as women nor should have access to any assistance in the eyes of those who carry anti-Black beliefs.

It's not unusual that anti-Blackness is accompanied by anti-immigrant opinions. Often, white supremacist rhetoric prevails in these instances by connecting racist language applied to Black women and families and applying it to immigrants and their children in a derogatory manner. Common, but inaccurate rhetoric due to changes in the 1996 Personal Responsibility and Work Opportunity Act (PWORA), places immigrants gaining access to social safety net benefits through the racialized term "anchor baby" who can easily apply for benefits, which is wholly inaccurate due to changes made in the 1996 Personal Responsibility and Work Opportunity Act (PWORA).[45] Pre-1996 PWORA allowed for states to decide if documented immigrants were eligible for access to disability and food stamps. Post-1996 PWORA, the legislation severely restricted documented immigrants from accessing benefits of any kind for five years. Under PWORA, if you are an unqualified immigrant (undocumented), you are ineligible for any kind of support from local, state, or federal government. However, the average American is relatively unaware of these nuances, because "native-born" American citizens never had to sit through immigration procedures, unless they were trying to help someone immigrate into the United States. For example, this excerpt details the disconnect by saying,

> But guess what? When they have their "anchor babies" those moms can apply for housing, food stamps, Medicaid, etc. etc. etc. in the name of the kid. Oh, not to mention the fact YOU/ME pay for the delivery and all the hospital costs.

Symbolic annihilation configures immigrant mothers as takers and abusers of the system and creates a situation where undocumented women are significantly underserved because of their lack of access to documentation and are consistently placed in harm.

The shift of rhetoric changed within the year 2015–2016, when a major presidential election took place. Americans, even though prided on their "nation of immigrants" status, showed that only a certain type of immigrant was acceptable. Post-2016, anti-immigrant sentiment increased and became a major talking point for anti-benefit assistant comments due to an election cycle wherein the executive branch formulated and promoted negative associations about immigrants. Racism in all its forms is one example where the "trickle-down" effect is apparent. Anti-immigrant rhetoric migrates down and is absorbed by the average commenter on these articles. Symbolic annihilation configures immigrants in one way, mostly by insinuating they are Latinx or more specifically, as undocumented Mexicans crossing the border, which is at present, the lowest reported form of undocumented immigration. This racist and xenophobic/anti-immigrant sentiment clearly defines an immigrant in one specific way—as an invading affliction that must be stopped. The willful forgetting of how the United States is built on stolen land through the invasion of manifest destiny is astounding. Often, common identification is that the words of an elected official lack an impact; however, it is important to note how easy this rhetoric can trickle down, as evidenced by the below comment:

> And just wait when we let all those caravan a holes in . . . more free stuff!!!! Socialism doesn't work here. With that said. I don't mind using tax payer money to air drop condoms and birth control on these populations.

This messaging and commentary about immigrants also map onto the bodily autonomy of who qualifies as "documented." The threads of symbolic annihilation are woven throughout this section via configuring immigrants in one specific manner—as bad individuals and stealing things from others, which does not stray from the long-standing anti-immigrant rhetoric that has plagued immigration commentary in the United States from the 1950s through to the present.

Intersections of Racism and Lack of Reproductive Autonomy

The following comments intersect racism via removing femininity from Black women and simultaneously use racist language that is often used in color-blind racist lexicon.

> Why has she had so many jobs? Does she keep getting fired and if so, why? And she can move if it's getting so expensive. People like you keep justifying bad decisions, laziness and irresponsibility. She is a welfare queen; why doesn't her BF get another part-time job or a full-time job? If she has such a hard time with childcare (which is a lie because she gets everything paid for) then why . . . have a second kid. She'll have a third and at least one will end up in jail or dead and you'll be right back here yelling "BLM!!!" when her laziness and your ignorance caused this. If you love her and the welfare people so much, why don't you offer up your home? Go ahead . . . I'm waiting for an answer that doesn't play the race/sex card . . . go ahead.

From the above comment, symbolic annihilation can help analyze and unpack their identifications and views on race. First, the notion of "being able to move" is squarely centered in color-blind racist rhetoric. The presumption of available affordable housing is at the responsibility of the person, not that people are priced out of certain areas that were formerly affordable, or other factors/barriers that families can face.[46] Second, what often is misunderstood is the childcare costs and how often women are placed at fault for this. For one, it places the frame of Black Lives Matter at the feet of Black women and families, instead of at the feet of institutions and structures, that is, disparate policing practices that affect different families in different ways and misunderstand the sociopolitical statement of Black Lives Matter. Issues of reproductive rights are at the heart of these comments, especially when Black women are having children, as well as the "subtle" notion of the absent or "deadbeat"/non-provider Black father running through this commenter's post. And the assumption that a heteronormative dual family is the best outcome, without considering that an LGBT+ relationship may be an option for this person profiled in the article. Another way relationships are explored are through the demonization of single mothers, as noted:

> Four kids—no husband equals poverty mother and four more dysfunctional adults. Any welfare program that awards irresponsible breeders more money for having more children is only contributing to the failure of our society.

The above statements are followed by the notion or perception that heteronormative relationships are the key to success, forgetting that families of color are often the recipients of harsher prison terms and police violence and may be barred from involvement in the lives of their children by stating that,

> Mother is 31, her son is 17. Do the math. No father or even a step-father in the picture. This is part of the poverty problem. Help is needed regarding birth control, education and job training.

Posts about heteronormative relationships, wondering about marital statuses, fatherhood status, or how having a two-parent man/woman household are the best for avoiding poverty appear above. These posts describe nuclear families as the best form of family formation. Connected to the construction of the nuclear family, traditional families, which highlight heterosexual, cisgender families, thereby erasing and annihilating LGBTQ, queer, transgender, and single-family households.

A key point is the use of the term "irresponsible breeders" in reference to Black women and Black families. Regardless of the economic barriers placed in front of Black women, the references to Black women and the family structure fail to even recognize the children or her as living, human people. The lack of recognition creates an easier avenue for their livelihood (and other similar families) to be annihilated in the context of this speech. Historically, Black women experience/d a history of white supremacist reproductive control over their bodies as they lack access to the same reproductive autonomy as white women.[47] Another example of this socially structured identifications occurred below by the statement:

Children need to be taught to refrain from having kids until they are financially stable and have the ability to support them. They also need to be taught to acquire marketable skills. I could get behind programs that provide free birth control to young women starting as early as age 11 if needed. Having numerous, early, out-of-wedlock kids is the surest way to remain at the bottom of the economic heap.

Not only does race but also class emerge in these comments. For starters, the personal and the public are disconnected. The idea that everyone has the ability and access to plan for a family seems grossly overestimated. Having access to appropriate reproductive care, doctors, and health insurance are key pieces and many communities do not have the same access to these services.

Next, we see the notion that young women are being tasked with the sole care of their reproductive systems. And subtly, the sociocultural aura of hypersexual women emerges because it references eleven-year-old girls as women who need to have their rampant sexuality controlled with birth control, instead of offering sexual education classes and information about how their bodies change. The assumption is that eleven-year-old children are unable to be taught healthy sex practices, like condoms or courses, but simply placed on birth control, without ever consulting the child about their changing body systems. Young boys are excluded from the conversation of their participation in reproductive health and care because childbirth is not a one-sided experience.

> Help the woman with the first child that is being raised with no father/and or husband . . . but then that's it. No help for the second, third, fourth, etc. It's good to be caring about single mothers and their children but let's use some common sense. Let's not support a lifestyle that isn't doing the mother, the children, or society any good. Honest, hard-working folk should not be burdened with having to support the litter of someone repeating the same mistakes over and over. . . . When I was on Unemployment . . . , I never considered applying for [welfare] and . . . people scamming the system to help support their bad habits . . . even though they are working.

The above quote brings to light the issues discussed in the Moynihan Report, which blamed the failings of the Black community and society—not on racist institutions, systems, or structures, but specifically on Black women and mothers, which these comments illuminate as still present in the current mindset of the public.[48]

The threads of symbolic annihilation are apparent throughout the comments. The simple desire to only control how specific people use their bodies in reference to everyone else is clear. Only certain individuals should be given the opportunity and ability to reproduce or engage in sexual activity. Instead of controlling sexual activity, having adequate, accurate, and accessible reproductive health information is important for anyone. Trying to remove that or highlight that issue for only one part of the population is key and highlights and erases people at the same time.

Bodies and Ability

Connected to welfare recipientship are ideas about "appropriate" body size and visible disability associations. While they are grouped together, this is not a statement that body size is a disability, only those commenters wanted to see the *embodiment of* disability. Perceptions of poverty in relation to fatness and being "overweight" is used as evidence that recipients do not deserve welfare benefits. For example,

> First woman can afford jewelry, a dog, and what looks like booze (bottles in background). She can buy her own food. The fat guy in image two lives with family. [Probably] not paying[any] housing expenses as he would pay if he lived on his own (if . . . anything). He also is an able-bodied male with no children. He doesn't need the taxpayers to buy his food for him. The third guy has a disability so should be exempt. . . . One can work, volunteer, or get an education for no money out of their pocket (save for maybe transportation) . . . to improve the situation. . . . There is no excuse for an able-bodied adult with all of their mental faculties in place to be asking . . . taxpayer [help].

First, it assumes that having possessions equates to not being in poverty. Second, the notion that having alcohol in the house assumes it is a luxury item versus a simple addition to a grocery list, namely because it cannot be purchased with SNAP funds. It presumes that people in poverty must fit a narrow window of poverty—destitute, with no belongings or items.

Not only do people who are poor need to "look poor" (i.e., not have smartphones, cars, nice cars, or accessories), they must now physically embody poverty with proper malnutrition. It appears that for many of these posters, a "skinny or not fat body" correlates to food insecurity. For example,

> I have seen true poor people around the world and they would call our poor rich. I know, I am evil for pointing out the obvious and being honest . . . let the hate begin. The poor starving examples in this article were obese people. Are none of you smart enough to see they are NOT starving. Hey look, that overweight woman is starving . . . really?!!

The other issue exposed in these comments is the notion/perception of visible disability. Here, someone who appeared to exhibit no visible signs of a disability (in a photo) signified that they were a fraud or lying. It adds to the mountain of negative experiences that people with different types of disability encounter. Also, it does not matter if he has a disability or not, poverty is a wide-ranging issue with a wide variety of causes by stating.

> These are able-bodied people. They're not people who are disabled—those people qualify for food, shelter, and cash subsidies. There are also food kitchens a-plenty.

People with disability need to demonstrate embodied disability—which annihilates other disabilities—those need not be immediately visually present. The narrow window of embodied disability is seen when people who use motorized carts—get up to reach an item—are seen as not "truly" disabled and frauds. People with disability must have visible signs and be completely immobile. The articles often withheld identifiable race or the story was a human-interest story that profiled the lives of particular recipients, often using Black women. Stories about lives of white recipients were rare. Symbolic annihilation focuses on the presence or absence, and, in this case, Black recipients are present and white recipients are not which helps maintain the façade that whites are self-sufficient (while accounting for the largest benefit assistance receipt),[49] which similarly annihilates their history with receiving government aided assistance.

There are ways to examine how power relations are a key component through each of the themes, and these online comments represent these power relations.[50] Already marginalized people are socially annihilated and continue to experience rhetorical annihilation because they appear to live outside a manner that the commenters in these comment boards find appropriate. Regardless of if the featured people do not read them, the commenters expressed their opinions in the way they vote, who they support politically and that trickles down to tax dollar spending. Commenters may not intend to support the power structure, but the use of phrases or words has that effect. Through the uses of the terms "breeder," "welfare queen," and affirmations of heteronormative family relations, the commenters post comments about recipients in which recipients do not deserve any level of humanity and their lives policed. While commenters may not be intentional in how they affirm power structures, that is, the sociohistorical process of media perceptions of Black women as welfare queens, their language use helps complete this process.

Symbolic annihilation woven through the articles and more explicitly featured in comments often appear in articles that profile Black women and mention birth control as a condition to accessing welfare benefits. Equating welfare recipients with out-of-control birth rates ignores the continued historical inability of Black women to access reproductive health rights.[51] Removing this ability to procreate for women of color is a continued racialized structure. While many representatives tried and failed to restrict the reproductive choices of women of color by linking benefits with birth control, it is not beyond impossible.[52] Having the power to potentially control and equate the procreation of children with Blackness and not apply that same horrendous policy logic to white women is an explicit representation of annihilation—figurative and literal. Also, language referencing color-blind racist and coded language for how (mostly) whites talk about race and can be read through their discourse on welfare beneficiaries, deservingness, ability, and

need to be monitored.[53] In addition, comments like the ones displayed illuminate the ways anti-immigrant sentiment and color-blind racist language intersect with the politics of annihilation and violent online discourse to create the
erasure or presence of problematic controlling images. Given the nature of
color-blind racism, much of the racism no longer is overt with specific slurs
but coded with other diversion tactics to hide racist intent. Intertwined within
the issues of color-blind, coded language, the study also found intersections
of body, fat phobia, and disability issues regarding perceptions of poverty.

These examples necessitate a critical examination because the comments
relate to how the average American is taught or shown to understand these
issues and were unable to locate power relations regarding who makes decisions that affect the livelihoods of the poor or working class. These critiques
about "recipients as burdens upon society" were aimed downward. These
groups often are large in number but lack the social, monetary, and advocacy
power that those who are wealthier or have liquid assets can advocate for
themselves. It acts as an example of the power of dominant ideologies of the
ruling class being accepted and reiterated by mass society.

The Center for Budget and Policy Priorities (CBPP) notes that there are
fewer people receiving benefits despite increasing poverty within the decade
of 2010–2020, which indicates that poverty is a larger and far more reaching
issue than most believe it is. A very related issue is the concept of inflation.
While costs of living have increased, benefits paid to recipients have not—
which results in the affording less at the grocery store. To be specific the
CBPP finds that "families have not kept pace with inflation and home rental
prices, so the benefits received by needy families enrolled in TANF today are
worth about 30% less than they were worth in 1996."[54]

How Does Food Insecurity Fit into This?

Perhaps while reading this chapter, some readers may have found a connection
to these statements above being said by a family member at a holiday party.
What does all this have to do with food insecurity? Well, as federal support for
state food access programs is changed, it affects how people access food. As the
requirements are changed for recipients due to how people feel about food access,
that creates more stress on how one accesses food, which impact health concerns
within all age ranges. The decisions made at higher levels affect people at the bottom, with those in higher income levels either blissfully unaware or very willing
to disregard the problem as individual failures. Therefore, as people are less able
to use their benefits at the grocery store, they are more likely to subsidize that
gap with food banks/pantries, which places those facilities into more precarity
because they need to have the ability to supply demand. Welfare benefits (pre-
COVID) account for 10–12% of the federal budget, which is smaller than many
of our other expenses.

Whether or not the public understands that their language usage upholds power structures, these examples show how this language is pervasive in society. However, with the use of screen names, one may conclude the commenters understand that their postings are littered with racist, sexist, and prejudicial language. Simultaneously, anonymity can also lend itself to notions of power. For example, commenters can support austerity, such as defunding social safety net programs and using problematic language, and are never held accountable for their speech. Language is fundamental to upholding different power structures, and while the identity of the commenter is unable to be revealed, the trickle-down notions from government actions regarding who deserves assistance and how the public views that assistance—often erroneously. The next chapter explores the historical legacy of welfare systems and how racism and classism impact welfare recipient access to services..

NOTES

1. Collins, *Black Feminist Thought, Black Sexual Politics*; Gerbner, "Dynamics"; Gramsci, *Prison.*
2. Aschwanden, "8,500 internet commenters."
3. Bourdieu, *Outline*; Gerbner, "Comparative"; "Dynamics."
4. Bourdieu, *Symbolic.*
5. Ibid.
6. Ibid *Symbolic*, 44.
7. Ibid *Symbolic*, 45.
8. Dow, "Welfare Queen."
9. Gerbner, "Dynamics; Tuchman, "Mass Media."
10. Collins, *Black Sexual Politics.*
11. Tuchman, "Symbolic Annihilation."
12. McLuhan & Fiore, "Medium"; Meyrowitz, "Worlds."
13. Meyrowitz, "Worlds."
14. McLuhan, "Medium."
15. Meyrowitz, "Worlds," 59.
16. Bonilla-Silva, *Racism without Racists*; Gilens, *Americans Hate Welfare*; Lieberman, *Color Line*; Lipsitz, 2006; Quadagno, *The Color of Welfare.*
17. Roberts, *Killing the Black Body.*
18. Gilens, *Americans Hate Welfare*; Roberts, *Killing the Black Body.*
19. Gilens, *Americans Hate Welfare*; Lieberman, *Color Line*; Roberts, *Killing the Black Body.*
20. Bullock, "Attributions."
21. Ibid.
22. Ibid.
23. Collins, *Black Feminist Thought*; Kelly, "Regulating the Reproduction"; Monnat, Critical Understanding; Roberts, "Prison."

24. Roberts, "Prison."

25. Rose & Baumgartner, "Framing the Poor"; Ramasubramanian, "Racial Attitudes"; van Dooran, "Welfare Reform."

26. Van Dooran, "Welfare Reform."

27. Abrajano, Hajnal & Hassell, "Media"; Ahmed, *US Immigration*; Farris & Mohamed, Picturing Immigration; Garand, Xu & Davis, "Immigration Attitudes"; Perry, *Cultural Politics*.

28. Ferris and Mohamed, *Picturing Immigration*.

29. Bonilla-Silva, *Racism without Racists*.

30. Marx and Engels, *Manifesto*; Marx et al., *Capital*.

31. Gilens, *Americans Hate Welfare*; Lieberman, *Color Line*; Quadagno, *The Color of Welfare*.

32. Aschwanden, "8,500 internet commenters."

33. Chang, "Segregation"; Meyer, *Racial Conflict*.

34. Meyer, *Racial Conflict*.

35. Bobo, "Race, Interests"; Prejudice; Bobo and Smith, "Laissez-Faire Racism."

36. Bobo, "Race, Interests"; Prejudice; Bobo, Kluegel, and Smith, "Crystallization"; Bobo and Smith, "Laissez-Faire Racism."

37. Bonilla-Silva, *Racism without Racists*; Bullock, "Attributions"; Collins, *.Black Feminist Thought, Black Sexual Politics*; Cooper, et. al., "Poverty"; Lieberman, *Color Line*; Quadagno, *The Color of Welfare*; Roberts, *Killing the Black Body*, "Prison."

38. Andersen, *Corner*; Gilens, *Americans Hate Welfare*; Lieberman, *Color Line*; Lipsitz, *Possessive Investment*; Quadagno, *The Color of Welfare*.

39. Holley, "Welfare Recipients."

40. Gilens, *Americans Hate Welfare*.

41. Mettera, "Subsidizing."

42. Bonilla-Silva, *Racism without Racists*.

43. Collins, *Black Sexual Politics*; Cooper et al., "Poverty"; Roberts, *Killing the Black Body*.

44. Cooper et al., "Poverty."

45. Singer, "Welfare reform."

46. Bonilla-Silva, *Racism without Racists*.

47. Roberts, *Killing the Black Body*.

48. Ibid, *Killing the Black Body*.

49. https://www.clasp.org/press-room/news-clips/americans-are-mistaken-about -who-gets-welfare; https://www.lexingtonlaw.com/blog/finance/welfare-statistics .html; https://www.thoughtco.com/who-really-receives-welfare-4126592.

50. Johnson et al., *Critical Content Analysis*.

51. Collins, *Black Feminist Thought, Black Sexual Politics*; Hooks, *Black Women, Ending Racism, Feminist Theory*.

52. Collins, *Black Sexual Politic*; Roberts, *Killing the Black Body*.

53. Bonilla-Silva, *Racism without Racists*.

54. https://www.cbpp.org/research/family-income-support/tanf-benefits-still-too -low-to-help-families-especially-black.

55. https://www.thoughtco.com/who-really-receives-welfare-4126592.

Chapter 3

Perceptions of Poverty

While the previous chapter talked about recipients from a non-recipient lens, this chapter focuses on the people in poverty and how they see themselves, which is going to differ from the governmental and popular conceptualization of the "recipient." Often when recipients are configured in the media, what is often lost is how poverty legislation (or lack thereof) can affect real people—those that do and do not receive assistance, given that something might happen wherein people would not normally receive these benefits, would suddenly need them. This chapter seeks to humanize the interactions that I had with recipients during their day-to-day experiences.

Outside perspectives of recipients often create this perception that all recipients are these takers, always trying to get something (which misses and dismisses the reality that corporations *actually* do this). However, in many situations that I experienced, there was more community, love, and solidarity within these groups than the perceived narrative often discusses. For example, when I was writing my notes after one day at the pantry, I noted that it felt like the "poor helping the poor." I reflected on that because it showed a level of connection and solidarity in a way that I think often gets missed in other groups. It's not to say that middle class or wealthier classes are missing a level of human connection but perhaps there's a lack of empathy based on this notion of bootstraps theory or the oft-repeated, "[insert group here] made it, why can't [insert group or individual here]" which is not giving true respect to the ways in which privileges and access to upward mobility function. It is true that the people I ended up working most closely with were Black and African American, but it highlights the highly segregated nature of Milwaukee.

Similarly, it highlights the ways in which reaching out and seeking help is seen as positive and can lift people up, as in if the community is stronger, the individual is stronger. For example, many of the individuals I met with were not just focused on themselves, but what can I do to help someone else. I saw this with the pantry volunteers and those who helped people at the pantry. When looking at programs and policies writ large in the United States, the group that is helped are white people—but because they've never had to "struggle" in the sense of being forcibly denied access to something, it appears that they were able to create this wealth all on their own—instead of that while they were able to create wealth, accrue assets and set up inheritances, other families were denied that same ability. Perhaps, outwardly asking for help might conflict with the whitened notion of "American exceptionalism" and the bootstrap ideology that so often gets used by whites of all classes, regardless of if they too use welfare and public assistance. So often asking for help taints the perception of how poor whites are viewed and view themselves—no matter that whites have been the beneficiaries of loopholes that are explicit and vague over the recent years. This will be explored further in this chapter.

In October of 2018, Ava, the church administrative assistant, invited me to the GPLC women's retreat to be held in a town near Lake Geneva, Wisconsin. She thought that it would be a great idea for me to be able to collect some of my data. Ava was one of the first people I interviewed and was excited for other women to be able to tell their stories about living in poverty and using benefit assistance. So, I went to this retreat that was led by Susan, a white woman who is also a church volunteer. Most of the attendees of this retreat were Black and Latina women. During the retreat, we ate together and created a community with one another. Ava thought it was important for me to attend this event because it was a way for potential respondents to feel comfortable with me and it would be a way for me to meet new friends who attended church. Most of the women who attended the retreat were living on the Northside, older, in the sense that they were just a little older than I. Most were married, widowed, or were single. In the morning on the day the retreat was to end, all the attendees received these folders that had inspirational pamphlets about leading a good and understanding life and how to live joyfully, and so on, which was helpful but for me personally, I couldn't forget the real tangible aspects of poverty. I thought, there are so many opportunities for people to express feelings of "joy" and "understanding" and many of those reasons are expressly personal. I asked the women at the retreat their favorite guilty pleasure, or what would they spend their SNAP on if they had a little extra. The answers were probably similar to what non-SNAP users take for granted. A few women said Ben & Jerry's, others said candy—but specified the idea of "good" candy—Ghirardelli, Lindt and Dove.

Before we were ready to leave, Susan gave everyone a stone—some were shiny, and some were old with effects of wind and erosion. We were told to hold these stones in their hands and place all their worry into these stones. And many of the women were excited to have these stones. However, there weren't enough stones for the number of attendees, so I gave my stone to a woman who didn't have one. It seems perhaps trivial, but I remember her asking me, "are you sure?" I responded with "of course, I will be ok." And I thought to myself, "wow, what a time for self-reflection" at this moment. During this event I was thinking, what does this stone have anything to do with the realities that these women face. But more importantly, as that thought popped into my head, another one emerged asking me to take a step back and understand my privilege. It also exemplifies a more important message. The women at this retreat came together in the community and many of them occupy the same socioeconomic status as one another. The shared meal was a potluck and when the meal was over, we all helped each other clean things up. We worked together and it was a real display of community.

At the end of the retreat, when we were all leaving, we chipped in altogether to clean up the space to leave the place in the same condition with which it was found. And this brings me back to the stones. The stones were probably collected from nearby or from a convenient spot, but even those stones have a story to tell. It mirrors the way in that not a single woman rejected the stones. Some traded with each other for ones they thought were prettier or were a color they liked, some told stories about a trip that whatever stone they got reminded them of and to connected them together. This simple gift—a river stone—with its own story to tell highlights the ways that these women all had stories to tell, each of them different but all sharing their struggles under the same program. The women I was able to share with were unique and had different gifts that they brought to the retreat, but they also told of various struggles that they faced—specifically trying to navigate and work through various barriers.

In many of my conversations with recipients and social organizations working to assist those in poverty, the same sentiment came up time and time again, in a variety of different iterations. When asked how they felt about being on public assistance in one form or another, recipients responded with a version of "I'm just trying to provide for me and my family." However, publicly nor at a basic level of government, this experience is rarely understood, and this is often not the perception that comes to mind and it's mainly due to a misunderstanding of the historical evolution of welfare as we know it. Many of the books that precede this one often focus on women who receive these benefits and by and large there are racialized and gendered constructions of benefit assistance that influence how welfare recipients are perceived.[1] If anything, the Pandemic of 2020 which followed the Shutdown of 2019 showed the precarious positions that middle- and working-class people found themselves. However, these perceptions are not always completely accurate in how we as a populace understand who receives them and how they are received.

Racialized and gendered notions and popular representations in the media function to stigmatize welfare recipients in ways that are detrimental to alleviating or remedying poverty.[2] To begin, the following pages try and tease out how representations of benefit receipts can lead to faulty perceptions of welfare recipients based on how government policies create barriers. Secondly, this gap examines the differing situations in which welfare recipients of all genders may find themselves and attempts to present a complete picture of benefit assistance.[3]

Similarly, during this time of writing there was also the Pandemic of 2020 which placed precarity and people close to precarity in a very unfamiliar position. The normative ideas of how we understand poverty were put under a microscope. Namely, there were almost 26 million and counting unemployment claims filed within a month and a half across the nation and that number continued to rise throughout the pandemic. While government officials were discussing the impact of the pandemic, there was simultaneously little care directed toward the average American and workers who were impacted by the pandemic. Service workers, such as fast-food workers, grocery store attendants, and others, were deemed essential workers. At the same time as being essential, they were also disposable. It almost felt like service level employees were stuck in a spot that they did not choose. Much of the rhetoric that surrounded these workers was via an association of being a superhero or unabashed heroism. However, these individuals experienced two sides of the same coin. They were somehow heroes but also expected to be stocking and restocking for the needs of an over-consumptive populace which precipitated the great toilet paper shortage of 2020.

It is important to note that while service workers—like grocery store attendants—could work, restaurants that did not have take-out feasibility were largely unemployed. This led to an overwhelming flood of individuals filing for unemployment, and in many cases, the system was ill-equipped to handle this large influx. For example, Florida, one of the states that had a large part of its economy stunted by this pandemic, ended up giving away the game and outwardly noted that their unemployment system was *supposed* to function as a barrier.

The pandemic exposed a variety of issues within the US economic structure. If we recall back in 2017, the tax cuts to wealthy business owners were given on the premise that these business owners are "wealth creators" and are the backbone of the economy. However, what society "hopefully" learned explicitly during the pandemic is that the wealth builders are the workers themselves. That said, the business owners/capitalist class pulled back the curtain on the bootstraps ideology because these essential workers create the wealth, but don't see the pay off—the capitalist always wins. The capitalist class can't live without these workers and so there was a big push to open businesses without having the pandemic even under control in any real way because it became clear that capitalists don't make their money, they need people to do that work for them.

Now, those essential workers, in the previous chapter, who were demonized and told to get a better job are now the supply line for those commenters who were previously posting demeaning sentiments. It is important to recognize the theoretical implications that are necessary to understand how the perceptions of recipients become something in the first place. Lastly, the chapter ends with a discussion of how the (in)ability to access food is related to the location and spatiality in the city of Milwaukee.

WELFARE: HISTORY OF ASSISTANCE

First, let's take a quick trip through the welfare benefit timeline. Often, welfare is thought of as one of the many social safety nets for people in need; however, there are a variety of issues that arise from how the institution was structured from its inception. Contemporary identifications of welfare often do not resonate with the original intent of the assistance—specifically noting the issue of race and class.

Welfare and benefit assistance programs are a rather "modern" invention in the United States. Prior to 1929, there were no policies or institutions addressing poverty nor upward mobility for Americans. However, after 1929, the importance of a social safety net became necessary as breadlines lengthened and poverty increased. In 1935, President Franklin Deleno Roosevelt created the New Deal in connection with the inception of the 1935 Social Security Act.[4] This Act was the first effort from the federal government to protect citizens from poverty. One of the policies emerging from the 1935 Social Security Act was the Aid to Dependent Children (ADC), later changed to Aid to Families with Dependent Children (AFDC),[5] and then to PRWORA, and its Wisconsin variant, "Wisconsin Works" or "W-2" in 1997.[6]

Before Clinton "ending welfare as we know it" with PWORA in 1996, it is important to take a step back to explore the welfare benefit development timeline. For Roosevelt to pass the original 1935 Social Security Act, he needed support from Southern Democrats, also known as Dixiecrats. In order to gain this support, the passage of the 1935 Act resulted in the exclusion of certain occupations, such as farmworkers or domestic labor, which were mostly held by Black, African American, and brown workers.[7] Due to these exclusions, these policies allowed states to limit the number of Black welfare recipients and essentially viewed Black families as "undeserving" or nonexistent as they worked in these excluded occupations.[8] This institutionalized racial and gender inequality was guaranteed via deals between Southern and Northern congressmen to pass many of the New Deal policies.[9] Prior to 1965, the face of poverty and the poor was white, and African Americans and Black people represented the invisible poor due to being actively written out of most of the legislation.[10] However, legislators negotiating AFDC considered widowed white women as the primary recipients and their sole job was to raise children, which differs from how we view work requirements today.

Given how racism was threaded through these social service programs and how people conceptualized who did what work, people and legislators felt that Black women always worked; therefore, Black women should not qualify under AFDC guidelines.[11] However, beginning in the 1960s, the roles of women were beginning to change, wherein widowed mothers were seen differently than women who had children "out of wedlock" and these social changes encouraged changes to welfare policies based on this distinction.[12] Therefore, the movement toward demonizing single mothers begins to take a turn. In post-civil rights popular culture and the changing dynamic of civil rights being theoretically accessible by Black and African Americans allowed for the emergence of color-blind rhetoric. For example, news articles began circulating contrasting images featuring Black people to illustrate news stories regarding waste, inefficiency, or abuse of welfare, juxtaposed with images of white people in more "race-neutral" or more deserving discussions of antipoverty measures which helped to ground recipient perceptions.[13]

After civil rights legislation hypothetically made various forms of discrimination illegal and Black individuals qualified for more benefit programs, the white majority came to believe that there were no obstacles to financial security for people of color except for a poor work ethic. Given the power of Color-blind racism—or colloquially known as "there's only one race, the human race," erases the actual longitudinal historical significance of how racism impacts the experiences of people of color today. White people began to conceptualize antipoverty programs with a more intensified racialized suspicion, even though statistically speaking, white individuals and families are more likely to be using these social services.[14]

After 1951, benefit programs such as the Federal Housing Association (FHA) loans, GI bills for returning veterans, and Social Security benefits once reserved for white women and men were now legally "open" to Black families.[15] However, this did not mean that benefits were easily obtained. Once Black families were added as potential beneficiaries, work requirements, such as minimum hours to receive assistance, job training, restrictions on the length of assistance, began to appear and there was a transition from welfare to "workfare," based on a racialized public narrative about not assisting a lazy, undeserving, poor population of color, which is flipped from the original conceptualization of welfare policies.[16]

It would be disingenuous to not mention the racializing rhetoric that emerged during the Nixon and most notably Reagan administrations. Not to be outdone by notions of "law and order," Reagan capitalized on previous manifestations of dog-whistle racism and doubled down with his creation of the "welfare queen"—configured as an inner-city Black woman living high on the hog on the government's dime.

This "dog-whistle racism" was thoroughly explained later in 1981 by Lee Atwater, who worked closely with both Nixon and Reagan regarding the emerging "Southern Strategy"—which is only the update of the Dixiecrats in 1935. This dog-whistle racism is related to the notions of color-blind racism due to the fact neither of these terms is overt, racist, or racialized slurs used. What happens is the evolution of "coded language" where people use words that are not seen as a slur, but do the work (i.e., thug, ghetto, ratchet, etc.). Due to the intense focus on Black people—with specific focus on Black women—white welfare recipients were removed as beneficiaries and Black women and families were the focal points.

This rhetoric not only placed Black individuals and families as the only welfare recipients but hid the fact that white individuals and families were able to use the benefits without receiving the same level of anger and backlash. With the increase of Black families receiving assistance and the downplaying of white families overwhelmingly receiving assistance, and the negative attention placed upon Black and brown Americans intensified via the Nixon and Reagan presidencies. Their rhetoric and actions exacerbated racial tensions and increased barriers for marginalized populations trying to attain upward social mobility. The racial perceptions that created negative welfare benefit implications will be discussed in more detail shortly.

Fast forward to 1996, during the Clinton presidency, where we first began with PWORA, it was considered a major welfare reform. At the signing of the "reform," Clinton proudly exclaimed, "it is the end of welfare as we know it," which ended the 60-year AFDC program and created TANF. TANF is a temporary program aimed at eliminating long-term assistance program usage (and introduced time limits on benefit assistance, work requirements for recipients, and the ability for individual states to figure out how to administer the program).[17] TANF became less associated with caring for people in poverty and more associated with workfare or increased work requirements to qualify for benefits. After the 1996 changes, stricter policies became more prevalent in not just TANF but also in unemployment, housing, and other safety-net benefits, as well as immigration policies and how we treat those in marginalized conditions.

RACISM: AMERICAN AS APPLE PIE

Societal constructions organize the ways racism can take shape in society and construct internalized perceptions about others. Bonilla-Silva characterizes racism as "a set of ideas and beliefs," which can lead people with constructed advantages to internalize racialized attitudes and attribute them to a whole group of individuals.[18] The empowered group that holds prejudiced ideas may engage in racially discriminatory action. Institutions and socially constructed norms work as a set of mutually reinforcing elements or a feedback loop, wherein institutions inform people and people inform the institution. Institutions and structures are not removed from human interaction but are structured by specific human interactions. Hamilton and Ture argue that we must distinguish between the individual or interpersonal actions of racism and the more institutional or legalized forms of racism—the coded racialized outcomes that can result from the normal operations and functions of American institutions.[19]

That institutional, systemic, and structural piece is wrapped up in what scholars might call the racial states, which define racially identified groups via a variety of bureaucratic and institutional forms and measures.[20] The racial state is not static, but a "political force" that employs economic, legal, and cultural structures that recirculate racialized patterns about other groups to secure their production.[21] For example, racial states, like the United States, define, regulate, govern, economically manage, and mediate racially identified groups and structures, determining who speaks for others and in what capacity.[22] The racial state often protects and supports white people differently than Black and Brown people.[23] White people, by structuring the racial state, have greater access to differing levels of power within these institutions, structures, and systems.[24] Power is not measured as physical strength, but more assertively describes how policing, incarceration, housing, income, and education produce disparate effects and problematic positions for individuals of color more so than for white people.[25]

However, white racism, regardless of intentional or not, only tells part of the story and erases the potentiality for how threads of racism can be woven. Racism requires power structures that are facilitated by white people. However, there are complications to how power can be solidified. For example, a study on welfare recipient perceptions concluded that most of the 236 (112 middle-class, 124 working-class European Americans living in Rhode Island) interviewees held anti-Black feelings toward recipients of color.

PREJUDICE AND IMPLICIT BIAS

Prejudice, the stepsister to racism uses tropes and controlling images but often lacks the power that is necessary to "do" racism. Sometimes these terms can be confusing and be conflated with one another. While again racism needs power, think about prejudice as a prong in the umbrella of racism. It doesn't carry the same reach as racism but uses the tenets that were set up by white supremacy, which gives racism its power. While racism is strictly used by white people, prejudice, and implicit bias to be enacted by non-white people themselves onto other marginalized groups, thereby allowing the tenets of white supremacy to continue without white people having to do any "work" contributes to the perpetuation of racist institutional policy and structure.[26] There are ways to mitigate issues of prejudice and implicit bias through social integration and contact—the more contact you have with someone from different groups, the less likely you are to hold prejudicial ideas and values.[27] The reproduction of these internalized prejudices and implicit bias occurs through holding dominant perceptions of people within the same racial category, such as believing them to be more likely to abuse welfare, be on welfare, be poor money managers, or have poor family structures. Therefore, the structure of assistance programs that are mediated through perceptions about race also works to recreate problematic perceptions about welfare beneficiaries.

To give an example of implicit bias, the same study of the 236 recipients found that welfare recipients were more likely to reject restrictive welfare-reform policies and use structural identifications for the existence of poverty, but they were more likely to view fellow recipients as being dishonest regarding deserving of benefits.[28] This contradicted some previous ideas because many people expect middle-class participants to hold harsher views; however, middle-class participants did view recipients as generationally dependent on benefit receipt without looking at how barriers can remain over time.[29] This study is relatively important, and because of its limitation, it only looked at the attitudes of white men and women to the exclusion of other potential recipients.[30] Therefore, the reason for the bias is that they see other groups as "misusing" benefits and therefore implicit bias exists.

According to the 2013 US Department of Agriculture data, which administers the SNAP program, "40.2 percent of recipients are White, 25.7 percent are Black, 10.3 percent are Latino/a/x, 2.1 percent are Asian, and 1.2 percent are Native American."[31] White Americans are symbolically removed from the image of welfare recipients—their positions are erased and, more importantly, hidden from view and allow for the repetition and continuation of inaccurate media representations of welfare recipients.[32]

The fact that Black families figure prominently as recipients in public perception, while white families do not, disrupts the ability to adequately assess the structures of poverty and benefits assistance. These false presumptions influence welfare case workers' attitudes toward their clients. This issue transgresses all boundaries of social services. For example, social workers were more likely to describe Black and African American women as hostile and aggressive without giving any context for these notes in their client's case files or making similar notes about white parents.[33] Connected with that, social workers also assumed that African American or Black parents had substance abuse addictions without making the same assumptions about white parents in similar situations. These feelings map onto public perceptions of drug abuse in welfare benefit populations and account for public support of drug testing for food stamps—regardless that these programs end up spending more than they actually find people using drugs. Mostly urban areas with high concentrations of Black and African American populations have higher rates of child welfare agency intrusion, while white suburban families encounter less such intrusion. Therefore, including the perceptions held by caseworkers or people who make decisions determining benefit assistance for people applying for cash and food assistance is an important detail left out from previous studies and how they determine fitness for benefits may present different socialized ideas about race and class.

In accordance with the widely quoted statement that the ruling ideas of an age are the ideas of its ruling class, those receiving government assistance do not fare well in public discussions.[34] By defining Black women as "welfare queens" and overwhelmingly dependent on welfare, without considering historical constructions of poverty, this racialization makes many welfare recipients, who are white, invisible.[35] Therefore, a reversal of roles occurs now—Black families formerly written out of the welfare recipient debate become the focus, and Black mothers are configured as "welfare queens."[36] While Black people experience high rates of poverty, white people make up most welfare benefit recipients; yet they are less likely to be seen as recipients by the public.

WHAT THE W-2 CAN DO FOR YOU

To connect these larger governmental issues to a more central focus, it is important to discuss the ways that the Wisconsin Works, or W-2 program changed how people access benefits and how that affected Black program participants. The cliff's notes of W-2 are simply seen as from "welfare to workfare" for women and children—the Wisconsin version of TANF and took more extreme steps to ensure this change. Most of the literature about welfare recipients is about how they experience the system, not the emotional and mental labor that goes into working with the boundaries of these programs. Therefore, a researcher at UW-Madison focused on amplifying voices and experiences with welfare benefits, specifically, Baldwin examines how Black women specifically navigate the changes in the Wisconsin W-2 program and how the transition from welfare to workfare specifically affected them.[37] She also used the opportunity to question whether the voices of Black women are heard, as well as, whether there was any concern for them among policymakers and the issues that they face.[38] Baldwin's dissertation[39] examines the success of the W-2 Wisconsin Works program through the voices of Black women themselves. While Baldwin[40] examines the W-2 program success and examined the effects through the voices of Black women, this work broadens the approach to how intersectional perceptions of women and men of all identities perceive themselves and others regarding the use of other benefit assistance programs.

SOCIAL CONSTRUCTION AHEAD

The following sections illustrate how we understand these social constructions and how they inform our perceptions. Because the contents of these following pages discuss perceptions, it would be expedient to revisit the sociological literature by Mead, Cooley, and Goffman.[41] Foundational theories about perception, the self and society, and the "looking glass self" all point to the ways in which people understand themselves, how they perceive others, and how people think others perceive them.[42] There is no self (I) prior to the social (we); structures of the self can take shape through daily interactions with others; people constantly modify actions to present a self-image and self-presentation as a response to the social.[43] Mead examines the ways in which the "I" part of the self is a response to the "me," which is a set of others' attitudes organized within the self. In this case, the perceptions of those who receive benefit assistance are shaped by how they think other people view benefit receipt. Much of the perception of benefit recipients are overwhelmingly negative, given the number of negative media reports and numerous attempts to restrict how people use their benefits.[44] Using these perceptions formulated through various interactions, including interacting with media, one forms a self-image and applies that to oneself and to others.[45]

Goffman[46] further extends Mead and Cooley's symbolic interactionism in his theory of the presentation of self; we organize our lives through encounters with others and manage impressions of ourselves in front of others. Welfare recipients need to convey the image of poverty, because if they do not, they risk being perceived as untruthful about needing benefits—such as judgments on car make and model, if the vehicle looks *too* nice, or if they themselves are dressed too fashionably and recipients need to behave the "right" way to be considered part of the "deserving poor." People receiving benefits must fit into a narrow window of what it means to be poor and exude the appearances expected of them. People who do not fit into this narrowly defined space, by having certain clothes, shoes, cars, cell phones, and the ability to buy certain food items, are deemed as undeserving and not the "right type" of poor.

During some of the writing of this book, I was unemployed and receiving SNAP assistance. In some ways, it felt very much like an "art imitating life" experience, as I shopped in various stores, both local and specialty, and felt the prying eyes of other shoppers awaiting to check out. I say prying eyes because I already know about the perceptions of how people look at those who use their benefits. While Mead, Cooley, and Goffman all discuss how the self and society interact, they did not go into detail about the ways gender, race, and other socioeconomic factors specifically affect how one views oneself, others, and how others might see one through institutionalized racism, classism, and sexism.

At the onset of the pandemic, I was joined by 80 million other people who were thrusted into unexpected unemployment. News reports circulated regarding the intense toll this was taking on the economy. To help cushion the impact, Congress in seeming reluctance, passed the CARES Act via the Pandemic Unemployment Assistance Program, which included many items but most importantly extended unemployment for thirteen more weeks (unemployment is available for 26 weeks) and for four months included a bump in the unemployment benefits that people would receive. This drew a series of objections from lawmakers, convinced that the unemployment bump would be more than what the unemployed person would make from their paycheck. The pandemic had a way of making people say how they really felt—in some ways highlighting the class inequality structure that exists but goes on denied in the United States. People were frustrated with the unemployment benefits increase; however, this is less a problem with unemployment and a more general glaring problem with how wages are not high enough for people to get by during their day-to-day lives. Over the course of the year, with the public expressing increased frustration about the pandemic, there was an increased focus on the "freeloading unemployed"—tens of millions of people who unexpectedly lost their jobs or were furloughed for an undetermined amount of time. While other nations provided extended care for their citizens, it took almost nine months for Congress to greenlight a $600 check to families—with more discussions about an additional $1,400 to make $2000, which is still yet to be decided. During this time, unemployment systems were overwhelmed with the millions of applicants applying for assistance.

This is a stark difference from the easy passage of the 2017 tax cuts and pandemic corporation stimulus by Congress members in 2020, the protection of the corporation, at the expense of American families. It is also exemplary of the wealthy protecting their own and pushing harmful rhetoric onto working- and middle-class families. It also places the same concern on how relief was rapidly released to people who were in far less precarious situations, and there was much less rapid movement for the average American. However, this bleeds into how poverty as an experience evolved over time.

WHEN SOCIOLOGY VICTIM-BLAMED: EXPLORING THE MYTH OF THE CULTURE OF POVERTY

The frameworks of poverty often revolve around various approaches, such as the culture of poverty, spatial mismatch which detail how perceptions and representations of welfare recipients involve problematic assumptions. Other than understanding power structures, these approaches provide one way to understand how people in poverty are configured and presented, but they nevertheless leave a gap by failing to fully address welfare recipients' actual experiences, which conflict with popular victim-blaming presumptions, as well as what this means in Milwaukee.

The "Culture of poverty" rhetoric is hypothetically race-neutral but often refers to an "underclass" of Black families that make poor decisions, based on problematic beliefs about people of color.[47] This supposed unhealthy culture was said to cause Black families to lack the social mobility to emerge from poverty and thus transferred to the next generation. Not that culture of poverty does not exist for white families, the framework that people use to discuss their lives is different.

Building off Lewis' culture of poverty work, Moynihan, a sociologist-turned-senator (and major sellout) who also worked for the Nixon administration, argued that the failings of the Black community were not due to the lack of available jobs or enduring issues of racism and discrimination for African American and Black families, but the increase of Black single mothers, whom he pathologized as the reason for the downturn of the Black community.[48] The Moynihan/Nixon connection is the foundation for the racialized rhetoric of that administration and the ones that emerged after it. Since at the time, most white people considered racism to be "over," due to the signing of the Civil Rights Act in 1965 and anything experienced by the Black and African American community was seen as a personal failing, not a systemic, structural, or institutional one. Since legislators believed that Black families were undeserving of assistance, the lives of Black families began to experience more intense regulation upon benefit receipt. Moynihan and Lewis failed to recognize that many white families benefited greatly from federal welfare programs—such as Federal Housing grants and the GI bill—and more white families were thus able to lift themselves out of poverty and increase their wealth and assets.[49] Over time, the media constructions of welfare as one of Blackness versus whiteness created an environment of "us versus them" pathology. In turn, belief in a culture-of-poverty theory allowed for those with a privileged racial status to enact problematic welfare legislation that perpetuated faulty popular representations, such as "if x group can make it, why is x group unable." It creates a foil that disrupts actual systemic, structural, and institutional change. Other researchers critiqued the theory of a culture of poverty or offered a blended explanation.[50] For example, William Julius Wilson, in his earlier work, believed that the reason for intergenerational poverty was not necessarily a cultural issue, but more prominently, the issue of deindustri-alization—the reduction in manufacturing/factory jobs, increase in service positions, and the lack of well-paying jobs in areas where there are high populations of Black workers.[51] However, his later work began to emulate a Moynihan-esque approach to why Black families experience poverty, without looking at the historical and enduring nature of racialized policies and discrimination.

SPATIAL MISMATCH

Spatial mismatch hypothesis emphasizes a mismatch between low-income households and suitable job opportunities, which mostly affected Black and African American populations and rural whites—for example, the techno-logical push from coal or oil production to more eco-friendly innovations.[52] Some other scholars argue that the issue is not so much a spatial mismatch, but more a racial mismatch—employers choosing not to locate where Black people live, which dictates where Black people are hired.[53] Wilson[54] con-nected the structural theory of spatial mismatch with cultural factors. For example, Wilson[55] contends that Black women headed households and low rates of marriage are some of the reasons for the downfall of the Black community. This analysis does not clearly examine the impact of racism or policies/legislation that disparately affect people of color, or wrestle with the mass incarceration or the high populations of Black and brown men behind bars. Other researchers argue that culture-of-poverty theory hinders the debate in discussing poverty—because it fails to grapple with any systemic or structural barriers that make getting ahead or out of poverty more difficult.[56] But why does any of this matter? What does spatial mismatch mean in terms of food insecurity and how people experience poverty?

MILWAUKEE: SITES OF SPATIAL
MISMATCH AND FOOD INSECURITY

Milwaukee, in relation to its population size, is named the nation's most segregated city.[57] While the history of segregation goes back to the Great Migration (1910—1970), particularly the post–World War II second wave when many African Americans from the southern United States migrated to Milwaukee, its continuance can also be partly explained through the decades of "urban renewal" displacing families and creating new neighborhoods of concentrated poverty.[58] Much of Milwaukee was shaped by the construction of new highways such as I-43, which bifurcated parts of the Southside and Milwaukee's Black neighborhoods. Businesses closed and forced people to migrate North.[59] Since spatiality is not naturally occurring but a phenomenon socially constructed through migrations, restrictive covenants, government and industry policies, and societal attitudes in different cities, a sociological examination of sites of encounters is important.[60]

Similarly, how cities come to terms with the reality of segregation related to racist and classist policies can be examined by analyzing the geographical location and spatiality of grocery stores. Therefore, connected to the segregation related to racist and classist policies, the geographical location and spatiality of where stores are located is also related to how people perceive themselves and others. Since Milwaukee is the most segregated American city, notions of spatiality and who is occupying that space may be particularly interesting. Nutritional redlining, where grocery stores are spatially located near interstitial areas (where white and Black neighborhoods blur) and access to healthy, nutritious food is placed at a distance.[61] Food insecurity is an issue that affects people in many cities. Previous work by scholars notes that Milwaukee's food insecurity has a long-standing history.[62]

Much of this history began with a Milwaukee Chapter of the Black Panthers, who met in the early 1970s to bring school breakfast and lunch programs to Milwaukee children. This program was not Milwaukee specific, but one of the goals of the BPP, established in Oakland, California, to help meet the needs of the marginalized communities, specifically those who are Black and brown. The BPP often gets mischaracterized in history books and in the common narrative; however, much of the work of the organization was to alleviate the effects that discrimination had on Black families. For the BPP and its equity measures, Black liberation would entail the liberation for all other marginalized groups. Therefore, with the oppression of Black people no longer in existence, it would signify the end of oppression for all other groups.

In terms of Milwaukee, the BPP was instrumental in bringing the idea of food insecurity to the broader community, which through the 1970s began a Milwaukee institution—HTF, a free and local food bank that services the Milwaukee area. Without the three BPP members and the listening ear of Pastor Joseph Ellwanger, who mused that without these three Black men, it was unknown whether people in the city would have known that child hunger was an issue and even less that there would be a breakfast and lunch program for marginalized and low-income youth in their schools. Many of the programs which are branded as government programs originally began via these revolutionary measures—like the BPP and concerned citizens taking up the charge.

It is important to explore the issue of food insecurity via the relationship that local geography and the inability to access quality foods have with and between each other. Therefore, the understanding of that spatiality arises from how people continually change and are connected with different power structures which can and should be disrupted through learning and engaging with others.[63] For example, instead of seeing the lack of grocery stores as a problem inherent to the Black community and Black community alone, a critical approach would examine everything that surrounds the outcome of hypertension and other health-related issues. The easy answer is just thinking that this is a problem within a community versus a neglect from outside a community. Elwood et al.[64] note that geographical conceptions of geography are constituted in three distinct ways: socio-spatial, epistemological, and politics of possibility.

I think that it is important to note that the data collection occurred in a different neighborhood than I lived, and I did not live in the community I was researching. As I was traveling around the city, it made being self-reflexive much more important because I was being welcomed into people's homes and they were sharing their experiences with me. Undoubtedly, I know that perceptions work in various ways and that taking time out of their day to have me enter their home was probably unfamiliar to them. However, it is important to highlight these key moments as support for how we all live in situations that may not be exact but are similar. Other researchers explore this engagement through sites of encounter or contact.[65] Geographers use Allport's contact hypothesis to how researchers can be more mindful of the shared space between strangers collecting data from participants.[66] Therefore, for researchers who may live in different areas than the people that are their participants, consistently remaining mindful of the role inequalities play in restructuring how race and gender often interact is vital.

This chapter explored the various ways in which theory can be present in data collection and how perceptions matter via the changing rhetoric of welfare benefit receipt. The theoretical lens helps us understand how power and language matter in how we can apply them to the geographical considerations that often impact groups differently. This chapter described the overarching national identifications of welfare programs and how it is applied in Milwaukee. The following chapters will explore how specifically this rhetoric occurs in Milwaukee, how it operates, and how different groups navigate what is often a very confusing road of red tape.

NOTES

1. Baldwin, "Stratification"; Gilens *Americans Hate Welfare*; Kingfisher, "Welfare Reform"; Lieberman, *Shifting the Color Line*; Lubiano, Black Ladies; Quadagno, *Color of Welfare*; Seccombe, *Cadillac.*

2. Gilens, *Americans Hate Welfare*; Handler and Hollingsworth, "Stigma"; Lewis, *Sanchez, Poverty*; Moynihan, "Negro Family"; Quadagno, *Color of Welfare*; Roberts, *Killing the Black Body*; Rogers-Dillon, "Dynamics"; Seccombe, *Cadillac.*

3. Baldwin, "Stratification"; Bullock, "Attributions"; Gilens, *Americans Hate Welfare*; Rank, "View"; Seccombe, *Cadillac.*

4. Lieberman, *Shifting the Color Line*; Quadagno, *Color of Welfare.*

5. Collins, *Black Feminist Thought, Black Sexual Politics*; Gilens *Americans Hate Welfare*; Lieberman, *Shifting the Color Line*; Roberts, "Patriarchy."

6. Baldwin, *"Wisconsin Works."*

7. Gilens, *Americans Hate Welfare*; Lieberman, *Shifting the Color Line*; Quadagno, *Transformation, Color of Welfare.*

8. Gilens, *Americans Hate Welfare*; Lieberman, *Shifting the Color Line*; Roberts, *Killing the Black Body.*

9. Fligstein and McAdam, *Theory*; Roberts, *Killing the Black Body.*

10. Gilens, *Americans Hate Welfare.*

11. Davis, "Birth Control"; Roberts, *Killing the Black Body.*

12. Gilens, *Americans Hate Welfare.*

13. Ibid, *Americans Hate Welfare*, 117.

14. Bonilla-Silva *Racism without Racists*; Gilens *Americans Hate Welfare*; Lieberman, *Shifting the Color Line*; Lipsitz, *Possessive Investment*; Quadagno, *Color of Welfare.*

15. Gilens, *Americans Hate Welfare*; Lieberman, *Shifting the Color Line*; Quadagno, *Color of Welfare*; Roberts, *Killing the Black Body.*

16. Gilens, *Americans Hate Welfare*; Lieberman, *Shifting the Color Line*; Quadagno, *Color of Welfare.*

17. Gilens, *Americans Hate Welfare*; Lieberman, *Shifting the Color Line*; Quadagno, *Transformation; Color of Welfare.*

18. Bonila-Silva *Racism without Racists.*

19. Ibid.

20. Goldberg, *Racial State.*

21. Ibid.

22. Ibid.

23. Ibid.

24. Bonilla-Silva, *White Supremacy; Racism without Racists*; Lipsitz, *Possessive Investment.*

25. Bonilla-Silva, *Racism without Racists*; Lipsitz, *Possessive Investment*; Roberts, "Patriarchy," *Invention,* "Prison"; Taylor, *From #BlackLivesMatter.*

26. Aberson, Shoemaker, and Tomolillo, "Implicit Bias"; Allport, *Prejudice*; Lee, "Making Race Salient."

27. Allport, *Prejudice.*

28. Bullock, "Attributions."

29. Ibid.

30. It would be remiss to think that every study can do everything about a large issue, like poverty.

31. Delaney and Scheller, White People.

32. Collins, Di Leonardo, and Williams, *Landscapes*; Collins and Gimenez, *Domestic Labor*; Edin and Shaefer, *$2.00 a Day*; Halpern-Meekin et al., *It's Not like I'm Poor*; Quadagno, *Color of Welfare.*

33. Roberts, "Prison."

34. Collins, *Black Feminist Thought, Black Sexual Politics*; Marx and Engels, *It's Not like I'm Poor*; Roberts, "Patriarchy," *Killing the Black Body.*

35. Collins, *Black Feminist Thought, Black Sexual Politics*; Collins and Gimenez, *Wages*; Edin and Shaefer, *$2.00 a Day*; Lieberman, *Shifting the Color Line*; Quadagno, *Color of Welfare*; Roberts, "Patriarchy"; *Killing the Black Body*; "Prison."

36. Collins, *Black Sexual Politics*; Lieberman, *Shifting the Color Line*; Quadagno, *Color of Welfare.*

37. Ibid.

38. Ibid.

39. Ibid.

40. Ibid.

41. Cooley, *Social Order; Social Organization*; Goffman, *Presentation*; Mead, *Mind, Self and Society.*

42. Ibid.

43. Ibid.

44. Bullock, "Attributions"; Diamond 1966; Gilens, *Americans Hate Welfare*; Halpern-Meekin et al. *It's Not like I'm Poor*; Kingfisher, "Welfare Reform"; Lieberman, *Shifting the Color Line*; Quadagno, *Transformation, Color of Welfare*; Rank, "View"; Seccombe, *Cadillac.*

45. Mead, *Mind, Self and Society.*

46. Goffman, *Presentation.*

47. Lewis, *Poverty.*

48. Moynihan, "Negro Family."

49. Bonilla-Silva, *Racism without Racists*; Collins, Di Leonardo, and Williams *Landscapes*; Edin and Shaefer, *$2.00 a Day*; Halpern-Meekin et al., *It's Not like I'm Poor*; Lipsitz, *Possessive Investment*; Oliver and Shapiro, *Racial Inequality*; Roberts, *Killing the Black Body.*

50. Edin and Shaefer, *$2.00 a Day*; Newman, *No shame.*

51. Wilson, *Declining, Disadvantaged, Disappears.*

52. Hellerstein, Neumark, and McInerney, "Spatial mismatch"; Kain, "Housing"; Wilson, *Declining*, *Disadvantaged*, *Disappears*.

53. Hellerstein, Neumark, and McInerney, "Spatial mismatch."

54. Wilson, *Just Race*.

55. Ibid 2009.

56. Gilens, *Americans Hate Welfare*; Gorski, "Myth"; Leacock, "Culture of Poverty"; Lieberman, *Shifting the Color Line*; Massey and Denton, *American Apartheid*; Quadagno, *Color of Welfare*.

57. Loyd and Bonds "Where Do Black Lives Matter"; Rosenblatt and Cossyleon, "Pushing the Boundaries."

58. Massey and Denton, *American Apartheid*; Niemuth, "Urban Renewal."

59. Niemuth, "Urban Renewal."

60. Elwood, Lawson, and Sheppard, "Geographical Relational."

61. Blauner, "Internal Colonialism"; Cho and Clark, "Disparities"; Eisenhauer, "In Poor Health"; Kwate et al., "Fried Chicken"; McBride, "Nutrition"; Schram, *Supermarket*.

62. Bonds, Racing Economic Geography; Heynen, "Monitoring Wisconsin"; Heynen, Kurtz, and Trauger, "Food Justice"; Jones, "March On Milwaukee"; Loyd and Bonds, "Where Do Black Lives Matter."

63. Elwood, Lawson, and Sheppard, , "Geographical Relational."

64. Ibid, 746.

65. Allport, *Prejudice*.

66. Valentine, Living with Difference; Valentine, Sporton, and Bang Nielsen, Language Use; Wilson, On Geography and Encounter.

Chapter 4

Food Insecurity in an American City

Like an unspoken marker, Holton Avenue runs through the heart of Milwaukee's northside and separates two different worlds, one Black and the other white. While hiding in plain sight, Holton Avenue helps visualize Milwaukee's unwanted honor as the most segregated city of America.[1] The food pantry where I met my participants is on the west side of Holton and when I would take the bus or drive through the neighborhoods, I would explicitly see the physical characteristics of the neighborhoods change, which are rooted in elements of Milwaukee's history. One day, after pantry, I was driving Wynette home, and my gas light popped on. There was a gas station at Holton and Center Street, and I pulled in. She told me that I needed to do this quickly because this station was dangerous and said, "ooh girl, you couldn't get me outta this car to get gas, nuh uh, no." As we pulled away, there was a front door littered with bullet holes and she said, "there's so many holes, you can't even tell which one is the peephole." I asked her why they were there, and she just presumed gang violence or a drug deal gone wrong. She consistently worried about my safety when I was doing my research. But this is only part of the story of how people live and navigate Milwaukee.

This presence and absence might geographically represent the notion of real and symbolic annihilation. Real annihilation is configured via the destruction of buildings, homes, and businesses. Symbolic annihilation manifests in Milwaukee's northside by being both present and absent in people's minds—in terms of how people might focus and erase its business and residential areas. Milwaukee's racial history gained attention with the marches across the 16th street bridge, led by the Milwaukee chapter of the National Association for the Advancement of Colored People, NAACP Freedom House, and Fr. James Groppi during the late 1960s, which are well-documented by Jones' *March on Milwaukee Civil Rights History Project*, and maintained by University of Wisconsin-Milwaukee Archives Library.[2]

This chapter highlights two neighborhoods as examples of Milwaukee's racial history and its change over half a century. Using information from the UWM Archives, Milwaukee Black Historical Society, US Social Explorer, and census data, this chapter attempts to show demonstrable racial change over time with geographical food deserts and food insecurity which create and maintain spatial mismatch and difference. Understanding the creation and maintenance of nutritional redlining is just as important as understanding barriers to housing and educational equality in a northern city.[3] Let us explore manifestations of how geography, poverty, inequality in terms of proximity to food insecurity play a role in the city of Milwaukee's past and present.

RESULTS OF URBAN INEQUALITY

Structural geographic inequities have at times disparately impacted Black and brown residents in the most horrific way. Klinenberg[4] wrote about a heatwave that occurred in Chicago, Illinois, in 1995 that disproportionately killed over 700 Black and brown people living on the south and west sides of the city, including a similar impact during the same summer in Milwaukee. During this event, local officials tried to downplay the aftermath; many of the bodies were stored in refrigerator trucks and families were unable to have access to their loved ones.[5] More importantly, this event showed an example of government breakdown, whereby crumbling or unattended infrastructure left residents and humans in dire situations. In addition to the issue of infrastructure, it also shows failure on multiple fronts because many of the deaths were seniors, but connectedly, many of the deaths were due to the abandonment of poor neighborhoods. There was a lack of access to cooling centers and personal air conditioners, nor were electrical/power lines maintained to combat the intense heat for residents in specific neighborhoods of the city.[6] This neighborhood abandonment (lack of infrastructure, reduction of welfare aids, etc.) by cities helps facilitate geographical sites of embodied inequality. As a result, hundreds of people died due to these intersecting institutional failures.[7]

As we will find in the remaining pages of this chapter, Milwaukee's spatial mapping and food insecurity emerged over time. While Milwaukeeans are not dying because of "starvation"[8] they are blocked from accessing fresh foods, vegetables, fruits, and so on which are important to ensure cardiovascular health and overall bodily health. In the context of food and nutrition, in Milwaukee, the spatial deficits in food access create the inability to access adequate care and help reduce life expectancy for Black and brown residents on Milwaukee's northside and create a situation where "racism is the unequal distribution of death."[9]

While the work that follows is not explicitly about death, it does show how institutional abandonment has detrimental effects on people, bodies, and food security. Roberts (1997) noted that health inequalities for Black, brown, and African American people are often seen via negative outcomes in overall health. These outcomes include maternal mortality, preterm birth rates and weights, and cardiovascular health. These are often compounded by Black and brown peoples' lack of access to doctors in their area, or doctors who believe the reported symptoms that their clients are experiencing.[10] Namely, this is less about the individual's health decisions and more about the environment and factors that racism and inequality which impact a person over their lifespan.[11]

Like the previous chapter discussed, Americans are unusual in the way poverty is manifested and maintained and how poverty discourse is internalized and discussed. Poverty is as much related to the economy as it is geographically created and maintained. Poverty and segregation are not just economic constructions but are also embodied, meaning that access to healthcare, clean air, and education, matter and can be visually mapped onto and into the built environment. Often the visuals lack the ability to explore and explain things like nutrition inequality and food deserts. However, to take it one step further, these figures do not simply display inequalities, they also visualize proximity to death.

MILWAUKEE: THE GATHERING
PLACE AND THE GOOD LAND

Geographically, Milwaukee is cut in half, east to west by the Milwaukee River and north to south by the Menominee River Valley, thus illustrated by the above map (see figure 4.1). Just like many other cities in the United States, it too was subject to various internal and great migrations over the years.

Redlining maps, as shown by figure 4.2, drawn for the city of Milwaukee show how social constructions of race and class are created. Redlining, or the process of deciding where and where not to give out home mortgage loans, was prevalent during the 1930s. Created as part of Roosevelt's New Deal legislation in 1933, the HOLC was the leader in and condoned legally discriminatory mortgage lending via the manner it graded neighborhoods in cities at the time. Studies show that these grading patterns hold through to today—with many areas that were described "hazardous" as now being Black and Brown areas and areas that were declining as low-to-moderate income neighborhoods.[12] The following figures explicitly detail these by designating each with a grade and color rating, typically exemplified by the HOLC map legend, wherein green designated an A which meant "Best," blue areas

Figure 4.1   Map of Milwaukee with the Defining Lines of the I-94, I-43.

were configured with a B which meant "Still Desirable," yellow areas were indicated with C which meant "Definitely Declining" and were flagged as a caution, and finally areas shown in red were associated with a D and indicated "Hazardous"[13] (see figure 4.3).

On this redlining map of the Milwaukee area, the areas that border Lake Michigan are considered the "gold coast" which refers to an area of substantial wealth along a coastal area, often with homes that are described as "mansions." This area, which includes today's Lower and Upper East Sides, at the time were labeled C and D, which indicate "definitely declining" and "hazardous" because at the time "lower class" homes and apartments were being made available to "lower class" individuals. However, it is interesting to note that these labels are created by class designations and depend on the class status of the incoming group and housing availability, which the HOLC configured as the Lower East Sides declining class status. For example, some

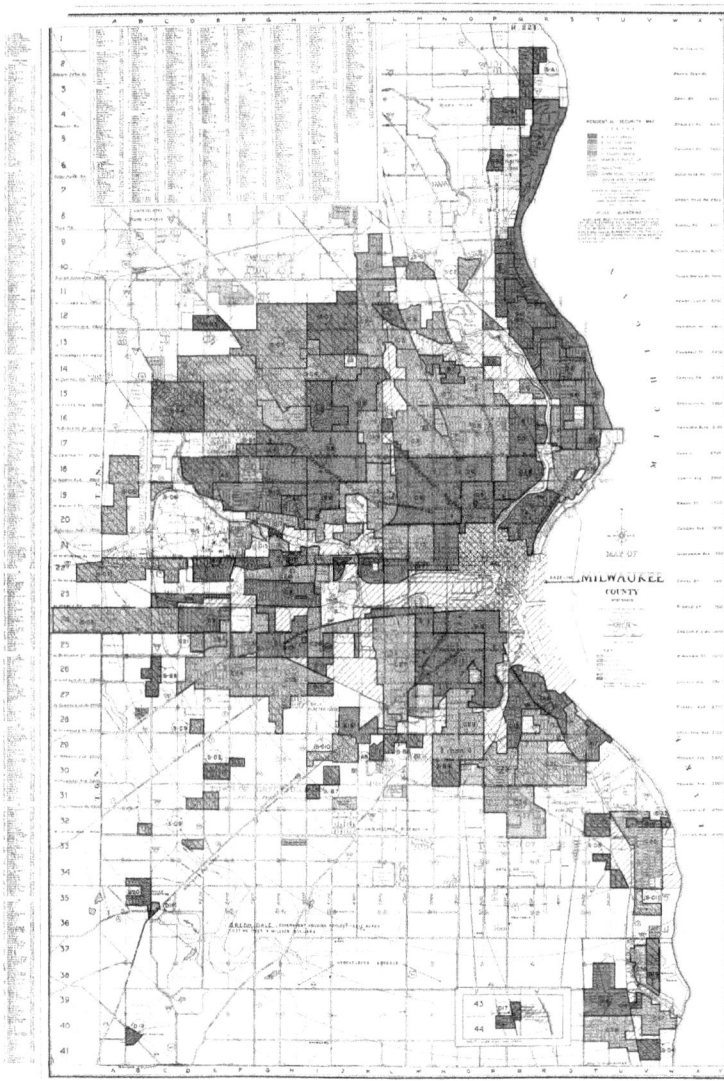

Figure 4.2 Map of Home Owner Loan Corporation (HOLC). Color-coded Map of Milwaukee.

areas are favorable toward Polish or Italian or German people if they were seen as professional or higher-class workers, versus unfavorable when the same groups were considered working class or low-wage workers. Therefore, whiteness was drawn in these figures along class lines versus racial lines. These lines change and factor both race and class if Black people and families were moving into the area.

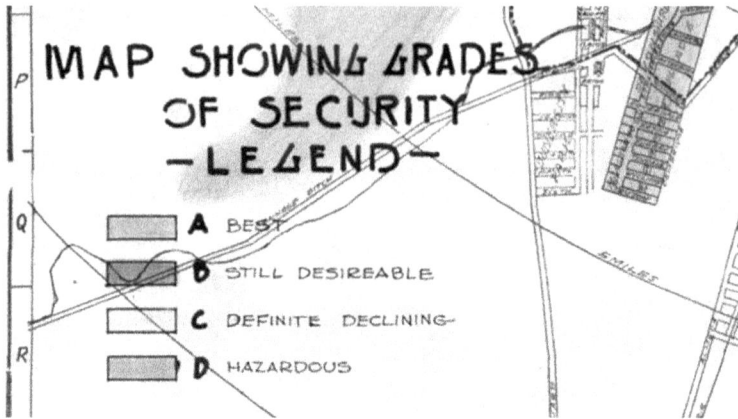

Figure 4.3   Legend for the A, B, C, D HOLC Map.

THE SOUTHSIDE

The southside has been distinctly ethnic, shifting from a predominantly Polish and Eastern European heritage, the HOLC documents claiming that "Mexicans are encroaching in the northeast," in the 1940s.[14] In this way, Mexican and Latinx migrants are seen as invading entities to the established Polish residents currently living there. However, today much of the old Polish history, Catholic churches, and other parks remain. However, perhaps more explicit is how the city and its residents cultivated the movement and enclosing of Black residents over time in Milwaukee.

While I was interviewing people in Milwaukee about its history with the HTF, I met with Reverend Ellwanger, a prominent former pastor at Cross Lutheran Church located just a bit southwest from GPLC, that in the early 1960s, the church and area were whiter. Ellwanger, originally from the south, was a prominent pastor who worked alongside notable civil rights leaders, like MLK and Milwaukee legend, Father Groppi. We met at his southside home on 16th, in an understated bungalow where he had lived since he moved to Milwaukee in the 1960s. It had a nice, welcoming feeling, filled with mementos, books, and plants. We talked about his career with MLK but I could see that he was probably tired of talking about who he was friends with and what he did in his younger years. I asked him, "what is the question that no one ever asks you, that you wish they would?" He replied, "No one has ever asked me about white flight. And what that does and how that affects communities."

When he first began his pastoral career, he was called up from the south to work in Milwaukee given his commitments to racial justice. As more Black families moved into the area, more white families moved out to places like

Menominee Falls, which is northwest of the city of Milwaukee, and which at present is still almost 90% white—essentially an anecdotal account of white flight. Ellwanger recalled that at first with the Black families moving in, they were not particularly attending the local church. Ellwanger made a few updates and changes to who appeared in the service, choir leaders, and the hymns that were sung. None of these fundamentally changes the way in which people "worship" but it was a way to blend worship styles. The church sought after him because of his ability to work with Black and white congregants; however, his white counterparts were more resistant to this change and effectively began their moves outward.

In the 1940s, evaluating the HOLC's redlining maps, the areas that are emphasized in the census maps are also the area identified as not just Black or, as written at the time, "negro," they were also described as Jewish infiltration (see figure 4.4).

Image D exemplifies how the HOLC went a step further and included not only anti-Black sentiments in their analyses of neighborhoods but also anti-Semitic sentiments. The HOLC did not just stop at anti-Black and anti-Semitic assumptions, they also included classist remarks about the individuals moving into the area. This is highlighted by their phrase "lower type Jews," which should give anyone pause, because at the time these documents were being collected and written in 1937, Jewish individuals and families were experiencing high levels of racist violence in Germany and abroad. Loewen[15] describes a series of restrictive covenants that were bolstered by anti-Black racism and anti-Semitism coupled with classism that paved the way for Jewish people to be included in restrictive covenants as well. Restrictive covenants essentially prohibited non-whites from purchasing homes from white home sellers.[16]

The HOLC was inconsistent in their anti-Semitism because, unlike Black and brown families, the HOLC could see through their "Jewishness" for some Jewish families if their class status was high enough. That does not make this better, nor should it be seen as a more "suitable" type of anti-Semitism, but it also showed that in some cases, closeness to the appearance of whiteness and having access to wealth was still considered better than being Black or brown and moving into or already existing in a neighborhood. This is exemplified in an HOLC document, Image C, which profiled an area on the northside of Milwaukee, on Center Street near Sherman and Washington Park (presently part of the Black northside) but not yet experiencing the movement of Black families northward. While in some cases, Jewish families were not seen as white, apparently this was mediated by "a steady influx of Jews of a substantial class" coming in and being noted as low-income areas. Loewen[17] notes that Black and African American movements in cities often followed Jewish families due to suspicions that these covenants would be used against

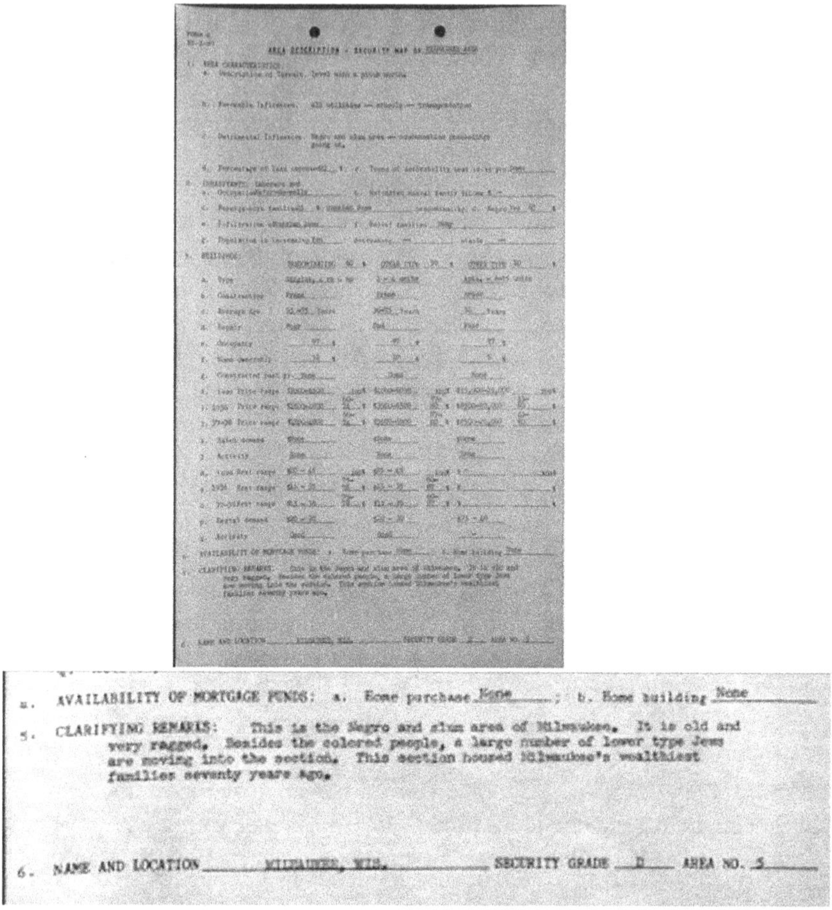

4. AVAILABILITY OF MORTGAGE FUNDS: a. Home purchase None; b. Home building None

5. CLARIFYING REMARKS: This is the Negro and slum area of Milwaukee. It is old and very ragged. Besides the colored people, a large number of lower type Jews are moving into the section. This section housed Milwaukee's wealthiest families seventy years ago.

6. NAME AND LOCATION MILWAUKEE, WIS. SECURITY GRADE D AREA NO. 5

Figure 4.4 HOLC Documentation.

Jewish families and essentially had to permit Black and African Americans to purchase their homes due to worries these restrictive covenants could be used against them.

THE WESTSIDE: HARAMBEE AND RIVERWEST

References to "west of the river" act as a geographical descriptor that helps construct perceptions of racial communities in the city of Milwaukee (see figure 4.5). Some researchers refer to Riverwest as "diverse," and it is, if you look at population percentages. However, if you break up the neighborhood

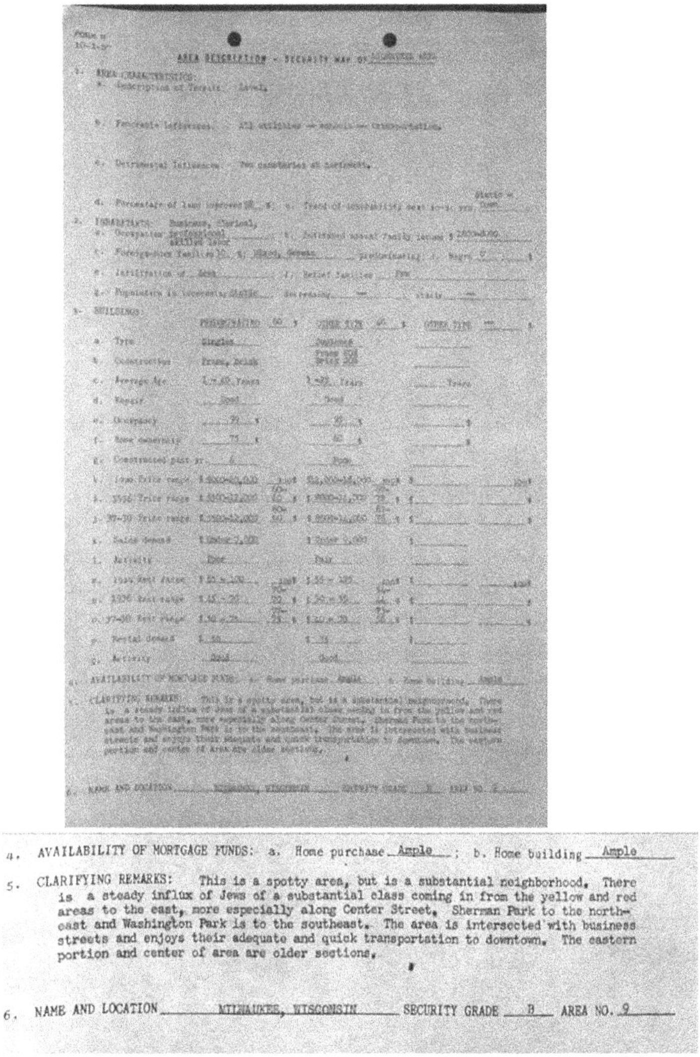

4. AVAILABILITY OF MORTGAGE FUNDS: a. Home purchase Ample ; b. Home building Ample

5. CLARIFYING REMARKS: This is a spotty area, but is a substantial neighborhood. There is a steady influx of Jews of a substantial class coming in from the yellow and red areas to the east, more especially along Center Street. Sherman Park to the north-east and Washington Park is to the southeast. The area is intersected with business streets and enjoys their adequate and quick transportation to downtown. The eastern portion and center of area are older sections.

6. NAME AND LOCATION MILWAUKEE, WISCONSIN SECURITY GRADE B AREA NO. 9

Figure 4.5 HOLC Documentation.

into its various census tracts, the viewer might notice the areas where neither white nor Black residents are moving into either tract.

Harambee neighborhood sits in contrast with Riverwest, with the defining line between the two neighborhoods being Holton Avenue. This definitive line of Holton Avenue highlights the stark nature of Milwaukee's segregation. While the study respondents live in various Milwaukee neighborhoods, many cited Harambee as where they spend or have spent a significant amount of their time. Many respondents noted that they had a history in the neighborhood, by either having family there or living by themselves at one point. Harambee is a representative neighborhood in terms of shops and residents that make up the rest of the northside. One might ask, how does this happen?

WHITE FLIGHT AND VISUALIZED SEGREGATION

Milwaukee, like Chicago, likes to call itself a city of neighborhoods, which is really just putting a pleasant face on racial segregation. Often these neighborhoods are historically created via redlining, white flight or restrictive covenants that governed residential areas over time. White flight, or the movement of white people out to the suburbs, led to high rates of deindustrialization and the creation of disenfranchised and abandoned areas in metro areas.[18]

Therefore, many of the neighborhoods that cities like Milwaukee pride themselves on are built on systemic, structural, and institutional discrimination and racism. However, much of this history remains unknown or unrecognized, particularly by white individuals. The theories of the Chicago School of Sociology place segregation, racism, and classism as natural outcomes of human existence due to people wanting to live near people who share interests, values, and perceived phenotypes.

Scholars often discuss white flight as a concept, but it becomes even more apparent when you visualize population change over time. Much of this is visualized via Social Explorer software using census data. Social Explorer is a web-based site that allows the user to create and analyze census data and other demographics using maps that date back to 1790. These maps also identify census tracts and how they changed more frequently for one neighborhood than the other. For example, prior to 1940, the census was just county-wide, but dating from 1940, census tracts were designated nationally. Because of the changes and increases in population sizes, census tracts were developed from other delineations of space and geographic mapping (census .gov). Census tracts are supposed to be relatively permanent; however, if there are population changes various tracts can be merged, split, or new ones can be created. If necessary, these arbitrary census tracts can be split into smaller tracts if they have more than 8,000 people and merged with a nearby tract if they have less than 1,200 people.

The neighborhoods of Harambee and Riverwest differ in a variety of ways and how these two neighborhoods have changed over time is dependent on a myriad of issues. Originally, the Harambee neighborhood was settled by German immigrants in the 1800s, but like many neighborhoods on the northside of Milwaukee, and other cities in the northern Midwest, it experienced similar events in white flight, with white residents moving out and Black and African Americans moving up and in due effects of northern de facto segregation.

VISUAL REPRESENTATIONS

The rest of this chapter is an attempt to visualize this discrepancy and to highlight the incredible segregation occurring within Milwaukee, compounded by the entrenchment of internal colonialism. Often, the concept of colonialism is where an outside force takes control over another area; for example, when the British Empire controlled India (as one example) or when the United States colonized Hawaii, Puerto Rico, or Guam. Blauner (1969) notes that internal colonialism emerges when an area, like a neighborhood within a city, experiences those same issues and is defined by clear and distinct boundaries and the lack of services that many other areas take for granted. Much of the discussion of Milwaukee is consistently about segregation, but Blauner (1969) adds to the complexity by noting that internal colonialism is related to keeping populations corralled in distinct areas. Therefore, the figures detail not only segregation but also internal colonialism of non-white populations as well.

DEMOGRAPHIC SHIFTS 1940

In 1940, Milwaukee was heavily populated by immigrants from Germany, Poland, and other eastern European nations, which we now collectively group as white. In what became known as Harambee, there was a significant white population indicated by the high concentration of white space from the census. While some of the census tracts transcend the border of Harambee (the rectangle), the white population was just over 50,000 white residents (white space) and just under 1,000 Black residents (gray space) (see figure 4.6). The rectangle area is Harambee and Riverwest and the street that splits Harambee and Riverwest is Holton Avenue. Harambee and the northside includes census tracts 63, 61 62, 60, 52, 53, 54, 55, 36, 35, 34, 33. This contrasts with over 20,000 white residents and zero Black residents in Riverwest at this time, which is east of the line, in census tracts 32, 56, 57, 58, and 59. In 1940, we find that the Black population in Milwaukee resides around the area of Walnut St (below 36, 35), which was locally known as Milwaukee's Black Wall Street or colloquially known as Bronzeville. In the figures that follow, they detail a shift northward due to the construction of Milwaukee's interstate system, which is not unlike other cities in the United States that demolished

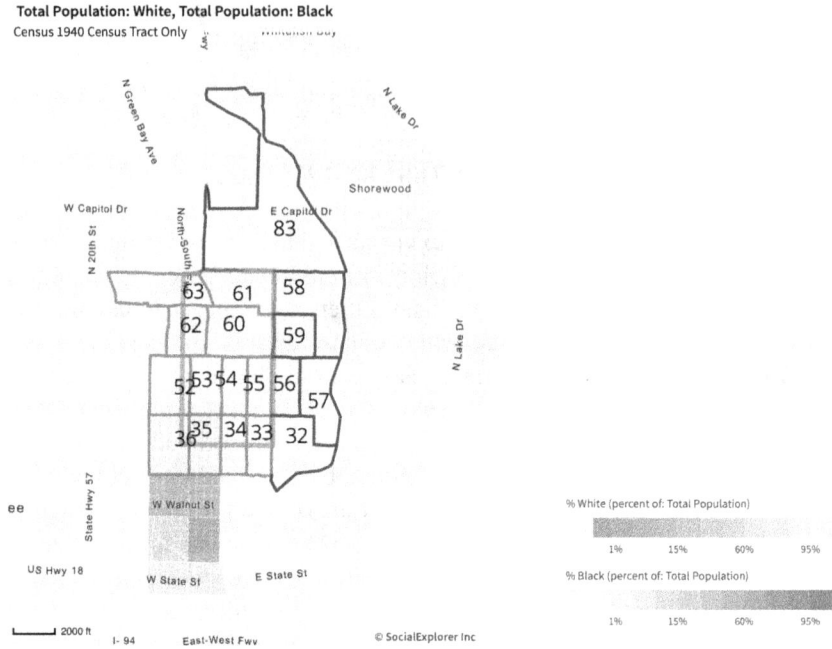

Total Population: White, Total Population: Black
Census 1940 Census Tract Only

Figure 4.6   1940 Census Map, Gray (Black Populations), White (White Areas).

Black Wall Streets to make way for city and suburban dwellers access in and out of the area. Over time, with each map, we see the visualized map of white flight or white families that fled from integration or the influx of Black families into the city and neighborhoods of Milwaukee.

Archival research at the Milwaukee Public Library revealed that the area of North Third Street (which was renamed Dr. Martin Luther King Jr. Boulevard in the 1980s), and Auer within the boundaries of the Harambee neighborhood, had a bustling commercial center. This photo from 1948, pictures a Walgreens, Kohl's produce store (which later became the Kohl's department store) and a well-connected streetcar system (figure 4.7). Not to mention that there was a Rapid Transit connection nearby that transported residents to northern nearby towns like Cedarburg, Sheboygan, and Port Washington (all predominately white). Other than the Milwaukee County Transit system, these modes of transportation within and outside the city no longer exist, which begs the question regarding the removal of these systems. It is also peculiar because these transit lines were removed after the demographic change of white residents to predominantly Black residents. This works to the same effect as Blauner's concept of internal colonialism—whereby a population is bounded by a dominant one with interstitial

Figure 4.7 3rd St (Renamed MLK Blvd in the 1980s) and Auer—Historic Photo Collection/Milwaukee Public Library. *Source:* Used with permission from Milwaukee Public Library.

areas (blurring) and then a clearly defined line that shows the demographic shift. Shown are the effects of white flight, as well as how to entrap residents within their communities and make it harder for them to cross its boundaries into other areas.

To visualize the above picture and place it in the context of a neighborhood, the intersection of 3rd and Auer is essentially the upper left area of Harambee (the rectangle) and movement to the northside of Milwaukee. However, consistent with HOLC documents detailing Black "encroachment," the demographic movement does show Black populations increasing in the bottom, almost middle of the map, which is indicated by gray/darker gray shading.

The decade between 1940 and 1950, there was a demonstrative demographic change wherein the Milwaukee Black population increased in the area that was considered Milwaukee's Bronzeville. Due to the increase of Black Milwaukeeans, the Milwaukee Green Book featured many local Black-owned or were businesses deemed safe for Black Americans. There were Green Books for most states and also a national green book, for motorists that wanted to safely explore the United States. The important part of this book is not just its existence but that the book details many places in Milwaukee and indicates that the new city had a developing and thriving Black Wall Street, with quality grocery stores, lawyers, beauty shops, and so on, within its borders. (This of course does not indicate that Milwaukee businesses writ large

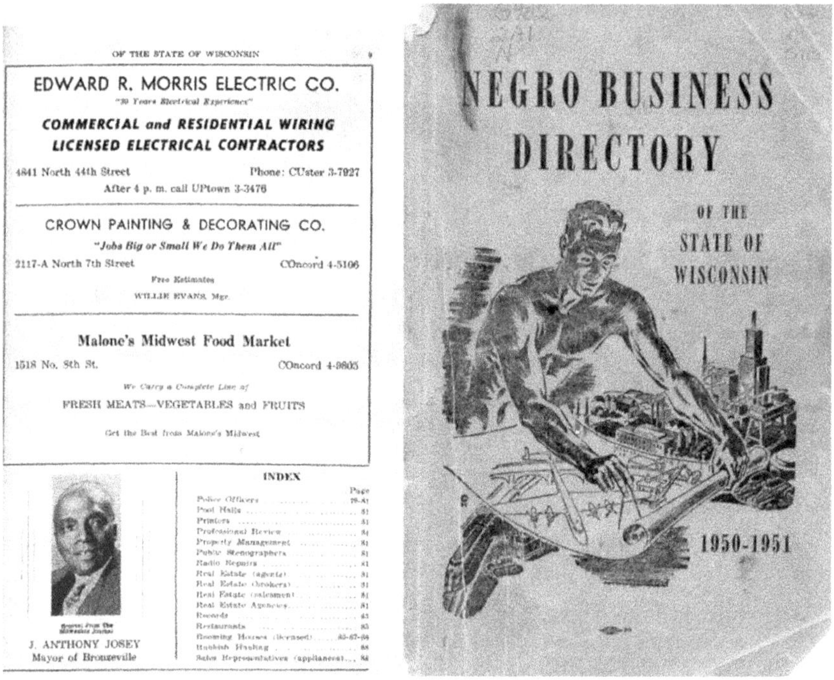

Figure 4.8   Milwaukee Green Book.

welcomed Black and African American residents—businesses simply served an emerging clientele and risks increased which resulted in Milwaukee producing its own green book [see figure 4.8]).

DEMOGRAPHIC SHIFTS 1950

Moving forward into 1950, Milwaukee's Black population shifted northward with the new residents staying a distance from the Holton Avenue Harambee/Riverwest border. There is a large population of white residents in tracts 33 and 34. The Black population moved into the area above Bronzeville for its proximity. The census data visualized from 1950 shows a direct movement directly north and the beginning of white flight from Harambee, with just over 45,000 white residents and 7,000 Black residents—which seems small—but from 1940 to the end of the 1950s there was a drop of 5,000 white residents and an increase of 6,000 Black residents (figure 4.9).

This map shows that Riverwest is just over 21,000 white people and a burgeoning population of 5 Black people. The description of the movement northward not only visualizes segregation and enduring issues of

Total Population: White, Total Population: Black
Census 1950 Census Tract Only

Figure 4.9   1950 Census Map, Gray (Black Populations), White (White Areas).

internal colonialism but also details the HOLC's redlining discrimination. The area where HOLC designated neighborhoods as declining was where Black and Jewish residents were moving northward (Mitchell and Franco 2018).

DEMOGRAPHIC SHIFTS 1960

As time moved on to the 1960s, Milwaukee experienced a growing Black population in Harambee but a relatively stable white population in the Riverwest area to the east in tracts 32, 56, 57, 58, and 59. In 1960, the Harambee Black population edges out the white population at over 26,000 people to 21,600 white residents. Therefore, in a 20-year timeframe, the white population dropped by over half and clustered in a particular area. Through this 10-year period, from 1950 to 1960, the figures illustrate Blauner's concept of internal colonialism via the boundaries built over time—the white areas acting as borders of "containment" for the emerging Black populations in and around these census tracts (figure 4.10).

Milwaukee in the 1960s was a relatively tumultuous place—like many cities across the United States and in the North and Northeast, there were

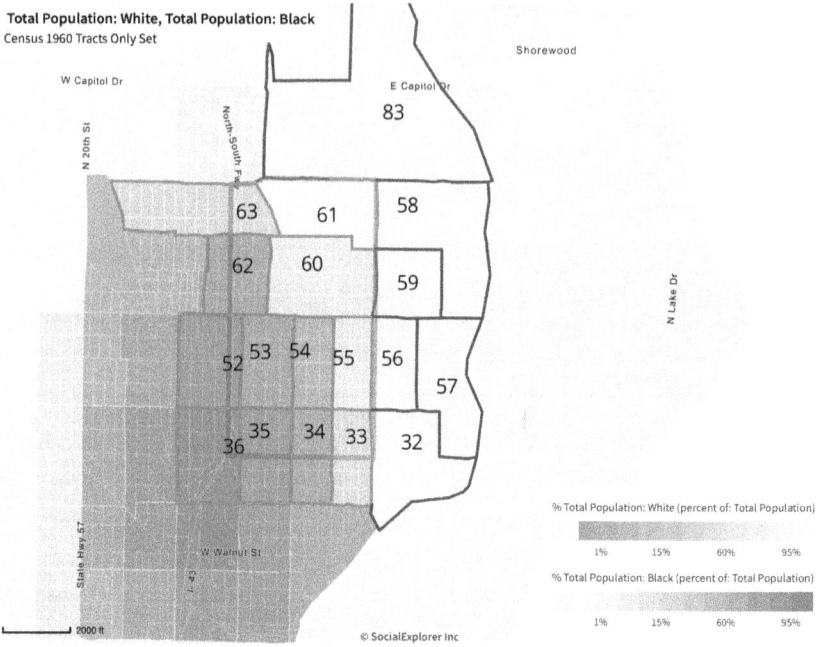

Figure 4.10   1960 Census Map, Gray (Black Populations), White (White Areas).

marches and demands for racial equality.[19] Local activists like Representative Vel Phillips, Lloyd Barbee, and Fr. Groppi advocated at the local and state level for fair housing, access to equal education and job opportunities. Just shy of 20 years from the above photo in 1948, Milwaukee also experienced race riots in the summer of 1967 along the same streets pictured. The summer of 1967 predates the marches for equality in Milwaukee and in cities around the United States.

GREAT MIGRATIONS

To understand these demographic shifts, people moving into Milwaukee had to move from somewhere else. During my participant interviews, I would often ask people where their families were from—were they native Milwaukeeans or were their families from other cities. Many of the Black interviewees would discuss how their families moved up from Louisiana, Missouri, Arkansas, Mississippi, Alabama, and Georgia. They recounted how their families met and moved northward—sometimes leaving behind more elderly residents. For many, they talked about how they themselves were children in the south and then moved up with their parents or they moved north with their spouses as adults. For most, Chicago was a layover point before they moved to Milwaukee. These migrations track how people moved from place to place up from the south, in search of better opportunities, livelihoods, and "safety" for themselves and their families. Safety is placed in quotations to highlight the issue surrounding de facto (feelings, thoughts, and emotions) and de jure (by law) segregation that also existed in northern cities regarding job discrimination, restrictive covenants, redlining, and, most recently, the subprime mortgage loan crisis. Not to mention, northern cities like Chicago and Milwaukee had various white uprisings protesting integration in education, transportation, and housing—so it is important to not paint northern areas as racial utopias.

During the decades between 1940 and 1970, Milwaukee, like other northern cities, was experiencing the Great Migration, or the largest demographic shift of Black or African Americans moving from the south up through to the north.[20] Like many other northern cities, Milwaukee was the destination point for many people who formerly lived in the south and sought better jobs and "safer" communities.[21]

Adding to the effects of the riots, instead of seeking to remedy community relations, shops decided to pull business out from the area and move elsewhere—essentially practicing business white flight. One example of this might be the store, Lerner Foods, which was located on what is now MLK and 5th at the most northern point of Harambee. Lerner Foods shows signs that advertise their available "Fresh and Smoked Meats" and "Fresh Greens Daily." The car models parked out indicate that this photo was taken at some point during the 1960s. The building that once was Lerner's still exists in the area, but no longer houses an important grocery store for local residents. Similar grocery stores dotted the northside of Milwaukee, for example, the Kohl's Grocery Store (now known as the clothing/housewares store) on 64th and Silver Spring, which is just west of Harambee but closed sometime later and replaced with a vacant lot (figure 4.11).

Therefore, the seeds of poverty were sewn as deindustrialization begin to affect the areas mostly inhabited by Black residents. Grocery stores with healthy foods moved out and chain restaurants offering fast, cheap food moved in. Transportation systems serving wider areas were disassembled. Governmental and economic actions were taken that directly but negatively impacted these areas and the effects of this are still evident today. These geographies are a creation of political and economic white flight. Disinvestment in the Black Milwaukee over time built into the large swaths of disenfranchisement that helped mold and sustain Black and white wealth gaps.

Figure 4.11   Lerner's Market, Green Bay Avenue (MLK Ave.)—Historic Photo Collection/ Milwaukee Public Library. *Source:* Used with permission from Milwaukee Public Library.

DEMOGRAPHIC SHIFTS 1970

The decade between 1960 and 1970 shifted the northside to how it looks at present—albeit at this time, smaller. Instead of being a relatively equal number of residents between white and Black people, whites accounted for solely 6,000 people and Black residents in this area account for almost 32,000 residents. The demographics do a complete shift, wherein the population numbers flip almost completely and what is clearly seen in Harambee and the surrounding northside is demonstrable white flight and the confinement of Milwaukee's Black population. What is also prominently featured in the below is a strong demarcation line, with the darker shaded areas being areas of higher Black population and the lighter areas containing prominent white populations in Harambee and Riverwest, along the line that borders the new census tracts of 71, 72, 79, 80, 107 which were formerly 32, 56, 57, 58, and 59. These arbitrary census tracts can be split into smaller tracts if they have more than 8,000 people; more people may move into an area or be merged with a nearby tract if they have less than 1,200 people (figure 4.12).

Figure 4.12   1970 Census Map, Gray (Black Populations), White (White Areas).

However, the 1960s posed new developments in terms of Black entrapment with two noticeable changes in the area. One was the creation of new census tracts—due to the drastic population shifts, new tracts were added to account for this change and will be discussed shortly. And the other was the creation of I-43, shown here in figure 4.13, which officially decimated Milwaukee's Bronzeville, with its large population of Black residents and removed thousands of homes. The construction area for I-43 was between 6th and 7th streets and the residents of the area were mostly Black and African American people with reduced power to try to stop a large interstate from bifurcating their neighborhood.[22] I-43 cuts through the western part of Harambee, which shifted families northward after they lost their homes and visualized segregation begins to be clearly seen.[23]

Along with the construction of I-43, the decade of the 1960s also include the infamous fair housing marches known as "200 Nights of Freedom" led by the Milwaukee Chapter of the NAACP and Father Groppi—which spurred violent white mobs to deter the marchers demanding equity in housing. The marches began on the northside and continued down 16th street to the southside, over the 16th street Viaduct—which was locally known as the "Bridge from Africa to Poland."

Figure 4.13   Construction of I-43, Demolition of Bronzeville—Historic Photo
Collection/Milwaukee Public Library. *Source:* Used with permission from Milwaukee
Public Library.

DEMOGRAPHIC SHIFTS 1980

As the 1970s ended, the 1980s brought new issues and challenges of deindustrialization and signal the entrenchment of segregation in Milwaukee, which
become more intense through the 1980s through the 2010s. Simultaneously,
the effects of white flight and deindustrialization become evident and left large
parts of northern cities with predominately Black neighborhoods that were once
filled with the opportunity are now areas that experienced high levels of deindustrialization.[24] Illustrated are the effects of white flight over time—visualized
via the expanding areas of dark gray (which indicate Black populations) and
the surrounding lighter areas, which indicate high proportions of white persons.

During these movements of white people out and Black families in over the
years of the 1940s to the present highlight the historical notions of the Great
Migration (or Great Escape) from southern de jure segregation to the intricate

Figure 4.14   1980 Census Map, Gray (Black Populations), White (White Areas).

blend of covertly overt de facto segregation and racism in the north. Many of the interview participants expressed memories of their family members moving from Louisiana, Mississippi, Alabama through Chicago—landing in the developing predominantly Black neighborhoods on the northside of Milwaukee.

Located on the northern part of Harambee, there was an AMC manufacturing plant (located just north of census tract 69) that offered stable wages and avenues for employees to have the potential to accrue wealth. In 1985, the plant closed, and thousands of jobs were lost. In its place, a Walmart was built, which pales in comparison to the wages and stable work prospects that the manufacturing sector once provided.

Since the *Brown v. Board of Topeka Kansas* decision in 1954, white Milwaukee residents resisted integration efforts in housing, schools, and jobs. The history of Lloyd Barbee, Father Groppi, Vel Phillips, among others, shows us that it took until the 1980s to "officially" integrate schools.

The map (figure 4.14) shows the explosion of the Black population (the increasing dark color) on the northside of Milwaukee. Even more apparent is the white flight (the lighter white area) throughout the building in the 1960s and through to 1970s, mapping on to Rev. Ellwanger's assertions and research about white flight and deindustrialization.[25] At this time, the population in the selected census tracts is approximately 87% Black, illustrating the demographic shift that occurred over just a few decades. Prior to the 1940s, the areas were predominately white for a very significant amount of time predating the turn of the century in 1900.

DEMOGRAPHIC SHIFTS IN 1990 AND 2000

What can clearly be seen over the last 40 years is the entrenchment of internal colonialism and the extent of the problem with segregation in a northern city in the United States. During this time, the population changes from almost 100% white in 1940 to almost 100% non-white in 2000. Both maps show an intensification of clear demarcations of racialized lines. The change in the maps from the 1980s through to the 2000s is simply done through the increasing demographics in these "established" racial boundaries. These maps (figure 4.15) are indicative of the severe residential segregation that exists in northern cities—much of which is ignored because it does not fit in with our understandings of racism being solely a "southern occurrence."

MILWAUKEE: AN AMERICAN CITY

Knowing that Milwaukee is one of the most segregated American cities is one thing, but seeing the change occur over time is another. The 2010 census details the population of Harambee as 80% Black/African American and 3% white. Given the moniker of being Milwaukee's most "diverse" neighborhood, Riverwest's white population represents 60% of those who live in the neighborhood while 25% of inhabitants identify as Black or African American. Even though the HOLC's active discrimination is long over, the remnants of negative home mortgage lending are still in effect. If Riverwest is examined as one whole neighborhood in terms of the percentage of inhabitants who are white and Black like above, it appears numerically to be diverse and more importantly integrated. However, if one takes a more critical look at the above Riverwest population maps, it becomes clear that the more northern and southern census tracts help sandwich the significantly whiter population. This area, in part, has not experienced dramatic shifts like other areas immediately to its west. While Riverwest isn't as white as it used to be, it certainly has not increased its Black population. Visibly missing from these maps are Latinx populations—which was not due to intentional oversight, but that Milwaukee is *so* segregated that Latinx populations are predominantly in neighborhoods that are south of the area depicted in these maps.

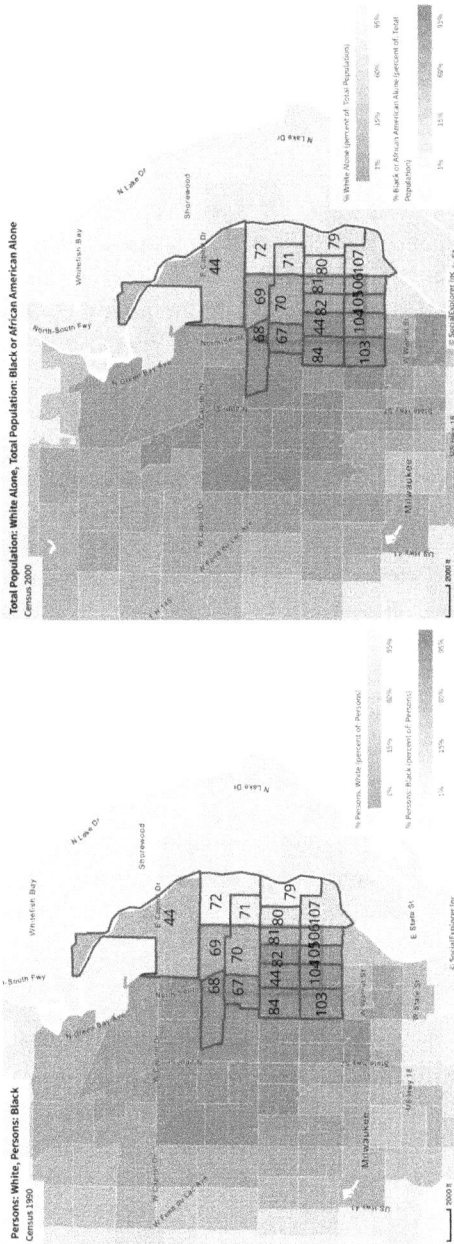

Figure 4.15 1990 Census Map, Gray (Black Populations), White (White Areas) and 2000 Census Map, Gray (Black Populations), White (White Areas).

ENDURING LEGACIES OF SEGREGATION:
COLOR-BLIND RACISM

Often when people learn about American racism, they learn about this facet of history with a geographical lens—the south. More importantly, a reader might think that there is no difference in the last three census maps for 1990, 2000, and 2010, but therein lies the uncomfortable rub that in 1990, 2000, and 2010 we see these strong racial lines drawn in residential areas during a time that is at least 60 years post-Civil Rights Act. However, much of the ignorance that accompanies modern racial issues is due in part to how we are informed and taught about policies that disparately affect marginalized populations. Often the question revolves around the notion of "self-segregation" that Black people self-segregate and that is why we see these long-standing issues with residential homogeneity.

The plausible deniability of overt racism via coded language or "outdated" redlining maps are present in current residential discrimination and segregation. Color-blind racism is the new racism where it supposedly does not exist—it essentially is all market forces or personal liberty and decisions. Bonilla-Silva[26] explained lasting segregation through the four tenets of color-blind racism. The four tenets are abstract liberalism, cultural, naturalization, and minimization of racism. Viewing post-civil rights legislation racism through these tenets, it becomes at least a little bit clearer as to how racism endures over time. For example, abstract liberalism is explained as individualistic freedom and the government should not make the public do anything. However, the government *does* make people do things they probably would not, if not for punitive action. Purveyors of abstract liberalism usually fall back on people who can move anywhere and there is nothing stopping you, except for yourself. This, again, forgets to mention the legacies of housing discrimination that are thought to no longer exist.

Thanks to the various Civil Rights Acts during the 1960s, housing discrimination is supposed to be a thing of the past. However, there are all sorts of workarounds to this policy, such as, "I can't tell you to not move to this neighborhood, but I think we should focus our search over in this neighborhood."[27] If we take this quote, and then map it onto all of the maps post-1965, we see that while on the books, housing discrimination is illegal, something is clearly going on to create and maintain these racially segregated neighborhoods.

Cultural racism is the notion that there is something innate in the fabric of a group that is not making them successful. In some cases, the idea of "credit scores" could be seen as this "lack" of cultural aptitude. Credit scores are a key piece to qualify for any type of loan—car, house, etc. And while credit scores are supposed to be "unbiased" when it comes to mortgages, the most recent housing crisis in the late 2000s showed us that even while keeping various components constant, Black and brown families were receiving subprime loans, instead of the more stable and preferred fixed-rate loans that did not fluctuate with the market.

Bonilla-Silva[28] also explains that color-blind racism can be explained through the concept of naturalization. Racism is just "natural" and it essentially "is what it is." This statement lacks the understanding of how legacies of discrimination affect the present. However, if we use our critical minds, opposite questions could be put forth that might get us to a more accurate answer for why systemic, structural, and institutional racism persist. Questions like, what about this neighborhood is unwelcoming to people of color? Or another one could be, why are white people so unwilling to integrate with others? For example, scholars note that even white liberals who oppose the idea of racism *still* engage in integration resistance.[29]

And lastly, color-blind racism allows these issues to manifest through the minimization of racism or explaining away issues of racism or verbal gymnastics. Instead of looking at the possibility of racial impact, the issue in question is diverted using a variety of other excuses. For example, during the subprime loan crisis of 2007, the focus was not on companies that called these loans "ghetto loans" or those who were receiving them "mud people" and understanding the way in which racism and discrimination appear.[30] The focus was on the people who "should have known" what "robosigning was" or that the document they signed was not the document they were originally shown.

SYMBOLIC ANNIHILATION

As the reader, you might be wondering how symbolic annihilation fits here. Well, if you've never had to think about how far you need to travel for a store, this chapter may bring you some pause. For many families, a grocery store is within a reasonable distance—stocked with fresh goods—and they are privileged in the fact that just a neighborhood away that same privilege ceases to exist. Therefore, Harambee and thousands of neighborhoods like it are simultaneously present and absent. The intersections of food access connect issues of race, class, geography, and government decisions. The movement or in some cases *forced* movement of people and the siting of certain businesses is an issue of governmental (in)action. Zoning ordinances are a part of city planning and neighborhood creation and can work to maintain inequality through enduring legacies of segregation and separation via ordinances and city management. What we find is that racism, segregation, and insecurity

Total Population: White Alone, Total Population: Black or African American Alone
ACS 2010 (5-Year Estimates)

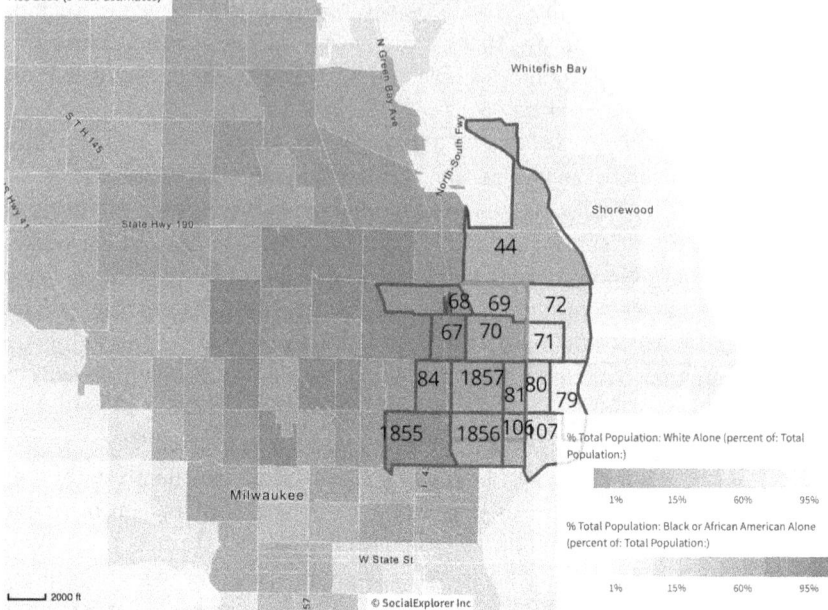

Figure 4.16   2010 Census Map, Gray (Black Populations), White (White Areas).

are not natural but woven into the fabric of a city through decisions and ordinances that affect people in different (often detrimental) ways.

We might expect that after the Civil Rights Acts were signed the opposite would appear in a city like Milwaukee and that the entrenchment of residential segregation would cease to exist. Given all of that, how does what appear in the previous maps happen? What might explain the appearance of these racialized boundaries is how political decisions either aggressively or passively encouraged much of this segregation to flourish. One of the main issues that should be noted is the lack of attention to the purposeful acknowledgment of how legacies of racism, discrimination, and disenfranchisement were never adequately addressed. Instead of tackling the issues that affect marginalized populations, new stumbling blocks were placed in the way of traditional upward mobility, like the war on drugs, increases in incarceration, housing issues, and continued job discrimination. For example, Pager[31] noted disparate impacts on people of color compared to the experiences of white people in the labor market. As she noted, a white man with a record would be three times more likely to be called back for a job than a Black man with no record. The inability to access employment to ensure standards of living and means that people of color are still experiencing various levels of discrimination are yet to be properly alleviated.

Eerily, the redlining map a few pages back can be overlaid onto the maps from the 1980s through 2010 and the nutritional redlining map that is to follow in the next few pages. Not only is there a racial disparity in housing between the neighborhoods, but the median home price in 2014 for Riverwest was also approximately $150,000 and for Harambee, $63,000—a difference of almost $100,000, just by crossing one street. Therefore, the ability to accrue wealth through homeownership in Harambee is completely different just a few blocks away. Harris[32] notes how whiteness equates to disparate wealth attainment since homes owned by whites often lead to wealth attainment. For example, a biracial family sought to sell their home and after removing family mementos was appraised at $135,000 or 41% higher than when it contained mementos of Blackness.[33] This devaluation of Blackness and valuation of whiteness seems to hold for the neighborhoods of Harambee and Riverwest. The median home prices in these two neighborhoods show how strong the connections between race, whiteness, and wealth are to neighborhood demographics.

For representation, in figure 4.17, each dot on the image equates to 25 people and the colors are as follows: red indicates white populations (this surrounds the gray spread in the northern part of the city, dark blue for Black populations, the large diagonal shape located in the northside), light blue for Asian populations (located in the southwest), and yellow for Latinx populations (just below the empty spot in the middle right of the image). The map of visualized segregation was constructed by Fischer in 2011 and details the racial distribution in Milwaukee via the 2010 US census. To highlight the segregated nature of the city, Latinx and Latino populations are in the southern area of the city. That is not to say that Latinos do not live in the areas profiled above but they are similarly segregated to the south. The city did not become this way by accident, but by the remnants of the HOLC and city policies that created what appears in figure 4.17. The absence of this knowledge plays into the continued lack of understanding of the historical discrimination and racism that have clearly long-standing effects.

WHAT DOES ALL THE ABOVE MEAN?

The above maps document Milwaukee's racial segregation that built up over time via federal regulations and white flight, which in the following maps details the lack of access to grocery stores selling nutritious foods.[34] While there are many claims recently that food deserts do not exist and poor people just "choose junk," the below maps work as an attempt to dispel that myth.[35] Milwaukee is one example of a city that has food access

Figure 4.17   Racial Segregation Map.

inequalities—what some scholars describe as food deserts wherein there is a lack of healthy and fresh food options. However, Kurtz[36] argues that "food deserts might better be called nutrition deserts, because the term encapsulates a lack of access to nutritious food, and often an over-exposure to unhealthy foods that are high in fat and calories and low in nutritional value." These nutritional deserts contrast with a "food oasis" where grocery stores are widely available.[37] Food is available in areas that lack a grocery store, but often the options lack fresh fruits and vegetables and if they do stock these items, they are sold at a higher markup than a regular grocery store. One example is Blast Foods on North Avenue, where there was a wide selection of sweets, candy, dairy, and processed foods, but no access to fresh vegetables or meat.

Figure 4.18 Rectangle Is Harambee, the Markers Denote Convenience Stores, Census Tracts 72, 71, 80, 79 Is Riverwest.

Grocery stores selling fresh foods are mostly absent from the Harambee neighborhood. Those that do exist are near or on the periphery of white neighborhoods, or what Blauner[38] called "interstitial" areas. Interstitial areas usually contain some demographic blurring before populations have a clear, defining line. Figure 4.18 is a close-up of the Harambee neighborhood outlined in rectangle. Another Blast Foods, located on the northside, similarly Black-owned offered the local community fruits, vegetables, and meats, but was forced to close in 2008. While they own several stores, losing just one in a neighborhood creates a significant impact. The church icon denotes Gathering People's Church, and the surrounding markers are corner/small stores that sell various items within the square. The icons outside the rectangle indicate small stores that carry specialty items, such as vegan/vegetarian or gluten-free products. One of these specialty stores is the Riverwest Co-op, located in census tract 80, a very small store that sells oats, vegan, and vegetarian items and with an attached kitchen. The other marker is Pete's Fruit Market (located in census tract 1856) on North Avenue, which sits at essentially the border of Harambee. The marker slightly hidden by the legend is a full-stock, chain grocery store, Pick n' Save.

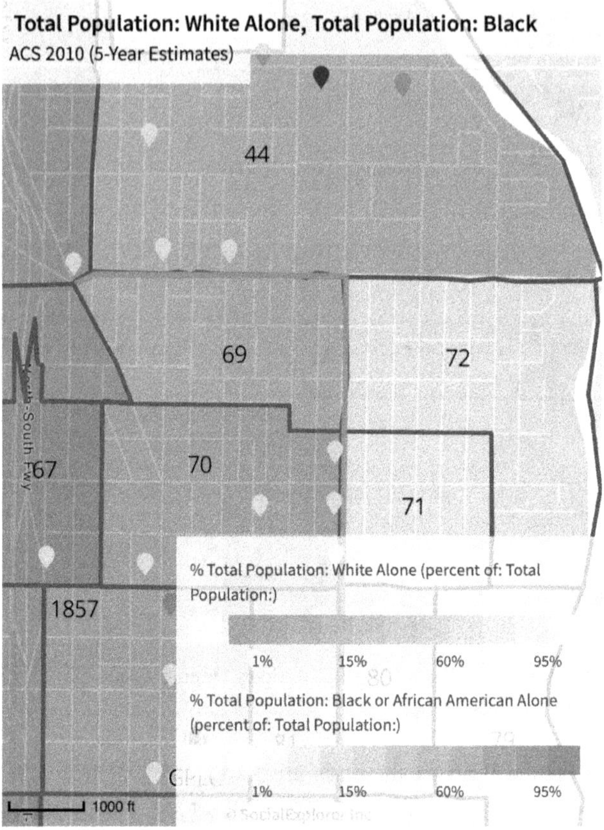

Total Population: White Alone, Total Population: Black
ACS 2010 (5-Year Estimates)

44

69   72

67   70

71

% Total Population: White Alone (percent of: Total
Population:)

1%   15%   60%   95%

% Total Population: Black or African American Alone
(percent of: Total Population:)

1%   15%   60%   95%

1857

1000 ft

Figure 4.19   Top of Harambee Rectangle, the Markers at the Top of the Map Are Three Grocery Stores.

However, figure 4.19 below details an area that is just a bit further north and just west of the village of Shorewood and details the location of an Aldi's Walmart and Piggly Wiggly, another full-stock grocery chain in the area, at the top of the image. These three are what people might consider a "food oasis" because the stores are near each other.[39] These low-cost food stores are in areas adjacent to areas with high rates of white residents. What should be noticed is the lack of red markers, which indicate grocery stores, in Harambee. What is important here is that the residents of Shorewood just need to dip into and out of the cusp of the northside.

Total Population: White Alone, Total Population: Black or African American Alone
ACS 2010 (5-Year Estimates)

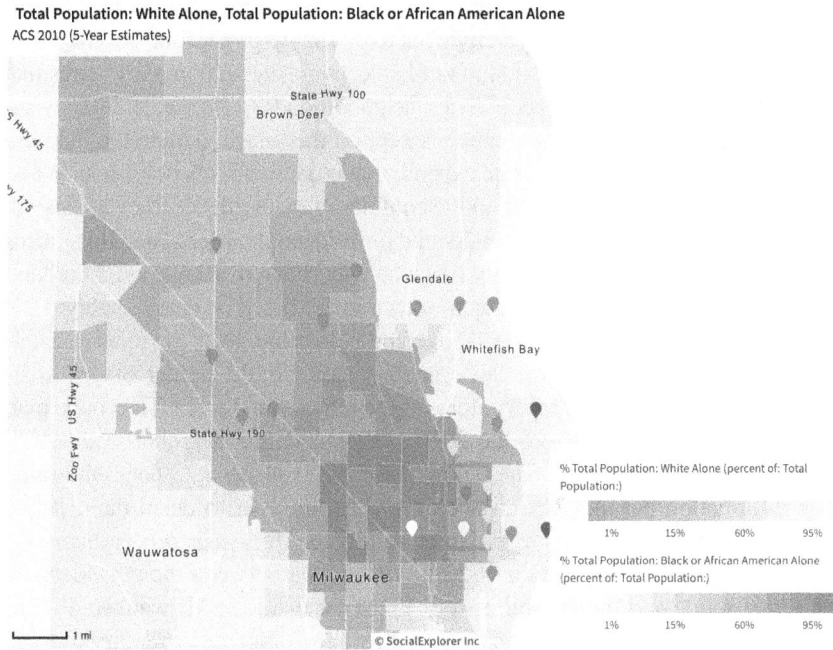

Figure 4.20   The Expansive Northside, with Harambee and the Markers of Grocery Stores.

NUTRITION DESERTS AND FOOD INSECURITY

However, the following part of the chapter details more explicit nutrition deserts that exists in the city of Milwaukee and the surrounding areas in the county. Living in a nutrition desert is an example of food insecurity. While there is a great deal of academic discussion of historical redlining in housing markets, these figures detail nutritional redlining, which is explained as the lack of grocery stores in marginalized areas.[40] Juxtaposed next to the image of the northside and the great distance that exists between residents and stores, the following figures detail access to three grocery stores, in relative proximity. The previous figures detail the locations of a Pick n' Save, Metro Market (an upscale supermarket), and another upscale supermarket Fresh Thyme; further north and northeast are another Pick n' Save and Whole Foods. Not pictured is the Metro Market, which is located north in Shorewood, the southernmost of the suburbs to the northeast of Milwaukee. Given the spatial area (which is almost identical to Harambee), on the east side, one cannot walk any long distance without running into a grocery store, chock full of fresh vegetables, fruits, and meat which differ from the neighborhoods to the west.

The below figure details the entire northside, complete with grocery stores that by and large outline Milwaukee's Black neighborhoods—and for context—visualized nutritional redlining. Harambee is kept on the image, outlined in the rectangle, to center the eye on the large expanse that is Milwaukee's north side. While there are three grocery stores within the confines of the northside, they are also in neighborhoods where there is an interstitial or residential buffer zone. This means there is a shift from a predominately Black neighborhood to a white neighborhood and there is some blurring occurring as they transfer based on directionality.

The key point illustrated by the above and below figures is the relative availability of the markers which indicate grocery stores in the lighter shaded areas and the significant lack of grocery stores in the gray shaded areas. The above map includes population data from the 2010 census detailing neighborhood demographics and grocery stores. The below figures 4.21, 4.22, 4.23 detail the same map information but includes distance measures in order to detail the distance between where someone might live in proximity to a full-stock grocery store.

Figures 4.21, 4.22, 4.23 detail spatial difference between the considerably whiter east side and the predominately Black northside in Milwaukee. Figure 4.22 is the same map as figure 4.23 but shows the distance necessary to even reach the grocery store. The three stars on the bottom account for 0.47 of a mile, so less than half of a mile. Said another way, in under half a mile, you can enter three very nice, clean, grocery stores with fresh produce and meat.

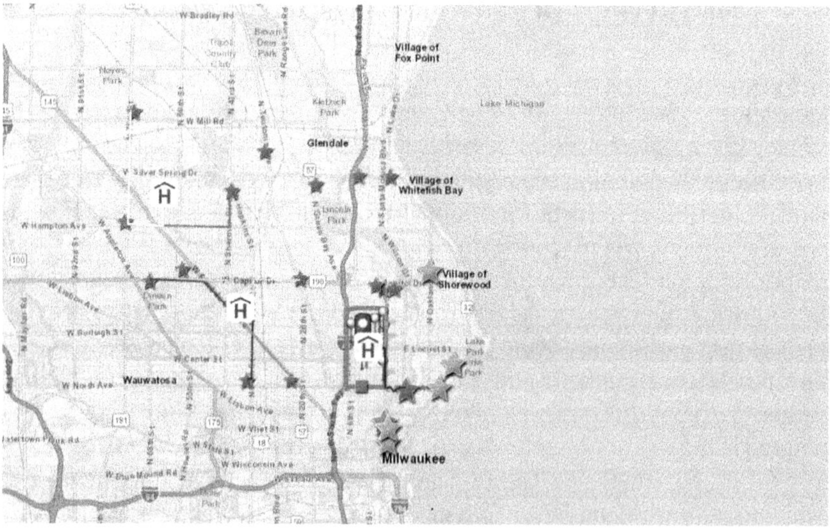

Figure 4.21   Distances in Neighborhoods from Grocery Stores.

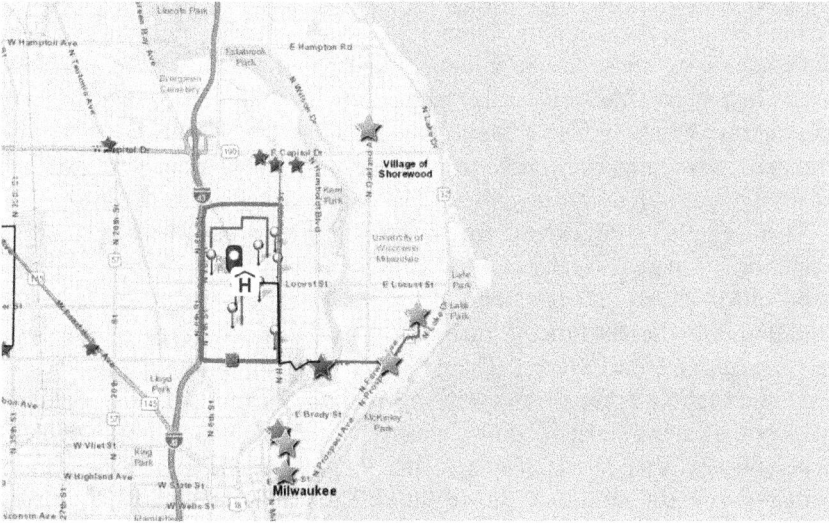

Figure 4.22   Eastside Grocery Store Distances.

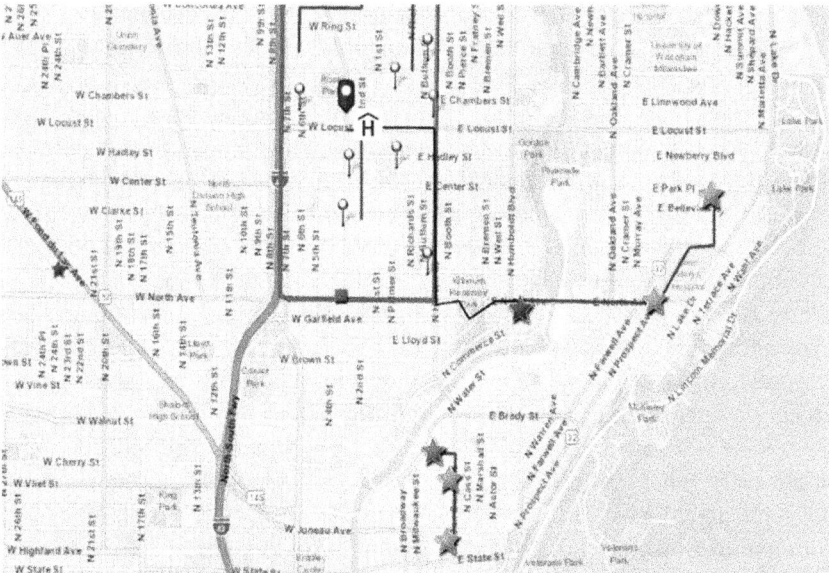

Figure 4.23   Eastside Grocery Store Distances.

Just about half a mile north, residents can access three grocery stores that also have fresh produce and meat within 1.3 miles. This same spatial makeup does not appear in the same manner anywhere else on the northside or in the Harambee area. For example, figure 4.23 includes markers for homes on the northside, to demonstrate the minimum distance it would take for someone to get to a store. The shortest distance is 1.6 miles and the longest in these examples is 3.5 miles. The 1.6-mile example is the one within Harambee (the rectangle) to the first star. These points were chosen at random as an example of what a nutrition desert might look like for residents on the northside.

There is really no excuse for the inability to access healthy food in Harambee as there is on the eastside or in Shorewood or any other neighborhood in Milwaukee. At one point in Shorewood, there was a Sendik's—an upscale market and a Pick n' Save before that particular Pick n' Save was remodeled to a Metro Market. There is an important distinction here. Pick n' Save and Metro Market are all owned by the same Kroger Company, but their marketing strategy and price points matter, in consideration to what neighborhood they are located in. For example, one might say that Pick n' Save is more budget savvy, cost-effective, has regular brands, and is a traditional grocery store—no frills. Their location matters as well—they are the only ones to appear in Black or brown areas. Metro Market is a level up from the no-frills grocery experience. Perhaps specific to Wisconsin, in the Shorewood and on the eastside there is a bar inside where you can eat and drink at the store, take a growler (can growler) home and during lunch hours a pianist serenades the shoppers. They often contained a sushi station, BBQ, or pizza counter, as well.

Inside the box that indicates the boundaries of Harambee, the relative distances are shown that there is "space" for three grocery stores or places that sell nutritious foods to be placed in proximity within the neighborhood. While I have quantified the access to healthy foods in miles, there are more things to consider than just distance.[41] The main issue is that areas with high proportions of white residents are convenient with a variety of grocery stores in either walking distance or a short driving distance. There must be a discussion about the affordability of foods and income of shoppers and if those shoppers have access to vehicles or transportation. If shoppers do not have personal access, via a car, lack of access to rapid public transit negatively impacts visits to grocery stores. But fundamentally, if there are no nearby grocery stores selling fresh fruits, vegetables, and meat in a neighborhood, that makes it hard for people living there to access them. And probably most importantly, what gets sold at grocery stores matters too. If grocery stores do not have ingredients that are necessary for the dishes that people in nearby communities like to make, it increases the work, effort, and expenditures just to get those products. Inability to access grocery stores therefore makes access to food pantries more necessary and important.

LACK OF FRESH MARKETS, BUT NOT COMMUNITY

I was interviewed by Wisconsin Public Radio about recent elections in the state, where many LGBTQ candidates won seats. There was a commercial segment in an upcoming news broadcast about Milwaukee's food insecurity problem. One way that local food markets have tried to "solve" this problem is via "mobile markets." These "mobile markets" are trucks filled with fresh vegetables and fruit and they come during a specified day and time to different neighborhoods and residents can purchase food from them. A local Milwaukeean was interviewed and said, "put the mobile market next to the corner store and see who wins." But why do poor communities need to choose between something for access? Predominately white communities can access both local stores and larger grocery chains without having to go through the pains of choice. Also, more deeply, why not figure out ways to build brick and mortar stores, that are available daily versus having these mobile markets that have schedules available in an online format that not everyone might have access to on a regular basis. Fresh food should be as readily accessible in Black neighborhoods as in predominately white areas or white adjacent areas. Simultaneously, within the confines of Harambee, these figures detail the existence of corner stores and convenience stores. For many, these stores are no pun intended, "cornerstones" of communities, where people congregate on a daily, weekly, or other familiar basis. These convenience and corner stores fill the void with the absence of larger grocery stores. They also detail the long-standing segregation and structures of discrimination that were built via institutional, systemic, and structural racism.

CONCLUSION

As evidenced from this chapter, the areas that surround and are within the neighborhood boundaries of Harambee once had several grocery stores as well as transportation that allowed residents to get their groceries. Over time, as the demographics changed, the access to foods and businesses that sold food with nutritional value changed. Therefore, the relationship of race to access goods and services is present but often hidden via other methods, such as interstate construction which became I-43. It also highlights connections of spatial mismatch and racialized spaces—with reference to the change in fresh foods and grocery stores, over a 40 year+ period. While combing through data, one archived photo of a razed grocery store noted that it was replaced with a Kentucky Fried Chicken.[42] In Shorewood, a predominately white, middle to upper-middle-class suburb east of the river and neighborhoods referenced above, at one point there were two grocery stores in proximity (about one city block) to one another. If a person wanted fast food, you needed to cross the river, by turning around and going back west. Essentially, you needed to leave the area to the east to access unhealthy options.

The purpose of this chapter is not to advocate for closing corner stores, but that other communities do not have to *choose* where they should be able to shop—there are options. This chapter highlights the fact that many places lacking fresh foods are predominately Black and brown neighborhoods and that nutritional redlining is linked to so many systemic inequalities. In Milwaukee during the COVID-19 pandemic, the maps where communities were the most affected would almost be overlaid with areas that lack access to grocery stores and healthy foods. This then is not an issue with a specific community, but what has been ravaged *upon* a community. Corner stores not only play a role within communities, but they also leave space for food banks and pantries that become indispensable to fill these gaps left by the absence of grocery stores. The following chapters detail the experiences of members of the community that live in or near Harambee and how they manage their lives while living in poverty.

NOTES

1. Frey, *Black-White Segregation.*
2. Jones, *The Selma of the North*; "March On Milwaukee."
3. Cho and Clark, "Disparities"; Eisenhauer, "In Poor Health"; Heynen, Kurtz, and Trauger, "Food Justice"; McBride, "Nutrition."
4. Klinenberg, *Heat Wave.*
5. Ibid.
6. Ibid.
7. Ibid.
8. Meaning the inability to access fresh foods directly impacts health and bodily issues.
9. Gilmore, "Fatal couplings"; Sundaram-Stukel and Pearson, "Wisconsin Life Expectancy."
10. Hoffman et al., "Racial Bias."
11. Hoffman et al., "Racial Bias"; Pulido, "Rethinking Environmental Racism"; Roberts, *Killing the Black Body*; *Fatal Invention.*
12. Mitchell and Franco 2018; Rothstein 2017.
13. Ibid.
14. Nelson, et. al., *Mapping Inequality.*
15. Loewen, *Sundown Towns.*
16. Rothstein, *The Color of Law.*
17. Ibid, 155.
18. Wilson, *Declining.*
19. Jones, *The Selma of the North*; "March on Milwaukee."

20. Geib, "Mississippi to Milwaukee"; Jones, *The Selma of the North*; Sernett, *Promised Land*; Trotter, "Great Migration."

21. Jones, *The Selma of the North*; Trotter, "Great Migration."

22. Niemuth, "Urban Renewal."

23. Ibid.

24. Wilson, *Declining*.

25. Ibid.

26. Bonilla-Silva, *Racism without Racists*.

27. This was an actual quote from a job I worked in Chicago in the late 2000s.

28. Bonilla-Silva, *Racism without Racists*.

29. Tatum, *Why are all the Black Kids Sitting Together*.

30. https://www.nytimes.com/2009/06/07/us/07baltimore.html.

31. Pager, "The mark of a criminal record."

32. Harris, "Whiteness as Property."

33. https://www.wbur.org/hereandnow/2020/09/23/home-appraisal-bias-racism.

34. Heynen, Kurtz, and Trauger, "Food Justice"; Kurtz, "Linking Food Deserts"; Morland et al., "Neighborhood Characteristics"; Shannon, "Beyond the Supermarket"; Slocum and Saldanha, *Geographies of Race*.

35. Schneider, "Grocery Chains Leave."

36. Kurtz, "Linking Food Deserts," 248.

37. Schneider, "Grocery Chains Leave."

38. Blauner, "Internal Colonialism."

39. Slocum and Saldanha, *Geographies of Race*; Walker et al., "Food Security."

40. Heynen, Kurtz, and Trauger, "Food Justice"; Kurtz, "Linking Food Deserts"; Slocum and Saldanha, *Geographies of Race*.

41. Heynen, "Monitoring Wisconsin"; Heynen, Kurtz, and Trauger, "Food Justice."

42. Kwate, "Fried Chicken."

Chapter 5

Outside the Pantry

Often, those who lack insight into how poverty is experienced also lack the understanding of the day-to-day experiences of it. The common thread is that poor people might be sad, always depressed, or unhappy in their lives. Researchers note that most recipients are not depressed because they are themselves "sad" but workfare requirements often mandate work, which is often menial, unstable work that lacks the mental stimulation.[1] It is not to say that emotions come into play, but issues of depression are not always related to the lack of economic capital. When I interviewed the women at the retreat in the previous chapters, many of them expressed a variety of emotions. At some level, they viewed their recipientship as a necessity to simply feed their bodies—"I need to eat and feed my family, this is a way to do this," and, at the same time, expressed levels of discomfort at being in a position that made it unfeasible to provide these items on their own. The women most often oscillated between being simultaneously proud and dismayed at the process.[2] The important part about that discomfort is not because they are a recipient, but the way the system treats them. By the system, they specified the social worker contact—where they feel like a number, a bother, or putting the worker at an imposition. This issue will be discussed at length in an upcoming chapter.

This chapter chronicles the close relationships with those from the pantry and how they navigated their experiences with poverty. Not only does it examine that, but also how race entered the interactions that we shared. But over time, the volunteer crew became a lunch crew—and I was invited over to Harold and Wynette's home to play cards and drink some beer and hang out. This chapter explores joy even while being economically disadvantaged and how people navigate these situations.

Wynette asked me one day, "Hey dear, after pantry wanna come over for a cookout?" And it felt great to be invited. These cookouts became a time for me to hang out, drink a beer, and learn about my newfound friends. They were always asking me questions about my research and what I was finding out about people. Often, Harold would ask me to pick up some beer and I asked him what kind he wanted. In a cute exchange, he asked me, "pick me up some Natural Ice" and I said, "ah natty ice." For some reason I figured that this was common knowledge. Harold stopped and looked at me and in his light southern drawl, he said, "no, natural ice." After a few minutes of these back-and-forth banter, he concluded that it must be something that white people say, because he had never heard it before. However, every time he would ask me to pick some up, he'd say, "gimme some of that natty ice" and smile.

Chapter 1 discussed the happenings during regular pantry hours, but this chapter takes a dive into the lived experiences of those in poverty and how our lives are more connected than we might think. While I was starting my work at the pantry, I had the opportunity to be a first-time car owner. What is important about this fact is over time at the pantry, she was important in getting people from place to place and to and from the pantry.

At first, Wynette and Harold were reluctant to talk to me at the pantry, but I knew that from the beginning. I wanted to make sure that my repeated attendance showed that I wasn't just a fly-by-night researcher. Building trust over time was important. I started volunteering in May and took almost six months for the pantry crew to start inviting me into their homes and I started to get invited to more and more after-volunteer activities. Harold and Wynette both lived in the same building. It was a medium-sized building with five floors that sat on the Milwaukee River. Most of the people who lived there were seniors, but they did cater to low-income individuals.

After pantry, I would take Harold and Wynette home and help them put their items in the building buggy (a grocery store cart from the nearby market) and then would go home. One day, I helped Wynette bring her items to her door. It was a nice brown brick building, with a common room on the second floor. She lived on the fifth floor, or what she called the Penthouse. We entered her apartment a litter foyer that became the kitchen. It had a large round glass table that almost took up the whole space. It opened into a living room that had a small couch and some toys for her grandchildren. When we would hang out together, we would spend time in Harold's apartment. Her bedroom was to the right and just held her bed which sat on the floor with a small closet and connected bathroom that you could get to in the foyer by the door. Harold lived on the fourth floor down the hall from where Wynette was, and he had a view of the river. His layout was different, and he had more space for accommodating guests. He had a large armchair that sat in the corner by the window and a large couch on the opposite wall. One could enter the living room through a hallway. His kitchen was diagonal from the door and his bedroom was on the other side next to the bathroom. A table was positioned next to the armchair, and we would play cards or dominoes at his apartment versus at Wynette's. On nice days, he would open the window and you could hear the rushing of the traffic on North and the flow of the river below. They both had good furniture, trinkets they picked up over time, and pictures of their family and loved ones that dot their apartments.

One of these times, I had to give Jenny a ride to her house to drop off her items—because some were frozen. Jenny happened to live deeper into the northside, and she asked if I'd be comfortable driving her. Harold sat in the front, he was having some back problems and it was easier to get out of the car and she gave me directions from the back. As we drove through the neighborhood, Wynette recounted a story of a young man who witnessed a drug deal, or some interaction go bad and then remarked about it on Facebook. He was later murdered in an alleyway near Jenny's house. They often talked about the dangers of living on the northside each time I would drive Jenny back to her house—many times noting that I didn't get "scared" to take them home.

"GETTING INVITED TO THE COOKOUT"

One day after a rather rough day at the pantry, it was mid-month and sometimes there can be tension between the patrons regarding line placement. Wynette invited me to a cookout at her building after I gave everyone rides home after the pantry. Being "invited to the cookout" is an important moment because it indicates potential acceptance into the group. One can also be uninvited to the cookout, if someone does something negative or not in connection with the group. Many of these cookout themes and memes involve white people calling the police on Black people just being with their friends or families outside, living their lives and they would not be invited to the cookout. Harold set up the grill on the sidewalk near the building and a few of their friends came out to talk and hangout with everyone. Jenny wanted to relax a little, so we finished cooking on the grill, and we all went up to Harold's apartment. There, Wynette taught me how to play dominoes, which I had never played as a game before. At the same time I was learning how to play dominoes, Jenny started to roll a blunt with the papers of a Swisher Sweet cigar. During many of my hangouts, the sharing of blunts was a regular occurrence, just like many social gatherings people do together.

Like many of the other nights I would hang out over at their house, they shared a blunt rolled from Swisher Sweet papers. They asked me if I had ever smoked before, which I answered yes, but I have never really experienced this communal manner of sharing, that is, without a one hitter or bowl. There is a method to unrolling the papers from the swisher and ensuring that they can be rerolled again. One takes out the original tobacco, unfurls the papers, and then replaces the buds and then between a soft but firm roll to make sure everything is sealed and then it is finished off with a lick, not unlike someone might make a hand-rolled cigarette. The process, however, is not complete. The whole blunt itself is sealed with a lighter along the seam too, and one end is burned before it gets passed to the first person. I found at any moment, the passing of the blunt to be a communal experience. It was important to me that Jenny felt I could share this with her, since also weed is a luxury. The fact that she was willing to share it with me was something that I did not take lightly. Other times when we went to the park, Jenny used a vape, to be less detectable in public.

It seems of special import to talk about the perceptions of marijuana use and race—with white people engaging the behavior at similar rates to Black/African American and Latino groups but far less likely to receive the stigma of smoking weed or be tangled up with the justice system in the same ways. Even with the legalization of weed, white people can open dispensaries, smoke in public, and be rather ostentatious; Black people are still ensnared in the justice system with police interaction, tickets, and jail time.[3]

In Wisconsin, where marijuana is not yet legal, racial disparities also persist in convictions for possession. Wisconsin Public Radio reported that "in 2019, Black Wisconsinites were 4.3 times more likely than their white counterparts to be convicted for having marijuana."[4]

Movies like *Pineapple Express, Half Baked* among loads of others place white users as dopey halfwits but in their hearts are good people who are just living their lives. White users get to engage in smoking and can giggle, laugh, and still be perceived as productive members of society who sometimes have the munchies. There is also a lack of negative perceptions on white users who engage in the activity, with the availability of edibles, gummies tinctures, and vapes. Black users though are unable to tap into this and are solely perceived to be lazy and lack the ability to partake in that positive stereotype, however, the friendship and conversation are absolutely the same. Every time I encountered, the substance was either at a party, a cookout, celebration, or blowing off steam after pantry, especially if it was a difficult day.

BIRTHDAYS

Wynette invited me to her son's 24th birthday party that was held in the common room of their apartment building. Here there were ribs, chicken, natural ice beer, and a large cake that was donated to the pantry, but we were not going to be able to use it in time for the pantry. Often if there were extra cakes that couldn't fit in the freezer, volunteers could take them home. Often if there was a large event, like a party or birthday, that volunteer would get first dips on that cake. To help out with the costs, I supplied the balloons, table decorations, and tablecloths, in preparation for the party. This was a moment I recall humorously, because I had never met D'Andro, but he was supposed to be on his way to his mother's house. Wynette was unsure of when he would arrive. In thinking about understandings of time, I was thinking very much in "white time" wherein if something starts at three, you get there at three, maybe 3:15, so it is not just you alone waiting for other people. While I arrived at 12, D'Andro did not arrive until 5, and we did not start eating until 6, which totally upends considerations about time spent with family. It made me think about all the events I spent during holidays with extended members of my family. It was very *time* conscious. Not that family wasn't important, but time acted as a construct for these events. For Wynette and the families I hung out with, time was seemingly irrelevant—and not that people were disrespectful of time, there was no reason that family should be relegated to a specific timeframe.

The part of this party that I loved the most is that there were no gifts exchanged—it wasn't about what D'Andro was going to get, but that all his friends, family, and loved ones were there to celebrate his birthday. There were no presents visible, but this party was not lacking in love nor laughter. People from the building came down, played on the piano that was almost slightly out of tune in the common room, friends were telling jokes, and the feelings of family reunions were shared.

WEDDINGS

At this point in my research, it was not unusual for me to be the only white woman in the room, and this event was no different. Unsure of what to wear, I was a little over-dressed for the event—while everyone else was a bit more relaxed in casual wear, nice jeans, and tops. Thinking that this was a more formal event, I wore a black dress with wedge heels. However, I walked in with Harold and Wynette and Harold took me around and introduced me to the people he knew—sort of as a—"I'm vouching for this person" way, people started to talk to me about where I was from and how did I know the newly betrothed couple. Wynette has several children, D'Andro, DJ, and Diana. Diana was engaged to Phil and they had a child together, who was just over a year old. They lived in their own apartment about 15 minutes from Wynette. She invited me to their wedding, which was at a field house located in one of the county parks on the northside. I picked up Harold,

Wynette, and Peggy, who was Wynette's sister. I had my music plugged in to my car and it was playing some nice smooth classic soul—Bill Wither's is a personal favorite. Harold started to sing along and asked me how a person so young would know this music. My father had all the old vinyl albums of Otis Redding, Bill Withers, the Isley Brothers, among others, so it was always in my musical lexicon as a child, and Harold found this utterly perplexing. It was moments like these wherein I was able to build a connection between myself and the people who were not just my participants, but also my friends. Therefore, these presentations of self routinely emerged in these small, fleeting moments. Diana and Phil had already got married at the courthouse, she wore a beautiful strapless gown and he was in white trousers with a teal blazer with a white lily print on it. The reception was just like the birthday at Wynette's common room—low-cost but high amounts of love. There was a cooler of wine spritzers and natty ice (natural ice) and for food there was a potluck of homecooked items, fried chicken, and a beautiful naked wedding cake. They set up the tables with pretty tablecloths and made reception gifts of candy white boxes with an intricate cut out on them. There was a small dance floor set up in the bay window area where they placed a boombox in the corner. Wynette was a quiet woman that really shunned any focus of our attention. Diana, however, was a bit more outgoing than Wynette and had the reception attendees encourage her to get up and dance. Eventually, Wynette acquiesced and danced with her daughter for a few songs. The atmosphere was relaxed and casual—which was Phil and Diana's style—proving that you need not have a wedding that costs tens of thousands of dollars if you are surrounded by those that love and support you.

WHITENESS AT THE TABLE

Mentioned previously in this chapter are the experiences of whiteness while conducting research in predominately Black spaces. Being cognizant of how race functions in a segregated city like Milwaukee is important. The following experience highlights this important detail. One snowy Wednesday in particular, Harold and Wynette and I were getting ready to leave the pantry. I pulled my car near the door, to make it easier for them to put the items, boxes, and materials in my trunk. As I sat in the driver's seat, I saw a Milwaukee Police car approaching at a regular speed and then before he approached my car, he slowed down considerably, and our eyes met. I recall having my face crinkle in a "what, dude?" expression—we need not have this interaction. Two Black people, plus me, were out living their lives and somehow that was still suspicious enough to slow down enough to examine the situation. I often wonder what biases were scrolling in the officer's head while I stared at him. I often wondered that it if was nothing else, other than I was a white woman, in a Black neighborhood and two Black people were in the process of getting in my car. I thought to myself, I've never had this experience before—wherein an officer would slow down while I was just going about my day, but this unfortunately is a common experience for individuals across marginalized statuses.

Earlier in the spring, Harold asked if I could take him to pick up his back brace in West Allis. First, we had to stop at their home to drop off the food and other items from the pantry. A few of the friends that I met at various parties were out front, taking in some sun and drinking a few beers. They shouted to Harold in the car, "hey, where you goin'?" Harold replied, "I'm going where the white people are (West Allis)." They yelled back, "aren't you with one?" implying me because I was the driver. Harold retorted, "nah, she's a good one." I asked for some clarification about what he meant by that, while also holding in my emotions. In each of these cases, they said you "got it," and so on. It struck me each time they said this because I do not know what Blackness is like, I lack that first-hand experience.

My "getting it" solely comes from community immersion, my studies, the literature, and friends I surround myself with who are also practicing antiracism in their lives. When I would be in the presence of others, either inside or outside the pantry, I would ask them for direction, whether I was cooking or how they wanted something organized, because in the situation, I was not the expert, they were. I "get it" from an abstract theoretical experience, but not a lived experience—and to claim otherwise is disingenuous.

Harold had a birthday party and invited me to it. I arrived and Harold introduced me to everyone as "his n***a" and like whiplash I turned my head and asked, "Are you drunk?" because I have never heard him call me this before and I understand what this word means in this context, as a term of endearment.[5] I've heard Harold and Wynette use the word before in a variety of ways, as nouns, adverbs, and adjectives to describe different people and situations, good or bad. I struggled with different ways to write about this interaction because as a white woman, I did not want readers to read this and assume that I thought I was special or that I thought I had a free pass in terms of this word. I spoke to various colleagues on how to describe this moment during my data collection. I wanted to include this interaction because of its importance and relationship to the work I was doing and the data I was collecting, but I did not want to use this moment as a way for the reader to think I thought of myself as "special" or "gloating." Understanding historical significance is key because power relations in the use of this word are inextricably connected. At the moment, I was a little taken aback. There are whole theses and dissertations on how one word can mean so much depending on the context, tense, location, and embodiment. At the same time, I also know that Harold saying this to me is no big deal from his point of view because it is just an expression. And as a white woman, I'm in no position to police a Black man on language, but I took him aside and asked him to clarify what he meant by that. He told me that he wanted to express that I was "his n***a, no bigga" and that I was his best friend, just like Jenny and Wynette were his best friends. It was a moment that I remember fondly because it represented a shift in the rapport built over time and describes the trust that Harold felt toward me and the formation of our long-standing friendship. While I was working at the pantry, I also worked at the library and after this moment and as I was writing about it, I was perplexed as to how to even approach the subject. I thought it was an important anecdote to show how trust was created over time, but I also didn't want to be even remotely connected to virtue signaling or writing as if I was "special."

At another cookout that summer, there was a friend of Harold 's whom I sat next to and he started talking to me about my work at the pantry and that I was a teacher at UWM. He confessed to me that he did not really trust white people, but when I came into the space, he noted that he felt that I "came with love" and that I was relaxed and did not tense up upon being surrounded by Black people. I told him something I've similarly told my class which is that [white people] have never done anything to earn people's trust, which either white people do not believe or would never say out loud. From this moment, Greg went on to tell me about his history with the army and the roommate he had in his 70s who had lynching photos hanging in his locker and [he surmised that] he probably supported the KKK. He went on to tell me that those images provoked such rage that he got into a fight with him, which after beating him up, Greg got a seven-day suspension, and the overt racist did not and his superior stated that Greg should just ignore the racist locker. After explaining the encounter, Greg said the man whom he fought educated himself and afterward informed me that he considered this man to be one of his better friends. Personally, it shouldn't have taken a fight for this white man to understand his racist tendencies. I also thought about the pain and discomfort Greg had while telling me this story and what he had to endure while also serving the armed forces of a nation that told him to just "endure" racism.

In the same conversation, Greg told me about how he met this wealthy white woman while he was stationed in California, presumably around the same time as the story he just told. He told me this deeply personal and intimate moment of his life, where he met a white woman who had considerable wealth. He described how in love with each other they both were. However, like many of these love stories in the 1970s, they often lack a Hollywood ending. Her father, who Greg surmised as racist, told his daughter that she could choose love or money. From Greg's perspective, he was the one that told her that he would be the one to leave. After being discharged from service, spending years in the armed services, he moved back to Milwaukee. There, after meeting and dating a Black woman for 6 months, he proposed marriage and they were married for 35 years. She had recently passed away from cancer. She had a nice car, a red Chrysler, which was just a few years old—she drove it long before her health deteriorated. The way he spoke about this car was as if she was still in the car. He talked about the updates, the improvements, and his habits in keeping the car fresh and shiny. It was his way of keeping the memory of his wife alive.

In some sense, the conversations that I had with Greg were deeper than I thought would happen at a cookout—in the sense that they were conversations about race and whiteness and not the usual cookout pleasantries. Throughout our conversation, Greg asked me serious questions about the lack of white historical understandings—as in, why are white people so ignorant about history? Or why are white people so willfully ignorant but try to project some knowledge about history? During the conversation, like many of the conversations I had with Black and brown folks more generally, it was a different type of flow—listening and engaging and being able to be self-reflective when considering the issues that race and racism have within the nation. For Greg, after he was about time to leave, we exchanged hugs and he told me that it was refreshing to talk about race and for once a white person did not get "offended," that it was real.

BERNICE

At the pantry, I met Bernice, a woman in her late 50s, and like many of the participants, she was originally from the south. She was a sweet woman, who had a warm and caring face. When I worked at the pantry, she was getting ready for knee surgery—so she managed the cakes and dessert section of the line and could sit to cut and monitor the area. The cakes that were delivered came from local bakeries if they were almost expired or a baker made a mistake, and they could not sell the cake. Like many of the other volunteers, she also lived on the northside, just east of I-43. One day, she asked me to drive her home because she didn't want to stay at the pantry. I helped load her items in my car and she gave me directions to her house. She lived along Center Street, which was a fairly busy street in a two-story apartment building that lined the street. From the outside, it needed repair and had a security camera positioned over each door. There was a tiny foyer littered with junk mail that separated the outside door to the area with the stairs and other apartments. She lived on the bottom floor—which she said was helpful because of her knee. She shared her apartment with her partner of 25 years. He was disabled but could cautiously get around the apartment without his motorized scooter. They never married, she didn't want to get married, but because they had been together so long, she often referred to Robert as her husband. The hallway leading to her door that had a few religious stickers on it had a strong smell of weed that lingered in the air. She often complained about how she felt unsafe in the building as there were a few break-ins in some of the nearby buildings. She said that she mostly kept to herself and had no idea who her new neighbors were, but because they too had religious stickers on their door, she felt like they might be ok people. As she opened her door, I was greeted by her husband and her small dog, named Sammy, that was very excited to see me and I helped her with the rest of her groceries. These drop-offs and pick-ups became a routine occurrence for us if Jane was unable to pick her up.

Mid-year, Bernice had her knee surgery at Froedtert Hospital, which was all the way out in the suburbs of Wauwautosa. Wynette asked me if I would take her there to visit. I asked Bernice how the staff was treating her and what medicine she was on, and after surgery, she informed me that she was in a significant amount of pain but wasn't necessarily getting the relief that she needed. We didn't stay for long; it didn't seem as though Wynette was comfortable in hospitals, but she wanted to see her friend.

MIKAYLA AND BRENNA

Mikayla and Brenna were the next group of people I again met through the pantry, but they were late arrivals as volunteers to the pantry. I first met them during the Thanksgiving community meal. It was the Sunday before Thanksgiving and participants brought an item to share. Idgie asked me at pantry that week before if I would be able to come help. There was no way I could turn it down. For one, it would be an excellent way to meet more people at the pantry and it also was a way to show the pantry staff that I was willing to help whenever needed. That evening, we served approximately 200 people with all sorts of Turkey, ham, casseroles, potatoes, yams, and desserts. I was a food runner—essentially prep staff in the kitchen and restocked items in the food lines. I began at 3:00 p.m. that day and ended at 8:00 p.m. and it flew by in an instant. While sometimes a little chaotic with people coming in to see Idgie, it made for a very homey and welcoming experience. Mikayla and Brenna came and helped pass out the food to the line of people that evening, and we met in the kitchen. We worked like a well-oiled machine, making sure to create space in the kitchen for any new food that might come in, as well as keep on top of the dishes so as to not let them build up. We also made sure that if people brought dishes from home that they got items back that evening.

Mikayla and her family began volunteering at the pantry around March and I gave them rides home each Wednesday after the pantry closed for the day. Mikayla often came with her two daughters, Brenna and Kylie. Mikayla is a sweet Black woman in her 40s that worked for years but took some time off when her daughters became pregnant. Mikayla invited me to her Memorial Day cookout at Keefe Park (which is in the section of Riverwest that as a more saturated Black population) and not knowing what to bring, I came with raspberries and blackberries. As I drove and parked, it became clear that I was one of the only white people at this park. As soon as I got out of my car and walked toward the table, in movie-like fashion, it almost seemed like a record came to a halt with a scratch and everyone looked in my direction. Never in my life, have I felt this before, and made me uncomfortable, so I can imagine how uncomfortable non-white or Black people feel when they enter a predominately white space.

While at the park, after getting over the initial new feeling of discomfort, I was settling in, with my wine cooler and good company. Shavonna, a friend of Brenna and Kylie, came by and was interested in putting together a blunt. She had parked right on a street whereby police might think a smoke-filled car was suspicious, but Mikayla said that she wanted to get the full-effect and I said, "Oh she wants to hotbox it." Shavonna laughed and formally invited me by saying, "you're invited to the cookout." (For those who may be unaware, hotboxing is where you smoke a blunt and keep the windows closed and fill the car with the marijuana smoke which often creates a longer lasting and more intense effect of the substance.)

During the cookout, Brenna's one-year-old son was walking between the picnic tables which were linked together with a thick metal chain. Still being unstable, he tripped on the chain and hit his lip on the table. He visibly hurt himself, but because he was around one, he still is not able to directly communicate what hurts, if he feels ok, etc. So, while Brenna said she thought he was ok, family members were worrying her, asking her if he was ok, if he was concussed, and so she asked if I would take her and her son to the emergency room at St. Mary's, which is on the east side of the city. After waiting a few minutes, they were seen and they reemerged a little later, with an apple sauce packet and smiles, with just a small bruise on his left nostril.

The idea of a "good" white versus a "bad" white came up in the course of my time with Wynette, Harold, Jenny, Mikayla and her children. For example, when Brenna's son tripped over a chain and I had to take her to the hospital, on our drive over, she asked me what I did and studied and I told her and she responded with "it's hard to trust white folks," but I was a good one because I "got it." I asked her what that meant, and she surmised that I "didn't take myself seriously, knew I didn't have all the answers and that I understood issues, racism, police brutality, poverty and where people are at" in their lives.

Highlighting the negative instances Black respondents often have with authority figures which can lead to increased distrust, during our ride back to her home, she confided in me some of the experiences she had when she attended school. She said she was a good student, and was on the road to success, but one day there was a problem at the school and the resource officers were called. She was in the process of walking to class when a resource officer came up behind her and slammed her face first into a block of lockers. This officer was so aggressive that she needed medical attention after the encounter. She specified that she never even had a chance to talk to the officer, but experienced this unnecessary use of force, when she was clearly walking to class. She ended up missing class, still graduating but her grades suffered because of this interaction.

After returning from the emergency room, they invited me up to their home where Mikayla and her family were eating and drinking wine coolers. The children were getting under foot and in the way, which necessitated much yelling, and eventually the children started to listen. Eddie, the little boy that tripped, was trying to get some ice from the cooler, but Brianna kept telling him to go away. Eventually, they asked me if I knew how to play spades and I did not, so they helped me as much as they could. Mikayla's cousin and his wife were at the party too and there is a spades etiquette that I was not formerly aware of, since I had never had friends that either played the game or played around me. The game works where you have two partners that play two other opponents, and you need to organize your cards so that you can quickly pull and drop your cards. The younger generation of players used speed as their bargaining chip. The faster you could deal, the faster you could make your books (number of bets you and your partner must complete a round), and the more game you could talk were all things that they would use to their advantage. The older generation used noise as their playing style. The more exciting the potential play the more ostentatious the card flip and slap on the table, with a sound that resonated loudly. The elder players similarly talked some game, but more frequently used the loud slapping of the cards on the table. The other time I went over to hangout, they were playing for money, gambling between family members. I did not play this round of games, namely because I did not have money and was very certain many losses would be in my future. They played with a minimal amount, about twenty dollars for each player. This time all the players were younger and just Mikayla was the veteran player, but she still held true to her delightfully expressive playing style.

While this was another average night, the conversations that we had around the table piqued my interest. Kylie was nine months pregnant at the time and very much looking forward to the birth. She often sat in the kitchen, that had access to the patio, sitting in the doorway, exclaiming that she couldn't wait until this ended. While I spent time with them, I had never met whoever the dad was, but it didn't seem very important to anyone at the table. While the father wasn't as important, based on the conversations I witnessed between her, and her brother Ben and the rest of the family was that the father was a lighter skinned Black man. Everyone in the room at the time had skin tones of a deep brown, including the children. Ben had a skin tone that was deep brown with short hair that was not a buzz but not so long. Ben was nervous that the child would be so light that their skin would exclude them from being able to claim "Blackness." Because of where I was in the kitchen, I was unable to have him clarify more, but the tone of his voice was sad that this not yet born child's skin tone would be too light. I cannot venture to say what Ben felt about this, but culturally understanding the benefits and privileges extended to lighter skinned Black people is not lost when think-ing about issues of colorism and beauty queues and general social experi-ences that are often driven by white supremacy and whiteness. Colorism and beauty queues promote idea that lighter skinned individuals fair better and are more attractive than their darker complected counterparts.[6] It could be the ways in which white's divided households up and darker complected individuals worked in the fields and lighter complected individuals were able to work in the house. That, however, is not a problem that Black people and people of color started, not need to solve but illuminates the ways in which skin tone stratification created avenues of wealth or accesses to *some* privi-leges. That socially constructed division is a byproduct of white privilege and white racism. I often wish I could go back and ask Ben how he understood what "Blackness" means to him, but I know that the significance is personal to each individual and is just as valid as another person's identification of Blackness.

Additionally, this chapter illuminates how the daily lives of recipients are not as different from individuals who are not receiving benefits. Many of us have parties, engage in socializing, and enjoy the company of others. Often, people in poverty are configured as depressed, sad people due to their present inability to access cash. However, this chapter discussed that there was a lack of sadness and an overwhelming outpouring joy.

This chapter covered some of the happenings outside the pantry and highlighted the important ways in which people navigate poverty. Through identifications of race and whiteness, family celebrations and daily errands, the ways in which my participant and respondent lives mapped onto the lives of every other person living in America might show that we are not all that different, no matter where we sit on the poverty line. The next chapter exam-ines how the average recipient understood themselves, others and how they thought others perceived them while receiving and accessing their benefits during one of the longest federal shutdowns in American history.

NOTES

1. Seccombe, *Cadillac*; Morris, "Welfare program."

2. Seccombe, *Cadillac*.

3. https://www.chicagotribune.com/news/breaking/ct-marijuana-legalization-parallel-worlds-20210415-4hydfuinvje27mtctklm7dq4r4-story.html.

4. https://www.wpr.org/report-black-wisconsinites-4-3-times-more-likely-be-convicted-possession-marijuana.

5. In this moment, one of my library coworkers, who is Black woman, at the UWM library chuckled when I asked her, how do I even write about this because for me, a white woman, even typing the slur is questionable. For Black communities though, this word has meaning between each other.

6. Crenshaw, "Mapping the Margins"; Ducille, "Dyes and Dolls"; Hunter, "Colorism in the Classroom."

Chapter 6

What Happens When a Government "Fails" to Act?

During my time working at the pantry, there was the "fortune" of working there during a full government shutdown that affected a large population of Americans. What would happen if the entire government shutdown or failed to act to adequately help Americans or is this inaction by design? What happens when people who rely on and need essential services are found without them? The preceding chapters examined the geographical disparities of Milwaukee and how people experiencing poverty manage their daily lives to survive. In 2007, a Loyola Chicago professor once told our class, "All Politics is Local" meaning that political action, no matter its place (local, state, federal), affects the lives of people in real ways. The years 2019 and 2020 were fraught with issues and instances wherein people in poverty, or those poverty adjacent, experienced issues with insecurity and precarity. This chapter explores how federal government (in)stability (which will be explored), as exemplified during the Shutdown of 2019 and the Pandemic of 2020, affected people.

THE SHUTDOWN

By the time of the shutdown, I was working at the pantry for almost eight months. By this time, I had the opportunity to build rapport with the patrons and staff and see how government mismanagement was really experienced. The information collected during these 35 days was through conversations with social workers, organizations, pantry patrons, and volunteers who all detailed a general feeling of anxiety and feeling invisible—that no one cared about them—that reverberated through their lives. The shutdown had many different effects on many different groups of people going through very similar experiences. First, the recipients who rely on these services for basic needs suffered. Second, furloughed federal workers lacked access to services (which will be explained later). Third, the actual social workers who needed to assist people and maintain a suitable level of calm and self-care for themselves were affected. Mirroring other instances of presence and absence, this chapter explores how millions of people needing assistance were made invisible by the intense focus on the 800,000 federal workers being affected by the shutdown, and how social workers stepped in to temper the flames of confusion.

What Is a Shutdown?

The first shutdown was recorded in 1879—when Confederate Democrats refused to fund the government unless voter protections for Black Americans were removed. Shutdowns, at their base, are usually connected to budget or funding issues—for example, spending on social services or health care. However, thinking currently, since the 1970s, there have been a total of 22 government shutdowns, with 10 of those shutdowns leading to furloughed federal workers. Therefore, the shutdowns during the most recent administrations are not new to US residents. What was different about this shutdown was the prolonged and damaged residuals that it left upon people and other environments. The supposed purpose for this partial government shutdown was to procure funding for a wall along the southern border with Mexico—supposedly to protect American citizens from undocumented immigration. However, many of the people hurt during the shutdown were people living within American borders. Perhaps unsurprisingly, the disbursement of information about what would happen to benefit recipients and the checks they rely on was abysmal at best.

The Shutdown Starts

The shutdown began on December 22, 2018—the longest government shutdown in American history, lasting 35 days, until it finally ended on January 25, 2019. Much of the news coverage stressed the issue of federal workers missing paychecks and being unable to strike or call-off work due to determined essential workers (remember this term for later). While there were 800,000 federal employees who worked without pay during this time, not all federal workers were granted back pay for the shutdown period, including workers in low-wage sectors like custodian/janitorial and some food services. The shutdown was a bigger problem than even its coverage by the ceaseless 24-hour news media cycle made it out to be. Many government workers simply lost wages during that time—their labor was exploited, and they were never repaid for that time. Similarly erased from this mediascape were the nearly 40 million cash, SNAP, and rent-assistance recipients—who rely on this assistance to feed themselves and their families. At the beginning of the shutdown, many of the patrons expressed various levels of unhappiness, but ultimately, they felt like it was a faraway D.C. problem. As the shutdown wore on the D.C. problem landed at their doorstep when SNAP recipients discovered that they would no longer be receiving their food and cash benefits for February. What started as a problem that recipients felt they could distance themselves from came right to them in the use of their Link, Quest, SNAP, and rent assistance. Since food assistance is federally funded but distributed by individual states, its name can vary by state. Therefore, the scope of the problem, once we include food insecurity and precarity, is significantly higher than just 800,000 federal workers. Given my long-term participant observation at a local community lunch and food pantry, the immediate effects of the shutdown were easier to understand.

"These federal workers might have to work for free? That ain't right," said Earl, a bald Black man in his 40s, who I usually saw during the first couple of Wednesday's each month. Earl continued to note that no one should be working for free and they should all strike—even though that was not possible. To be certain, during the early days of the shutdown, the recipients at the pantry shared what other Americans felt that this was a blip and would end soon since shutdown activities were not unfamiliar to most of the public. In some respect, Americans have been socialized to think of these events as rather common. The most recent longest shutdown national parks and furloughed some workers but it failed to last as long to affect a good number of Americans. That isn't meant to minimize the impact, but just to note the shutdowns in the Obama administration felt far more manageable and controllable. It should also be noted that at the management level—meaning executive branch—there was far more understanding and control over emotions than perhaps what is experienced now or in 2018–2019.

At the beginning of the shutdown, the pantry patrons were relatively unconcerned with how this was going to continue. This should not be read as meaning that they did not care; they were just made unaware of what benefits would be cut depending on the length of the partial government shutdown. Therefore, community discussion started out framing the issues as merely bothersome and focused on the federal workers, expressed sentiments as, "because at the beginning of the shutdown in December, around Christmas time, the forthcoming benefit issues were unknown."

As the shutdown wore on, there was more focused and pointed frustration about the current commander in chief, Brenda, a usual patron referred to the president's demeanor in this process as being a "headass." Other patrons expressed similar sentiments of frustration, in the terms of the administration being "rude," "cold," and in general, no one really had any positive things to say, nor did they think anything was worth making people work while not getting paid. Many of them continued to state that they thought all the workers should walk off the job (which was of course not possible), the only thing federal workers could do was just call-off/call-in or just be understandably grumpy at work.

During the shutdown, I had made two trips to visit family outside Milwaukee, and the TSA expressed a level of exasperated irritation regarding their situation. However, this exasperation had not yet trickled down to the recipients, until the early part of January. At this time, the news media was finally beginning to report that cash and SNAP/food assistance would be significantly impacted. Depending on what an individual or family receives, the amount dispersed every month is dependent on social worker assessment, W-2 (another type of social welfare assistance), and other evaluations of assets which range from $15 to over $300 and the type of car a recipient has (if any). I asked participants to state an amount where they could buy groceries and fill all their needs. Depending on family size, they stated between $150 and $350 per month. I thought about how much I, as a single woman, spent on groceries per month and even with my cost-cutting measures, it didn't seem as though the costs the recipients spent were outrageous by any means.

Many of the patrons that use the pantry are recipients of multiple types of aid, whether it be cash, food, W-2, Women, Infant and Children (WIC), and rent assistance. In the days after the announcement that welfare assistance would be stopped, it was revealed that not only would food and cash assistance be halted but rent assistance would be affected as well. The level of precarity was increasing and the situation that seemed so far away was now affecting people in ways they thought impossible. Several patrons expressed frustration in food line, akin to, "What does he want to do? Starve us?" At this point, pantry patrons and people who received benefits writ large were unsure of what is to come for the remainder of the month and on into February and tensions began to rise.

On social and news media, landlords were releasing documents about how if they did not receive their rent on time, they would begin eviction notices. Many landlords added to the stress by sending notices to their tenants detailing eviction procedures if their rent was not paid on time. While the USDA and Housing and Urban Development (HUD) prohibit landlords from evicting residents during times of government-caused instability, it does not mean that they will refrain from trying it. In Milwaukee County alone, one in eight Black families experienced eviction—with Desmond noting that Black men get locked up and Black women get locked out. Around 1.4 million households are supported by these programs run by the USDA and HUD and because of the shutdown, thousands of contracts were not renewed, which placed about 40,000 people in housing precarity.[1] After one particular landlord was informed that she could not evict her tenants by several state legislative members, she not only failed at taking responsibility that she lacked knowledge on the program she participates in but went so far as congratulating the tenants on them and "thanked them for their *help* and that their voice matters!" It is almost comedic to scare people for their livelihood and then thank them because of one's own ignorance. At a time where people were experiencing uncertainty whether they were going to lose their home, this feels particularly callous.

Not unlike other situations handled by the Trump administration, the shutdown was mishandled and created exponentially more chaos than was necessary. More people were placed into a situation of precarity and families and environments were harmed or people were forgotten. The shutdown caused avoidable inhumanity because of the incredible non-communication and miscommunication. In terms of how people were finding out about their benefit situation, many people were being emailed or contacted electronically, versus by mail, which is how most poor people who might not have regular access to the internet get their notices. It is a little different with younger recipients because access to these more technological services is not so far out of their reach. However, for older recipients, many were kept in the dark about how this process was going to be handled. They expressed this frustration toward the president and were angry that they were being used as pawns in his power game.

The Pantry during a Shutdown

The worry and anxiety read on the faces of the patrons. They felt unclear and unsure of how they would make these next few unknown weeks and months work in terms of food and housing. During this time, I felt more compelled to ask about their mental and physical health and what they were doing to cope with the situation. While the faces of the pantry showed their emotions, the energy in the pantry felt frenetic and panicked. It was not unusual for patrons to ask for extra plates, foil, or other items to transport food home and when the announcement came down about their benefits, they only became more insistent about accessing these supplies.

During the time of the shutdown, the number of patrons using the pantries noticeably increased. At the pantry, there is the capacity for 25 families of various family sizes, typically from single people to a family as large as 8. For lunch, the volunteers serve approximately 25–30 and as few as 15 people. Depending on the time of the month, the pantry often accommodates everyone who walks through the door and places their name on the list. Benefits are disbursed on a schedule that depends on the last two numbers of their social security number throughout the month. Consequently, when the disbursement hits on the first of the month, there are fewer people signing up for the pantry. As the month goes on, each Wednesday sees increases in pantry participation. During the shutdown, because benefits were irregularly distributed, it meant that people were placed in a precarious position. During this time, our community lunch served about 40 people—which is a significant increase and resulted in running out of food both at the community lunch and in the pantry cabinets.

Social work agencies, like one under the direction of HTF (detailed shortly) noticed an increase in foodshare applications that correlated with an increase of anxiety when they were unable to have their needs met. Since there was no formal procedure during the shutdown, workers at HTF were given evening progress reports on what happened federally that day and what that would mean for recipients and applicants tomorrow. Detailed in the following chapter, the social workers would come into the office with similar concerns about the challenges each new day would bring them during the shutdown.

Tension Increases

On January 16, 2019, Jenny shouted to get the attention of the pantry patrons to explain to them what was going to happen with their benefits after talking with a representative from HTF. For many of the attendees, all of this was new information. The shutdown and the suspension of benefits that accompanied it displayed extreme shortsightedness and lack of preparedness that seems to be rather unique to this current administration. At this point, Jenny informed the crowd that the last disbursement of benefits would occur on January 19th and that there would be "no benefits for the month of February or maybe not even in March." While the pantry is a small subset of recipients, they found out from a woman who was not a social service worker that their last benefits would be distributed in the next four days. The crowd was informed that whatever they received on their card in the beginning of January would be the same amount that they received during their usual disbursement and that there would be nothing else after that point, until the shutdown ended.

Anxiety is an experience that can affect a person's well-being—like increasing heart rates and causing cardiovascular troubles.[2] Not only can anxiety affect stress levels of the body, but it can also affect one's emotional sense of self. During the 35 days of the shutdown, there were a range of emotions expressed, beginning with general annoyance at what they considered a temper tantrum by a grown man to increasing anxiety. Feelings of anxiety increased because of the confusion and lack of knowledge about how they were to simply provide food for themselves. For example, when Jenny was given the responsibility of informing the pantry of how the benefit distribution was going to be structured, the pantry erupted in questions and "what the hell?" and other exasperated exclamations.

Due to the lack of communication, Jenny was saddled with answering questions about which she had no authority, information, or ability to manage the emotions of 40 people who were expressing their various levels of despair, confusion, and anger. These feelings were accentuated further by how they thought people perceived them during the shutdown. For example, many of the patrons discussed not feeling cared for, when one patron stated, "[Trump] doesn't care if we live or die" and "how are we supposed to eat?" as the people asked if there was any remaining food that they could transport home from the pantry. The impact of the shutdown, which felt so far away just a few weeks prior, changed into feelings of despair and precarity washed over the patrons, and the reality of the situation sank in.

Pantry Function

While food pantries are a source of food for people experiencing food insecurity and politicians tell people to use them, they have limited resources by themselves. Many food pantries in the Milwaukee area either buy their food from Feeding America or use HTF, which is a *Free and Local* food pantry that started in 1974 by Black mothers who wanted children to have access to food in schools. However, both services operate under the USDA, which was one of the federal departments that was hit hard during the shutdown. Therefore, the level of precarity was practically unnoticed by the Trump administration, thinking the food pantries have access to unlimited resources and can adequately cope with the influx of individuals overwhelming pantries around the city.

Pantries, like Feed the Need, often operate on limited budgets and food supplies. Many of the 40 million people receiving benefits utilize many different food pantries and methods. Federally, many politicians unaffected by the shutdown either could not understand why people were panicking about their missing paychecks or food access and told people to either buy groceries on "good faith credit" or to seek out local food pantries—this would not be the only time that the administration would display a lack of empathy. Wilbur Ross, who is (at this time of writing) the Trump administration's secretary of commerce, could not understand why federal workers would even need to use food banks—why not just take out a loan—without understanding that at some point, those loans were going to have to be repaid with interest.[3]

Working the Food Line

While I was serving in the food line, Harold usually covered the meat, Wynette handled the vegetables and starch, and I usually distributed the salad or bread rolls and drinks. During these days during the shutdown at the pantry, the atmosphere in the pantry was frantic. Often in the pantry, the patrons would give each other a good ribbing and would poke fun at each other, during the shutdown, people were generally less amicable to each other than in days and months past. What did not help and was exponentially increased were the numbers of patrons during this time using the pantry and eating community lunch and added stress to the limited amount of food available at the pantry. When important resources become scarce, what is perceived as "social decorum" significantly decreases.

While people were worried about their next meal, athletes from Clemson University in South Carolina were invited to meet Trump at the White House given their football win and were served what many found to be an inappropriate style of food for the reason of the celebration—it was tables upon tables of fast food, burgers, and other high calorie items, rumored to be Trump's favorite. Freddie, a patron who comes rather sporadically looked at me, and I could see the worry in his eyes, and asked, "What are we going to do? How am I going to eat? I know those Clemson kids are eating that fast food and I think Trump should buy us all food to get us through this. He's an idiot." Coupling the mounting confusion and mismanagement, Earl expressed dissatisfaction with how the Oval Office and associated parties were executing their plans. First, I find it comforting that Earl expressed concern for the whole group rather than just for himself during this time of heighted emotions. Second, he also directed his anger, not at other recipients or federal workers, but at President Trump, while also expressing jealously that the Clemson students were fed fast food, which is fraught with connotations itself—because at least it was something.

Freddie, however, was not the only concerned pantry patron, as everyone that I spoke to that day were even more on edge, especially about their placement in the line to get into the pantry and open tables in the main room. Tensions were sometimes high in the pantry because having first and early pick of the materials that were set out in the main area and in the pantry created a sense of competition, and now with this added stress, people seemed hasty and expressed this unhappiness with their neighbors who tried to get in line and pick these items first.

The SNAP Gap

Just because the shutdown ended on January 25th does not mean that everything resumed as normally scheduled and this chapter only touches the surface of how people accessed services—the next goes into significantly more detail. Various agencies—social and environmental—reported damage inflicted upon people and environments because of the shutdown. The "SNAP gap" ordinarily refers to how the monthly budgeted amount does not cover all of people's food expenses, so they try to fill that need via pantries or money that might be useful for something else. For example, if they get $160 in foodshare but really need $200, they must come up with that $40 from somewhere. Perhaps $40 seems inconsequential, but it could mean that some other necessity must be pushed off to the wayside. However, in terms of the shutdown, the meaning signifies a temporal gap—indicating the length of time, which varied between 30 and 60 days—where recipients could be without any type of benefit or assistance.

Even though the announcement of benefits came on the 16th—wherein the 19th would be the last benefit disbursement of whatever recipients received in January—the benefits would have to tide recipients over through to mid-March. While the mainstream news discussed the eventual payment of back worker pay, additionally, 40 million people were placed in a precarious situation and held in limbo as to when they will be able to access food, cash, and rent assistance.

To add to the notion of precarity, Feed the Need was added to the 211 lists during the shutdown. The 211 number is Milwaukee's nonemergency system that functions as a helpline for people who are facing insecurity in Milwaukee of any kind. Milwaukee residents can call into the information line and be connected to services in the city—food, housing, and other social safety net providers. The only issue is that a person must have access to a phone and know that they would need to call 211 to be connected. At Feed the Need, everyone is a priority, and 211 is not necessary to use the pantry, but this helpline does help reach out to people who may be underserved in their communities.

On January 25, 2019, the shutdown ended, with credit given to the Federal Aviation Agency and Flight Attendant Unions efforts to close LaGuardia International Airport, a major airline artery that affected millions of travelers flying in and out of that airport. What became clear after the shutdown ended was that for many Americans, they were used as pawns in an unnecessary game. Not only were 800,000 federal workers placed in precarity, but 40 million people had their benefits and access to resources severely curtailed and a deeper exploration of this will be detailed shortly. The shutdown was the result of a man who simply did not get his way and was forced to concede by the power of unions. The impacts of the 2019 Shutdown were an unknown foreshadowing of the events to come in 2020.

The Pandemic of 2020

At the time of writing, COVID-19 is creating all sorts of barriers and, honestly, highlighting the ways in which our systems writ large are unable to adequately care for those it is affecting. The 2020 quarantine occurred after the shutdown of 2018–2019, but even so, highlights some connecting points. For many patrons, the pantry is the place where they get their meals and how they provide for themselves or their families if they need to make ends meet in the meantime, which is referred to as the SNAP gap. The pandemic and resulting quarantine created a barrier for those who relied on the pantry and the community lunch. At the time of writing, the community lunch is suspended. However, for half the time, the pantry is operating in what Ava called "pandemic mode" where people call in on Wednesday to register to receive curbside bags between 11:00 a.m. and 1:00 p.m. This adjustment allows for smaller families to receive one bag and larger families two bags to make the resources last and thereby feed more families. They were also providing a delivery service to those who were unable to get out and come to the curbside option. Across from GPLC there is the community garden where recipients are also able to get a big bag of produce. Before the quarantine, families would only be able to use the pantry just once per month but now with the "new normal" families are allowed to use the pantry more than once.

Prior to the pandemic, the pantry only had capacity for approximately 28 to 30 families. During the shutdown, the pantry was almost completely wiped out by the new arrivals to the pantry seeking food items. During the pandemic, pantry and food bank shelves were stretched to their limits because of the unprecedented increase (at least in current terms) in demand for food access. For example, Consumer Reports that one in five American families used a food bank or pantry for the first time because of the inability to afford or provide food for themselves or their families, with unsurprisingly, communities of color being disproportionately affected.[4]

Outside of the experiences of the usual pantry patrons, the extended pandemic impacted millions of families in very real ways. In many ways, the pandemic showed just how close most Americans are to poverty and having to use social safety net options. For example, in 2020–2021, people were held as political pawns in the fight in Congress of how much and when to receive payments. The rhetoric that often surrounds welfare recipients shifted focus to not just poor people but working- and middle-class individuals and families.

CARES Act

The Coronavirus Aid, Relief and Economic Security (CARES) Act distributed at minimum $1,200 to taxpayers with additional payments of $500 if taxpayers had children back in March of 2020. With the CARES Act, there was a boost to unemployment checks of at most $600.00 to the amount distributed to the applicant. This assistance was incredibly important as it helped people experiencing a crushing financial blow that was out of their hands. It was not all sunshine after these payments because in May of 2020, then-president Donald Trump motivated individuals to "fight" mask mandates and effectively flipped positive changes and increased likelihoods that the American people would stay in lockdown for much longer.[5]

In July of 2020, as those extra benefits were set to expire for unemployed individuals but with no change in the economic situation, people were still left in a precarious jobless situation. Those benefits were extended at almost the last minute to those receiving unemployment. However, what it did show was that instead of caring for individuals, the common rhetoric in the news media was getting people back to work and that additional stimulus packages were unnecessary. The same Congress members' lack of empathy for average and regular Americans failed to be transferred to corporations and industries who over time received substantial bailouts. In many respects, the American people bailed out corporations' numerous times, but have yet to cash in, so to speak on that reciprocity.

Almost 10 months later, with the end of the pandemic seemingly nowhere in sight, members of Congress met again to contemplate additional stimulus packages to American citizens. This stimulus dispersed in December of 2020 through the Consolidated Appropriations Act,[6] limited payments to $600 per person and $600 for each qualifying child. This stimulus was far stricter and placed those over 18 in a bind because even though they are dependents of their parents, the cut-off age was 17.[7] While the payments were helpful, they were markedly different from the trillions of dollars given to corporations either in the form of bailouts or tax within the 10-year period.

Due to the lack of assistance, many families applied for social safety benefits—like unemployment, food stamps, and child care in record numbers not seen in recent history. What this meant is that social service agencies are exorbitantly overwhelmed because of overall government inaction. Millions of Americans found themselves relying on food banks and social workers more so than ever before. What seems to be missing from the debate is that all of this could be avoided. The pandemic did not have to hit families in this same, disastrous way.

Just two months after the last stimulus, the most recent stimulus payment comes in the form of the American Rescue Plan,[8] which includes payments of $1,400 for individuals and an additional $1,400 per eligible child. The caveat for this payment was that it lowered the income caps to receive the payments than previous payments. Again, like the other payments, American families had to fight for the ability to receive some level of assistance from their representatives.

Congress with the approval of the Biden administration, taxpayers with incomes under $80,000 received $1,400 and people with children received an additional amount. However, the pandemic somewhat changed how some of the American public viewed assistance differently. I am caution to say "after" the pandemic because at the time of writing there are still variants and booster shots and people who are refusing to think of others because of ill-informed conspiracies regarding vaccines. It's important to note that this issue was curated and formulated by the previous administration—the resistance to wear masks, reopen public places, and the vaccine distribution.

Like many events in the United States' legacy through to its present, marginalized individuals are impacted in economically disparate ways. Workers in jobs deemed essential struggled because even though they had to work, it also meant that fewer people were probably going to be using their services. For example, people who once had jobs that were impacted by the pandemic started driving for rideshare or food delivery services. While these services do offer flexibility, what is not necessarily transparent is that you still need to pay taxes on these wages. Therefore, a person would have to make enough for themselves to live, plus save for tax time. Therefore, while these services were deemed essential, it is also possible that during tax time, people are perhaps now aware of this particular issue.

For example, Pew Research finds that nations looking from the outside view the United States handling of the pandemic as quite poor.[9] Other nations, such as Canada, gave people enough subsistence for the possibility to stay home and not worry about paying their rent, affording food, and other expenses. This is the exact opposite manner that the United States handled the pandemic but is exactly in line with contemporary views and policies on poverty. The United States within its borders holds 4% of the world's population, but 20% of its coronavirus cases.[10] We also have surpassed an amount of death that outranks some of our deadliest wars—at the time of writing it is over 600,000 people. If there is anything the pandemic uncovered, it is that Americans are far closer to poverty than they initially thought.

It seems particularly important to discuss how inaction was more so a function of the previous administration. The Obama administration handled various large-scale epidemics, and they failed to reach the shores of the United States in the same way that COVID-19 did in 2020. There were fundamental disruptions to how we as a nation dealt with large-scale pandemics and it began with eliminating the pandemic task force—which appeared to do a good portion of guiding previous presidents against these viral issues. There was also general misinformation regarding masks, vaccines, and general health precautions that led to people either not believing it was real or disregarding real facts as being a conspiracy. There were, of course, a minority of politicians who appeared to care for the constituents of the nation, but it took convincing to get the rest of the legislative body to agree with their positions.

CONCLUSION

This chapter acts as a microscope into recent events in US economic history—the Shutdown of 2019 and the Pandemic of 2020. While many might see this as solely an economic event, this shutdown impacted people in ways not previously experienced. While shutdowns are not new to the United States, the duration of this most recent shutdown resulted in lasting effects that changed how people view their government operates. The mass confusion led to recipients feeling disrespected and forgotten. Social workers were left feeling tired, overwhelmed, and overworked. Neither their experiences nor their stories were told to the millions of people watching the news or keeping tabs on the federal governments processes during this time. It left people symbolically erased from the focus. This chapter expanded the scope of the persons affected by the shutdown, which was significantly larger than the oft-reported 800,000 furloughed federal workers in the 24-hour news media cycle. This chapter also introduced a local food advocacy organization in Milwaukee, HTF, which will be discussed at greater length shortly. In combination with the recipients and federal workers trying to qualify for benefits, the following chapter details this struggle and the issues that social workers often encounter working with various populations in the Milwaukee area.

NOTES

1. CBPP.org.
2. Martin and Ferris, "Food Insecurity"; McBride, "Food Insecurity"; Olson, "Nutrition and Health"; Sims and Rainge, "Urban Poverty."
3. Lynch and Paletta, "Furloughed Workers."
4. https://www.consumerreports.org/food/americans-turning-to-food-banks-during-the-pandemic/.
5. https://www.pgpf.org/blog/2021/03/what-to-know-about-all-three-rounds-of-coronavirus-stimulus-checks.
6. https://home.treasury.gov/policy-issues/coronavirus/about-the-cares-act.
7. https://www.pgpf.org/blog/2021/03/what-to-know-about-all-three-rounds-of-coronavirus-stimulus-checks.
8. https://home.treasury.gov/news/featured-stories/fact-sheet-the-american-rescue-plan-will-deliver-immediate-economic-relief-to-families.
9. https://www.pewresearch.org/fact-tank/2020/09/21/americans-give-the-u-s-low-marks-for-its-handling-of-covid-19-and-so-do-people-in-other-countries/.
10. https://www.cnn.com/interactive/2020/health/coronavirus-maps-and-cases/.

Chapter 7

"I feel like a rat in a race"

The Benefit Experience

"I feel like trying to get benefits is like a map that winds around that leads you back to the beginning to start all over again." Like a constant scavenger hunt, the experience with benefit assistance is comparable to being in an endless maze. For millions of people, it is a necessary step for a person to provide for themselves. For others who are fortunate to not need those services are closer to situations of poverty than most would like to admit. Most Americans are just two missed paychecks away from poverty—and this became clear with the chaos created by the Shutdown of 2018–2019 and the Pandemic of 2020. Interviewing the participants led to several different experiences that sometimes differed from the perceptions of social workers who provide this assistance and care. While these participant interviews capture different experiences, they also capture similarities. Whereas the public perceives recipients as "takers" and lazy, this chapter tries to detail a more accurate snapshot of the average recipient. Almost everyone became this "average" recipient because of the lack of support from federal institutions and in many ways were made invisible. Participants crossed age, race, educational attainment, and geographical areas, but all say the same thing: these programs help me eat, but I am still unable to meet my needs. The following explores how the 26 recipients, who are different from the pantry volunteers, whom I interviewed navigated the Wisconsin SNAP/Foodshare,[1] manage and navigate poverty, and how 15 social workers and state workers managed burnout, changing, and unclear state regulations, and perceive assisting people in need during times of relative security and times of uncertainty.

BACKGROUND

Before exploring the interviews from both the recipients and case managers, it might be important to look at what Eubanks[2] calls "automating inequality." Eubanks[3] impetus for her research was due to her experience with insurance claims systems and associated digital platforms and the impact it had on her husband accessing medical care. The software flagged them as "fraud potential" and stopped their claims, without contacting them about the investigation. Eubanks noted that without the vast resources that they had, they would not have been able to fight the reduction of services. Therefore, this creates a far larger issue: if one does not have ready access to privilege and resources in applying for social services, they might drop off from applying. One of the examples of automated eligibility software debuted in Wisconsin in 2015 is Foodshare Employment and Training (FSET) program. Like some other governors, then-Governor Scott Walker wanted harsher restrictions and mandated new work requirements to receive SNAP benefits. The problem is that much of the program was not deployed in a clear manner and people who could be eligible, that is, homeless people and students, were told they were not. From the introduction of FSET to qualifying for benefits, recipients must meet the work requirements in one of three ways: "work 80 hours, or take part in FSET, Wisconsin Works (W-2), or certain programs under the Workforce Innovation and Opportunity Act (WOIA) for at least 80 hours, or work and also take part in an allowable work program for 80 hours each month."[4]

Many researchers covered the W-2 programs in Wisconsin and how it affects people living in poverty and receiving benefits.[5] However, fewer engaged with state programs that are individual to each state, which by itself makes the SNAP program mired in confusion and unable to operate successfully. This perhaps is the goal: make a program so inefficient that it seals its own demise or shows inaccurate results of a program's success. Eubanks[6] noted that a similar problem of how online software is meant to "help" make things more efficient, but often fails, perhaps on purpose, in that goal, as did previous "remedies." For example, I met with Rachel from the HTF, who formerly oversaw helping get teams out into the community and helping them sign up for benefits. She noted that FSET was good in theory but awful in practice. When you look at the FSET website, it shows that people are getting jobs above the minimum wage. However, Rachel explains that this is an incomplete picture because it only captures jobs attained but not jobs kept. What this means is, it captured data that someone attained employment, but not what type of employment, such as temporary work that was not to last for very long, day work, and other short employment. It also did not record starts and stops, only initial employment. For the purposes of the public, Rachel noted that state legislators were showing that the work requirements were beneficial to taxpayers because it looked like the program is working but people were potentially unaccounted and more than likely falling through the cracks. Rachel noted that during the rollout of the FSET and work requirement program, homeless people were ineligible for assistance, then after some lobbying at the state capitol, the SNAP requirement changed, but homeless people coming to apply for the benefit were still being told that they were ineligible.

Not only were there work requirements placed on people trying to access food security, but they also had their habits, purchasing, and amounts able to be deducted daily from an ATM monitored. State and federal governments routinely seek to monitor what they eat and how they spend their dollars, which the Electronic Benefit Transfer (EBT) system already tracks.[7] Wisconsin not only wanted to have more restrictive purchasing policies on meat, seafood, and items with sugar, but they also wanted to drum up support from taxpayers regarding drug testing recipients. The negative stereotype of the drug-addled recipient followed through to actual legislation (Gritter 2015). The problem is that the programs effectively spend more than they save, as they only find a small population of individuals testing positive. Depending on the source used, Wisconsin tested between 42 and 80 people out of 1,800 and found between 1 and 5 people having tested positive for drugs, and they spent approximately three thousand dollars during the initial rollout.[8] Other states instituted similar policies, tested millions of people and found that less than 5% of the population tested positive, but they spent almost a million dollars.[9] However, people who engage in doing drugs are caught in a bind because many statewide drug treatment programs are similarly underfunded. And at a basic level of humanity and apparently revolutionary concept, no matter what, food access is a human right and people who do drugs deserve food and nutrition in their bodies. Again and again, we find the "actions" of governmental institutions end up causing far more troublesome issues by their resistance to assist families in need or more directly fail to understand the realities of poverty.

The limits of the benefit eligibility system were further tested during the Pandemic of 2020 and the resulting economic factors from that event. States that created fewer restrictions on benefit eligibility and unemployment had a far easier time accommodating the unprecedented increase in claims. States like Florida, however, had the opposite problem due to the actions of the former governor. During the time of Rick Scott, he created policies to effectively make the process of obtaining unemployment benefits and SNAP benefits increasingly more difficult, which led to long lines of people at the unemployment office—completely in opposition to distancing rules to keep people safe from contracting the coronavirus. What this did was place people in a precarious economic situation in a precarious health situation.

Throughout this chapter, the thread that weaves all of these stories together is how people are forgotten in different ways regarding benefit management. Traditional recipients, new applicants, and social workers often receive negative connotations without understanding the external impacts placed upon them. During the shutdown and the pandemic, people forgot people who relied on these benefits and then additionally focused on people receiving unemployment as being grifters and takers only looking for a handout. Social workers were overwhelmed with callers and recipients wondering where their benefits were and being frustrated when there were errors or long wait times. However, just like the public configured recipients, social workers also engaged in placing recipients in a negative light but also giving some the benefit of the doubt.

Social Workers/Case Managers

As researchers note, the roadblocks set up to restrict access to government assistance often impact marginalized communities in harmful ways.[10] A social worker from another social service organization that directly assists houseless individuals find stable housing and work denotes the terrible trials and tribulations they must go through to access assistance. This worker I interviewed surmised that the process for the homeless, who admittedly was not part of the original project, is a long and winding road to finding stability. In the most basic way, Bridget explained that for her organization to help someone in need they cannot just come into the office. They must first call the Milwaukee Help Line which is 2-1-1. From there, they are routed through different programs that might be available to them. They can help the person access a bed in a shelter for a night. If they are reaching homelessness, there are rent-assistance programs, you must have a set amount in your bank account to receive this assistance. For example, when I was trying to access benefits in Illinois, I made $100 over the maximum income limit, but I did not have the $1,200 required in my bank account to qualify for rent assistance. Similarly, people who have just *become* homeless often cannot access all the services from this agency and must find alternative accommodations like one-night hotels. For agencies like this one in Milwaukee to assist anyone, under federal guidelines, someone must be homeless for a consecutive number of months. Therefore, just to recap, for social service organizations to assist someone here in the United States, they must already be homeless for some length of time. Eubanks' (2018) research is mirrored here due to all the hoops and ladders someone must endure to receive some level of assistance. This winding and confusing process is like the maze that people trying to access SNAP must navigate, which will be discussed shortly.

While FSET is a free program, it is still one of the requirements for benefit receipt. Jenny from the food pantry consistently found this program pointless and unnecessary. She had a job, worked over 80 hours, but her wages still put her at poverty level, all while trying to raise teenagers. Her case manager informed her that if she wanted the benefits, she had to search for a job, that "[she] already had." The other problem is that you must already qualify for Foodshare to even start FSET. Eubanks[11] describes similar challenges that Rachel and Jenny echoed above, when she examined the automated process in the similarly Republican-run state of Indiana. While the goal for Indiana was to improve the Department of Health and Human Services, it created more hindrance in proving people assistance.

Social Work Process and the Shutdown

Like the issues that people in poverty or near poverty face, the end of 2018 and the beginning of 2019 brought additional problems with how the system of benefit-assistance functions. As described in a previous chapter, the shutdown created additional problems for people who were not considered previously. When the shutdown began at the end of December 2018, there was a highlight of concern about how federal workers would be impacted. There are several layers to this problem. For one, the news continued to detail approximately 800,000 federal workers, such as Transportation Security Administration (TSA), National Park Services, and other important roles that help the government function. Second, due to the long duration of the shutdown, some federal workers missed their next paychecks. However, not all federal workers were entitled to back pay after the shutdown ended nor were people given a timeline of when they could expect their paycheck. Third, while some would receive a late paycheck, there were thousands of workers that essentially worked for free during this 35-day period. Regardless of their paycheck, all workers had to continue to report to work.

To qualify to receive benefits, you must show pay stubs from the previous month, and depending on each state, there are different income maximums. Therefore, if you made over the maximum last month, a person applying for benefits would have to wait for at least two paychecks to even apply for benefits, not to mention the waiting period for approval. Therefore, a person has to be in an even worse position to qualify for cash and food assistance. Therefore, the safety net that is supposed to exist, simply does not. To deal with this problem, government officials directed people to utilize food banks and food pantries to survive. It was clear from working in a food pantry that the people running the government had very little information on how food banks, pantries, and community lunches provide meals for people. It is from the help of organizations like HTF and the USDA which were at risk of shutting down additional services as the shutdown dragged on. One official suggested that workers go to the store and ask managers for an I owe you (IOU) to be paid, once they were. It is almost as if government officials lack the knowledge of how grocery shopping functions. Another suggested using credit cards, payday loan advances, and other high-interest loan sharks to help workers through what many considered to be an unnecessary shutdown. During the shutdown, media outlets focused and made visible the plight of the 800,000 federal workers who would be lacking income and perhaps having financial trouble. However, made invisible were the workers who would not be receiving back pay during this time. Made even more invisible were the 30–40 million recipients, profiled in the shutdown chapter, who also would lose benefits that they so depended on. How does this fit into the larger problem of social workers and social services?

Working under Confusion

Imagine if your paycheck was suspended for an undetermined amount of time? Audre, a social worker I interviewed, noted that there were individuals who never considered themselves to ever be put into a situation where they might need assistance, and given how the benefits system is structured, they lacked the support necessary to avoid economic problems. Audre noted that there was no communication on how the benefits system was supposed to function during this time, which made it almost impossible for social workers to do their jobs effectively, or at least with minor issues. Associated with that, people who were already receiving benefits had no recourse and were terrified of what might happen and how they would continue to survive and feed themselves and their families. Audre detailed expressions of anxiety, fear, and frustration with the misinformation that was being given each day the shutdown went on. Similarly, Audre stated that each of us is one or two paychecks away from poverty and many of the people that she saw come through the door during the shutdown felt forgotten and erased. For many people who experienced the effects of the shutdown, Audre noted how the people were relatively confused about how the process functioned. For example, the social workers at HTF were given daily updates about SNAP and other benefits assistance. They also had to manage people either coming in for the first time or people worried about the continuation of their benefits, but both were worried about how they would simply survive.

I had the opportunity to interview social workers from several different organizations and the common thread through how those workers interacted with white colleagues and clients and colleagues and clients of color. For example, at a social service agency that served the homeless or recently homeless population, many of the white social workers commented on how their workplace was wonderful and had limited frustration with how things operated. Conversely, Aubrey, a Black supervisor from the same organization, detailed a picture significantly different. She detailed experiences with white managers and specifically with white males who were resistant to understanding notions of privilege. She noted that the Black workers and workers of color found white allies and were able to bring attention to some of the issues that they found could be remedied with some workshops and speakers on different subjects.

Aubrey detailed one of their first workshops was on whiteness and white privilege. She noted that many white people, but specifically white men, were particularly frustrated by the assumptions or their unrecognized privileges. She noted that many of the people objected to recognize that their privilege by using the usual rhetorical gymnastics of whiteness, by stating that they grew up poor, are currently poor, or lack various abilities to do certain things. This is usually where white people have particular hang-ups about being confronted with notions about privilege.[12] Largely, these phrases of rhetorical gymnastics work to bar learning possibilities by protecting white fragility—essentially shielding white individuals from having to consider that there are privileges to whiteness. Aubrey eventually had to take a break from the committee working to set up these workshops simply because of the emotional labor she felt she was putting out for her white colleagues, but not receiving the same support from them. Mark, a white man, who was a rare "ally" in trying to bring more equity to the workplace had a different perspective. I placed ally in quotations because he felt that the committee was trying to do many things, too quickly. Therefore, like many calls for equity in the past, this mirrored white resistance to Black and brown equity.[13] It also recalls Bell's[14] assessment of interest convergence—white people or those with power will only support something if they see themselves also benefiting from that change. The issue is that there is no policy change where white people would lose anything. Bobo[15] noted that whites would vote against policies that would in fact help them, if they thought people of color were going to get preferential treatment. Reyna, a petite white woman who was a worker at a local agency described her former agency as a Jekyll and Hyde operation—where the customer sees happy faces, but the work–life balance of the worker is anything but balanced. While there weren't explicit "quotas" to sign people up for benefits, there were implied quotas for the workers.

Symbolic annihilation appears in a variety of ways throughout this chapter—how the social workers engage with recipients and how other social workers approach their own coworkers. For many social workers of color, the experience of actively being invisiblized occurred frequently in their own workplace—especially around issues of race and class that are intermingled in the work that social service agencies facilitate.

At a different agency, Aubrey noted some of the same issues with how some of her colleagues worked with their clients. Like how I needed to build rapport with my research participants, the same is true for social workers, especially if one is particularly interested in assisting them. It does not mean that her white colleagues were unable to offer the same level of service. She noted that some of her white colleagues excelled at listening to people's concerns and trying to do the most to help them. There were, however, colleagues who lacked that quality and handled these cases differently. I asked her how she felt the colleagues succeeded in building the same level of rapport as her. The first thing she said was that you just need to listen because many of the individuals that walk through the door hardly get heard. Then, instead of offering what you think they *should* do, offer up a plan to work together to achieve goals. If the goals are jobs, housing, food, the case/social worker, and the client come up with a plan *together.* That process of achieving these goals together creates a space for assistance and self-reliance. Then they meet every two weeks to assess the plan and adjust where necessary.

Connecting building rapport to job success and self-care are important, and is a process not often taught to students when they are in process of learning how to be social workers or caseworkers. Self-care is not a new concept, but being open to talking about job stress, mental health, and how these things can affect your body is. Melanie, a white woman from the northern part of Wisconsin, and recent social work graduate now working in the field, noted that the education she received did not include proper classes or practices in self-care, without which often leads social workers or people who care for others to methods that are not necessarily healthy and can lead to a faster rate of burnout. She also worked in Green Bay first and then in Milwaukee and had the ability to speak to two different local populations receiving assistance and how she felt about those cases.

Aubrey described some level of satisfaction with the ways the organization she worked for handled the sometimes-intense workload and emotional labor they might have to do each week. Before her promotion, her old supervisor would take them out for lunch or away from the office. When something negative happens to one of the clients, grief counselors are provided for emotional support at any time. Now as a supervisor, she also works with her team and asks them what they would like to do for a particular event. She has taken her group out to spa days, lunch, and some team-building events.

In some cases, some of the social workers I interviewed did not have any social work education and had wanted a career in something people-related, like marketing, which is the story of Abigail. I met her one day at Starbucks, surrounded by folders and paperwork. She noted that her supervisor allowed them time away from the office if they needed some air or a different location. She, like some others I met, did not seek out social work but simply fell into it and found a career that felt rewarding. Bill, who was a tall, skinny, white man with a few tattoos and an infectious laugh, became a social worker because he struggled with addiction in his 20s and 30s and knew that other people did too. Audre, who I previously mentioned worked at social service agencies, focused on workers and voting rights, but she was always focused on working jobs where she could directly assist people in need.

Not Always a Rosy Picture: The Common
Perception of Social Workers

However, not every moment is a Kodak moment, and social workers are real people who live in a world where social constructions exist. Melanie, for example, knew people were simply looking for assistance but often wondered why they could not just get it together and get off assistance. To her credit for her honesty, she stated she felt more often this way when she had white clients but still invokes notions that benefit recipients are dishonest. Another social worker noted particular feelings regarding people who were "homeless." I place homeless this way to highlight the way they discussed people in this situation. Per guidelines that pertain to homeless persons, they do not need to verify an address. This social worker stated, "you get homeless calls to do the renewal and you hear children in the background, so they clearly aren't homeless." For this worker, the mere perception that there was background noise indicated to this worker that there was an element of "fraud," and this person wasn't really "homeless," but homelessness accounts for a variety of statuses. Another younger worker, a "novice" as she said some of the more veteran social workers called the new workers, stated that sometimes when you are new into the industry, you are more "wide-eyed and bushy-tailed" and have a sense of optimism that you are going to help. However, she stated that older workers take this as a weakness because, over time, they say the new workers will learn that "some" people are just trying to scam the system. She ended that thought by saying that she understands that people who are more senior have obviously seen more, but often that original optimism gets replaced with a more hardened sense of self because people can forget what poverty looks like or place themselves outside, as she stated, "I made it, so why can't you?"

One of my first interviews was with a social worker named Fred. I met him in a quaint coffee shop in the suburb/town of Waukesha, Wisconsin. Waukesha is a western suburb of Milwaukee that is predominantly white. Fred, a white man in his late 40s of average height greeted me in the coffee shop that looked like a converted old home. He seemed a little nervous to be interviewed, which is to be expected, but over time, loosened up and began to speak a little more freely. He spoke to me about his job, commuting from Waukesha which is predominately white and has larger pockets of higher socioeconomic statuses, how he handled stress, the process, and how many clients he usually has under his control on a given day—which can be between 50 and 100. Some caseworkers expressed that they might have approximately 1,400 cases, depending on what is happening with people's lives and economies. During the interview, Fred kept using the pronoun "they" to describe his clients or clients in general. At the end of the interview, I asked him, "when you say 'they' who are you talking about?" Often, when speaking about an othered group, white people (but not exclusively) will code their language by using they and often it is seen as quite disparaging. This is different from when someone requests the pronoun "they" to be used for their gender identity. When I asked him what he meant by his use of the word "they" and he chuckled nervously and said, "I guess I never noticed I do that. I guess I am talking about Black people."

White/white-identifying people account for 63% of the population, Latinx populations account for 13–14%, and Black and African American populations account for around 12%, among other populations that currently live in the United States. Depending on the state, the percentage of white people that receive welfare can vary from 38.9% to over 40% and the percentage of Black and African Americans that receive assistance is 39%[16] If we looked solely at these percentages and not the population rates that they come from, we might assume that Black and African American populations receive more assistance than other groups. However, when taking into consideration population size, African Americans account for 12% of the population. White people in the United States are a larger group of recipients simply because they account for a larger proportion of the population but receive less focus due to some of the work by legislators in the past, that is, Reagan labeling Black women in particular as "Welfare Queens." After one meeting with a social worker at an agency in Milwaukee, she slipped me meeting notes that detailed their demographic numbers for people receiving/requesting assistance which totaled 29% of African American/Black, 47% Latino, and 50% white. She told me she wanted to change the perception that all welfare recipients were non-white. When placing these numbers within the population demographics, it becomes clearer that whites have a large share of recipientship.

Social workers are often be placed in a bind because while they work for the state to help people in need, the state is in a simultaneous desire to reduce welfare role numbers, often to the detriment of the people that need assistance. For example, while talking to Audre, she detailed that she employed several former state workers from the Maria Coggs Social Service Building. She referred to the state workers as "ineligibility workers" due to some hoops and extra proof that a social worker might make a client provide. She named social workers this way to drive home the point that social workers often would be tasked with proving someone was ineligible versus showing them they were eligible. Audre told me an anecdote about a former military service member who was trying to get enrolled in various assistance programs like SNAP and the social worker had the individual supply of several different things, and sometimes multiple papers with the same information. This does not mean that all social workers are vindictive and out to kick everyone off from receiving benefits, but it does illustrate that there are discrepancies in how the state workers think the program works, from how the HTF access workers describe the program and how social workers in private offices think the program functions. The situations profiled in this section exemplify how social workers can engage with symbolic annihilation on recipients that they are supposed to assist.

The Recipients

Some of the recipients I interviewed were college-educated, with extensive degrees, from various age groups (18–70) and from various locations all around the United States who ended up living in Milwaukee. Other members of my recruitment strategy had some or no college, worked service jobs or found themselves on disability or had retired. I posted my recruitment materials at the coffee shops, unemployment offices, food banks, pantries, local churches, and by word of mouth. The common perception of recipients often configures an uneducated, poor person that lacks the desire to be gainfully employed. This does not really mesh with how recipients exist. The average recipient is a spectrum of education, location, gender, and background. While the previous section examined social workers, this part of the work profiles people who are trying to navigate a very confusing and convoluted system in which they feel is set up to hurt them or provide them with the barest of minimums. They expressed their feelings that it is set up in a way that is antithetical to the way they experience poverty. A difference of one hundred dollars over the income maximum does not mean a person or family is immediately out of living in poverty. Many of my participants used the phrase, "to rob Peter to pay Paul" to explain how they made their living expenses work each month, or if something unexpected emerged. In the rest of this chapter, respondents recount their experiences with the system and their case managers, how they navigate poverty, and how they shop at the store and make ends meet each month, and how they themselves would fix the benefit-assistance system.

Many of the respondents recalled having tenuous relationships with their benefit social workers. Or they only spoke to them when required when they would have to fill out or update any paperwork. For the most part, many of the recipients recalled that the process was never really the same, nor did they always have the same case manager. While sometimes they found their case-workers to be nice, they also recalled moments where they felt simply like a number, as was the story of one of my respondents named Ashley. When she waited at a southside Milwaukee social service office, she recounted several stories where she felt there was an adversarial attitude toward the respondents. Jenny from the food pantry always felt as though she was getting the run around because she would tell the case manager that she had a job, but the case manager kept telling her she needed to sign on to FSET, the program described at the beginning of the chapter, even though she worked over 80 hours per month. Jenny was never one to keep her feelings to herself about how she thought these social programs "did not" work.

The following sections detail specific themes that emerged from the interviews that I conducted. From the interviews, I would take notes and listen to what the participants were saying. Over time, during interview after interview, I noticed that experiences between recipients were creating these various themes. While this is not an exhaustive theme list, it does allow for the ability to track those recipients who may not be so different from non-recipients or people who should seek benefits but not knowing the process. These themes indicated things that resonated between recipients and commonly experienced events.

Race

One of my first interviews I held was at a local coffee shop on the east side of Milwaukee. She had found my advertisement from Fuel, a coffee shop in Riverwest I used to frequent. Natalie was a young, blonde, white woman in her early twenties who moved to Wisconsin and received benefits for food each month. I asked her about the experiences of being a white woman, the group that by and large per population size are most recipients to receive these benefits. She noted that when she went to the grocery store, it was not that she felt unsafe or nervous, but she felt as though people thought she shouldn't have it. As someone who similarly in two states has been a SNAP recipient, those feelings are echoed—however, in Oregon I felt that less but there is a historical legacy to Oregon's origination story—as an exclusively white settlement because they could not be a slave state given the dispersion of slave and non-slave state legislation. Natalie, however, was a bit of a nomad and different from my other recipients. She moved away from home and had access to family members that could help her, but she had a wanderlust outlook on life—which is admirable. For respondents that did not identify as white, they discussed feeling comfortable shopping in stores where the clientele matched their racial presentation. They also limited their time spent in stores to ones that were generally closer to them or in an area like where they lived therefore, they experienced less issues with the cashier or felt no qualms about using their cards. And for the most part—no one cared if someone saw them using their card because they were getting food and it didn't matter a bit to them.

Taking these experiences, white and Black recipients highlight a complex and deep issue—access or inability to access class privilege. For example, even though white recipients use the benefits, their class position is not threatened. Black recipients, on the other hand, are not thought of outside the receipt of these benefits. More broadly, even though white people receive a larger portion of the population and therefore a larger share of welfare/benefit recipients, they do not receive the negative attributes of benefit recipientship. Jay-z came out with a recent song about how he has all these items, is ungodly wealthy, and lives a life that people could never imagine—and at the end of the day, people still see him as a Black man.

Restrictions and Shopping

Where the respondents differed among each other was how someone spends their benefits and the issues between what they want to buy and what they can buy in the stores. At a women's retreat for GPLC, I interviewed six women who had wildly different opinions about how they spend their benefits. Mary, a Latina woman in her mid-50s, held a very common idea with how people should spend their benefits. Like many older women, she felt that SNAP benefits should only be spent on staples—bread, milk, flour, beans, meat, and other non-perishables. These recipients received between $15 and $150 per month to spend on food.

I asked many of my respondents, including these women, how they plan out their shopping experiences and they detail a procedure that requires planning and time. Therefore, there are neither impromptu trips to the store nor are things purchased outside the items that they clip from the papers or their lists. Being poor takes effort and time and significant energy to do things that people who have reduced monetary concerns need not spend additional mental and emotional labor.[17] The places that people most often frequented were Walmart, Aldi's, Piggly Wiggly, or Pick n' Save. They also either had to secure rides from people with cars or take public transit.

Moving toward more technologically based programs, recipients can monitor their benefits either by calling the toll-free number on the card or there is an iPhone/Android app where recipients can load their card and find out their card balance. Many of the older recipients simply called the number and the younger recipients used their phone app. The recipients I spoke with were particularly vigilant about when their benefits would drop for the month—which is dependent on the last digits of their social security number—to be either the 1st, 15th, or end of each month. Knowing the balance was incredibly important because it allowed the respondents to see if there was any money for extras that they could splurge on during that month, since if on the off chance they did not use all their money, it could rollover from one month to the next. Raquel, Alexa, Marina, and several others talked about how even if they did know their balance, they still were anxious at the checkout counter, especially if the card failed to go through the first time. In my interviews, when women would go shopping, there was more accountability for their SNAP card, but this was not as common when men would go shopping. Alfred, a Black man in his late 50s, noted that sometimes if he went over, he would simply pull things off the list and then the workers would just need to put it back. Often, shopping is coded as feminine in contemporary America, therefore, men either lack the expertise or *pretend* to lack it to protect notions of masculinity.

Most women I interviewed were far more budget-conscious than most of the men. Antonio, a Latino man I met at the pantry, was very precise with what he would need to purchase because he often had family that would come by to eat, and he wanted to make sure that anyone who came into his house would have the opportunity to eat. He randomly shopped at the pantry to bulk up on items that most saw as kitchen staples. That way, he said he could purchase other items at the store, like larger cuts of meat or more fruits and vegetables. He found these "splurges" to be something extra that he could provide his family during various months of the year, especially if there was a special occasion like a birthday, anniversary, or holiday.

Anxiety and Fear

When I asked my respondents about how they felt when they shopped, they identified a variety of emotions from relief that they had the ability to food to anxiety like previously mentioned, as well as, a feeling of disappointment because many stated that they never thought of themselves as never in need, or people who would ever be in a position to need assistance. Ricardo, a Latinx-identified person noted when I asked them how they felt, they stated, "struggle, like I and others are definitely trying hard, it's not like, in my case and I'm willing to bet other people are not trying to live off the government its more as of, what I'm doing right now is not cutting it, it's not meeting my needs of my daily expenses." Millie, a Latina woman who moved to the United States 25 years ago, expressed disappointment with what she referred to as the "American Dream." She stated, "I am trying hard, I worked, I had children and they were followed by the police and yet I still cannot make it, and this is not where I thought I would be at this stage of my life." Being critical of the place you are is at its base a notion of freedom, which she was happy to have, but felt that America was a place of contradictions that some had the privilege to ignore or the unwillingness to recognize.

Disappointment

Many described feelings of personal disappointment. Anika, Freddie, and David among others said they did not want to or enjoy being poor or to rely on receiving these benefits, but they allowed them to eat. David infrequently attended the food pantry and sometimes worked the kitchen to clean up after food service was complete. He, like many of my recipients, had a college degree, but he was unable to attain the job he had studied so long for during his younger years. I asked him about what he did previously, and he detailed a story about how Milwaukee changed over time, echoing the same deindustrialization theme discussed by Wilson.[18] David talked about how he had been at one point gainfully employed with a good job, benefits, and pay. Where the Walmart is currently on capitol, there was an AMC car plant, which closed in the mid-1980s among other good manufacturing jobs. The respondents that I spoke to who were Black discussed that much of their later-life stage poverty was due to economic deindustrialization in the area versus issues of generational poverty. For the respondents who identified as white, their entrance into benefit assistance was accompanied by some sort of health-related issue or job loss, but neither group saw benefit assistance as something they would experience. They feel as though they failed to access the promise of a middle-class life that was yanked from through deindustrialization from corporations and employers who do not hire them despite their skills.

Responsibility

When I asked how they felt about shopping for themselves, the respondents felt that at least they could provide for themselves. My next question was always, what about other people, "How do you feel when other people use their cards?" Many of the respondents cited that they didn't judge other people for relying on benefits because they knew what they were probably going through—they were just people trying to feed themselves and this is one way to do it. Some of the other recipients stated that the new EBT cards that looked like debit cards reduced the stigma that they once felt before when they had to use the actual stamps in the booklet. Now, it is harder to identify a recipient in the store, unless you notice their card with the dark green color, yellow and white lettering, and if they pay for household and personal items with cash or a different purchase altogether. Similarly, I asked if they ever looked in other people's carts and compared themselves, to which a majority said that it was unimportant what people bought because it is just good to feed yourself. There were about five women I spoke to who had particular objections were the older women, and in particular Mary, who frequently exclaimed, "how do they afford that! I scrape by with my small amount and struggle with just the basics." Mary, among a few of the respondents who were particular about what people *should* be able to buy. Mary was probably one of my more "conservative" respondents because she was opinionated that people receiving benefits should be grateful for what they are able to get and should not have access to nicer foods—like better steaks and seafood. She rationalized this not in terms of spending but perceptions of how someone *appears* to be grateful. Mary along with some of the other women were more restricted in what they cooked—they themselves placed harsher restrictions on themselves than the state did—since they stated that they felt lucky that they were even able to provide this meager food for themselves.

Can You Fix a Broken System or Is the System Working as Intended?

Related to perceptions, it was important to ask the respondents what they wanted other people to know about experiences of poverty. Like David and the other respondents stated above, every time I asked this question, people just wanted other people to have a better understanding of what poverty is like and how they think it could be remedied. They were surviving the only legal way they could, but they would all prefer to have jobs that paid well enough to support themselves and their families. All the respondents desire from others and government figures is for them to first understand how poverty functions, second, to listen to them, and third, make sustainable changes that helped improve their lives, not make them more difficult.

Participant Led Change

The respondents had several ideas about how to "fix" the system because they were disappointed with how it currently operates. For one, they all advocated for an increase in the standards of living simply because of the way prices are increasing, they are having to spend more of their benefits, but they fail to go as far as they did previously. They also advocated for the ability to purchase whatever they needed—ending the restrictive policies on purchases. For example, if a person solely receives SNAP/Foodshare, they are unable to purchase hygiene products, toilet paper, dish soap, or anything that might help with personal health. Instead of dividing social service programs into three directions like WIC, cash assistance, and Foodshare, where there are only some purchases that qualify, they desired to see less red tape and oversight over their purchases. If they are supposed to be "searching for work" why make buying personal products more difficult. When I asked per month what would be sufficient for food, they stated between $250 and $400 would make a huge difference in how much they would be able to buy for their families. After a conversation I had with Charles, a respondent in his early 60s, I started to be more vigilant on what I spent monthly for myself, a single woman living in a neighborhood that had access to several grocery stores, that is, Aldi, Pick n' Save, and Walmart. I found that I spent around the range that the recipients specified—even shopping at stores that provided discounts. The most important statement that the respondents noted, however, was simply that they wished people had a more realistic understandings of poverty. Understanding that the media played a role in configuring how recipients are configured, Sam, a supervisor at a state benefit office, noted that the actual amount of "welfare fraud" was a negligible 1–5% of all benefit recipients.

Social Work and Quarantine

While writing this, the quarantine was in full effect and illuminated the income problem that we have in the United States. However, this time, instead of just people receiving benefits being affected, it brought the problem to people who are poverty adjacent. Most Americans are at minimum two paychecks away from poverty. The quarantine showed how the safety net as a "thing" does not actually exist. Without government involvement, people would be evicted from their homes en masse, people were unable to pay most of their bills and there were massive layoffs. The added pressure, just like in the shutdown, was that there was no end to the quarantine in sight. For many, it meant not only losing your job but also your employer-funded health care. The cracks within the system were illuminated by the lack of preparedness on how this affected actual people. And just like the out-of-touch response during the shutdown, government officials similarly felt that a one-time $1,200 "stimulus check" would be enough to hold people over for 10 weeks. The feelings and emotions of uncertainty for individuals and families increased while already experiencing anxiety.

In conclusion, the stories of people receiving benefits and those responsible for giving the benefits are intertwined. Some of the people who went into social work/case management had experiences of being on welfare and wanted to assist others in need. Other times, social workers who had been around the office for longer sometimes looked down on the new workers, as novices, not willing to see their clients as potentially engaging in fraud. As for the recipients, while the public perception is created and transformed over time to signify one group as one entity, from this collection of interviews, the "welfare recipient" *is* college-educated, trying to succeed, doing all they can, and trying to get by—which is not unlike anyone else, recipient or not. Service providers also assist recipients with options—in the case of HTF—which not only operates as a food bank but also a service point for SNAP and other types of assistance. HTF as an organization is explored more in the following chapter.

NOTES

1. Foodshare/SNAP are nutrition programs, and the name depends on the state you are in.
2. Eubanks, *Automating Inequality.*
3. Ibid.
4. Wisconsin Department of Health Services 2018.
5. Baldwin, "Stratification"; *"Wisconsin Works"*; Gilens, *Americans Hate Welfare.*
6. Eubanks, *Automating Inequality.*
7. Mulvany, "State to Spend"; Sandler, "Block Reconstruction."
8. Gomez, "What 13 States Discovered"; Gritter, *Food Stamps and SNAP.*
9. Gomez, "What 13 States Discovered."
10. Baldwin, *Wisconsin Works*; Eubanks, *Automating Inequality.*
11. Eubanks, *Automating Inequality.*
12. Bonilla-Silva, *Racism without Racists*; Lipsitz, *Possessive Investment.*
13. King Jr, "Letter from Birmingham Jail."
14. Bell, Brown v. Board.
15. Bobo, "Prejudice as Group Position."
16. Census.gov; Cole, Welfare Recipients.
17. Ehrenreich, *Nickel and dimed;* "Expensive to Be Poor," Weese, "Costs So Much to Be Poor"; Wellington, "Being Poor Is Expensive."
18. Wilson, *Disadvantaged.*

Chapter 8

Hunger Task Force

Your Free and Local Food Bank

When I was digging through the research on food insecurity in Milwaukee, at the pantry I asked what service we used for our deliveries. Pastor Patricia said, "Hunger Task Force, they have free items that we can get for the pantry." Unlike Feeding America, a large nationwide food bank, Hunger Task Force (HTF) is Milwaukee and Wisconsin specific and can offer many of its services free of charge. I thought to myself; this would be a great organization to speak with in terms of how they provide these wonderful services. I simply emailed their information account, very much thinking that I would never hear from them or if I did there would be no way I could get any useful information out of them. It was within one day that an education representative reached out to me and invited me for a tour of each one of their facilities. I could not believe my good fortune.

Food banks provide a lifeline for people who are experiencing food insecurity in ways that are almost too numerous to comment on. Throughout 2019 and 2020, food banks around the country have been keeping families fed when without them they would go hungry. Most food pantries survive on donations, via monetary and material items, as well as funding from the USDA. Previous chapters attempted to untangle the web of social work, benefit recipients, and pantries but all those things still need another component. Much of the food that comes into the doors of recipient homes or pantries is made possible by local food banks and organizations that collect donations from the community writ large. Hunger Task Force, Milwaukee's Free and Local food bank and advocacy organization, provided pantries, like the Feed the Need pantry profiled in chapter 1, the ability to fill their shelves. This chapter goes into more detail about the origins of a food bank and anti-poverty organization in Milwaukee that provides food to residents, how they came to be, their history, and their current operations, and what that means for recipients. The chapter also examines how the threads of symbolic annihilation and violence weave their threads within these organizations.

While some might read this part as rather critical of organizations that assist those in poverty, it goes without saying that many people are able to access food through the programs that are provided by the Hunger Task Force and similar organizations, but it would be remiss to not mention that even organizations that are well-intentioned need to keep working on themselves. Why would organizations hide their origins? What purpose does that serve and who is that accommodating? While their intentions are good, often organizations that are led by majority white leaders struggle with how to make those intentions actionable and less tinged with white savior syndrome.

A FOOD BANK DURING A GLOBAL PANDEMIC

While not a perfect organization, food banks like HTF were necessary during the shutdown, and even then, depending on how long the shutdown was to drag on, they were at risk of running out of food. A little more than a year later, Hunger Task Force is pressed to help thousands of more families than they anticipated during the pandemic. They created an interactive map where people could map the nearest pickup location for any items. In the image below (figure 8.1), there are locations specific to the senior stock boxes, meals

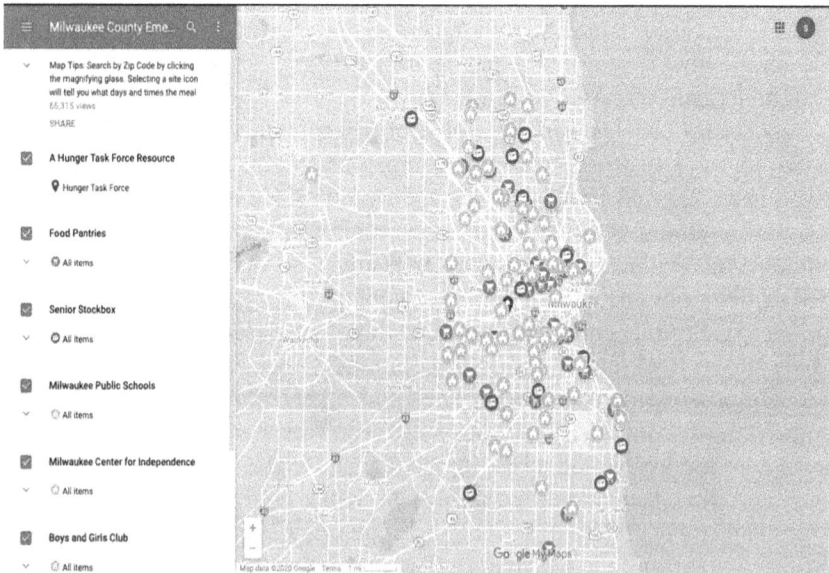

Figure 8.1   Milwaukee Hunger Task Force Food Bank Network.

for students and children, and location that service the broader public. During the time of the pandemic, their network still provided for the pantries that rely on them for their goods—like Feed the Need.

Hunger Task Force is not alone during this time. Food banks across the nation were at capacity with the overwhelming and skyrocketing need of community members and families. Some food banks and pantries noted that cars lined up for hours before they opened for access to food for themselves and their neighbors. For a nation that prides itself on being rich and prosperous, it took one pandemic to show the cracks in this façade.

In the Beginning

Per the organization's website, Hunger Task Force began in 1974 as the Concerned Citizens for School Breakfast, after the actions of community members advocated for children to have access to lunches and breakfast in schools. This remains a consistent problem for school children, especially ones that receive less funding than other schools within and outside their districts. For example, current legislators tried to create programs where children would be required to do janitorial work to pay for their school lunches—essentially saying that poor children lacked work ethic when we know that is demonstrably not the case.[1] In its history, the Hunger Task Force tried and tries to maintain its food advocacy work for people in the state of Wisconsin. For example, it released a report on its School Breakfast Program for the 2016–2017 school years. Per Hunger Task Force, "in Wisconsin, 1 in 6 children live in poverty . . . and [ranks last] in the nation for offering school breakfast to children."[2] The School Breakfast Program includes one fruit or vegetable, whole grain-rich item, and a milk carton. The School Breakfast Program began in 1975 and is funded through the USDA.

Is That It?

Since research can also mirror detective work, I wondered how poverty organizations fit into the larger picture and who these concerned citizens were. As the above paragraph explains, the formation of the Hunger Task Force was due to advocacy by a local parents' group. This description seemed intentionally vague, and it felt important to dig a little deeper into the origination of this concerned parents' group. In this research, I began contacting residents who either had ties to the community during that time or knew people who were active. I also researched the University of Wisconsin, Milwaukee Archives, which hold the Hunger Task Force notes and advocacy initiatives beginning in 1974 through 1996. While at some level, this is frustrating, it does lend itself to some interesting things that might come up from it. "Concerned citizens" aside, what lead me to explore this path was that through anecdotal conversations about Hunger Task Force, people alluded to the fact that the people being referred to as "concerned citizens" were local Black community members. The idea that Black women specifically or Black people more generally were erased from the historical timeline of this anti-hunger organization increased my interest in the topic. It appears too many people knew something was amiss but were not exactly sure where they learned this information. It also seemed pertinent to this research which is an exploration of symbolic annihilation regarding people of color white-washed from history.

Heynen and Witt[3] note the formation of the Hunger Task Force through the efforts of the local chapter of the Black Panthers meeting with Reverend Ellwanger from Milwaukee Cross Lutheran Church. The Panthers were seeking a space for their breakfast program. After this meeting, Ellwanger was confronted with a problem that needed a solution. Therefore, the Citizens for Central City School Breakfast Program (CCCSBP) eventually became the Milwaukee School Breakfast Coalition, which evolved into what is now known as the Hunger Task Force.

Removing the History from the Task Force

Before we can understand the Milwaukee Panther chapter, we must understand how the BPP nationally came together, since their history is tarnished with white fright and misinformation. Given the perception disseminated by the media, most white people have a very different feeling about the BPP. It is no secret that the BPP operated with a "by any means necessary" framework, of what some might consider militant. However, that perception of militancy overshadows the important social justice work the party completed for Black communities specifically and people of color more generally. Even with the original party breaking up a few years after Hampton's assassination, much of that hostility toward Black liberation groups lingered and is mirrored in the perceptions of the present-day Black Lives Matter movement. Many researchers highlight the connections between the COINTELPRO surveillance of the 1960s–1970s on the BPP and the current FBI surveillance of Black Lives Matter supporters and members that is ongoing. Some researchers note that the BPP was not particularly organized nor had a long duration. However, given that it was incumbent on Hoover to create whole task forces to monitor, infiltrate and destroy BPP chapters in cities like Oakland, Chicago, Milwaukee, and Winston-Salem, it seems that at least in terms of the FBI, the group piqued their interest. At the time, it seems important to mention that the United States was still engaging with the USSR and in the Cold War, so any organization that was critiquing capitalism and using socialized methods to do it was going to be investigated more thoroughly. However, the BPP had two strikes not only were they anti-capitalist, but they were also Black.

Service Programs

The BPP had several main points that collectivized them as a group. Most importantly, they focused on providing services that were missing in the Black community. Many of its social service programs were quite popular and were creating change in communities in ways that the BPP and the communities they live and work in felt the federal and state government assistance was lacking. Heynen[4] noted that the Black Panthers had approximately 65 survival programs running for their community. They were titled survival programs because the BPP felt that the US government was not concerned with the survival of Black people. Heynen[5] noted that he felt that the official US policy was to pacify the community, not sustain the community. Some examples from these 65 survival programs included: Child Development Centers, health classes, ambulance, prison shuttles, access to clothing, dental care, plumbing and home maintenance, a newsletter, and the School Breakfast Program, among others.[6]

Food insecurity is a health problem and in the 1960s and 1970s, the BPP were trying to find ways to combat this issue that affects millions of children still today. The BPP was observing a community that while there were some initiatives aimed to assist those in poverty with health care, many Black Americans were still lacking in quality care. Therefore, the BPP launched community health programs with people on-staff ready to assist Black people and those in poverty with health care, screening for diseases, such as sickle cell anemia and other issues deemed prevalent in the Black community specifically and communities in poverty more generally. They also began helping students in the school with breakfast, which assists greatly with academic achievement and better and more positive health outcomes.[7]

Many of the programs, like school breakfasts, that were started by the Black Panthers eventually were made into national programs—due to the pressure placed on government officials and via cooption of these programs because of their overwhelming success with poor and low-income Black and African Americans. One example of this is in California, where the original Black Panthers were founded had future president Ronald Reagan as governor. At the time, the Panthers were gaining followers and support for their programs. Reagan had his hand forced to accept some of these BPP-lead initiatives, but clearly reversed them during his presidency, undercutting a lot of plans that have made a positive difference in the lives of those experiencing poverty.

Symbolic Annihilation

Symbolic annihilation is the simultaneous presence and absence of something or group wherein controlling images are created, maintained, changed, or destroyed. To give weight to how popular these breakfast programs were, during the peak of the School Breakfast Program, it is estimated that the BPP and associated volunteers were feeding approximately 250,000 children nationwide.[8] Heynen[9] notes that Hunger Task Force owes much of its existence to the Milwaukee chapter of the BPP and that meeting with Reverend Ellwanger. Without listening to the BPP and their ideas about alleviating hunger insecurity and the support of local community members, Ellwanger himself even stated that he was unsure if the Panthers did not contact him who knows how long for there to be a food bank or pantry in Milwaukee. While the BPP was not directly involved, plans were put into motion because a relatively well-connected pastor was able to bring awareness and attention to the issue of food insecurity and Milwaukee children now had the possibility of school breakfasts.

Given what is known now, one would be unaware of that tangential history, even if fleeting, from their website. For example, referring to the website history, it states that the HTF emerged from a group named Concerned Citizens for School Breakfast, but this is not exactly accurate. Speaking with Audre, a community organizer with familiarity with HTF, gave me a sense of the organizational history. I wanted to get to a knowledgeable source namely because every person I spoke with outside of the organization alluded to this BPP history, but it was completely anecdotal. With this information, I was curious how people within the organization understood its history. This connection is not discussed readily, but people do treat it as a secret fact that gets talked about in hushed tones. This hushed sense is seen not only in how it is discussed within the organization, but that they changed the original organization name.

Audre noted that the reason why the history, tenuous at best, is not discussed is because of the perceptions of white people might have that donate to the pantry. Bluntly, Audre asserted that if white people knew that the Black Panthers were connected to the organization, they might reconsider their donation. The Hunger Task Force owes its presence in Milwaukee to the meeting of Ellwanger and the members of the BPP—without which could have delayed the development of such an important organization. HTF note that they assist a majority of Black and brown residents, but just like the grocery stores, they have no physical presence on the northside. The HTF service centers described below that provide benefit access assistance, food pantry/bank preparation and grow locally sourced food are all located on Milwaukee's south side, including one location in a rural suburb just southwest of the city.

May the Force Be with You

Given this interesting and important history, and that the pantry where I volunteered relied on Hunger Task Force as the free and local Milwaukee food pantry and organization that works closely with those in poverty, getting in contact seemed of high importance. To my surprise, I received a response quicker than I expected. Mark invited me to visit the facility and check out the farm that supplies many of the pantries and individuals in the Milwaukee area more specifically and Wisconsin more generally. Mark led some of the educational instruction programs for students around the Milwaukee area. As a food educator, he develops and uses simulations through the statewide program, *Food for Today*. This program focuses on food insecurity using various vignettes where participating students assume an identity that is based on a real person and must make ends meet with breakfast, lunch, and dinner with the allotted money. Mainly, the program brings many students together to discuss poverty while also breaking down the animosity and negative perceptions toward poor people or individuals that use food assistance.

During my tour of the main distribution facility, Mark was adamant about their advocacy and how the right-wing public disagree with the work that the organization does because they believe it is too political. While the Hunger Task Force does not have a stated political stance, simply advocating for food *security* equates to the belief it leans more left than center, given that much of their advocacy predicates calling your representatives, via examining their archives at the UWM, much of their advocacy focuses on keeping the heat on more right-wing, benefit-cutting or amnesty focused Republicans. As some archives detail, in a letter written by Dan Canadeo from Waukesha, Wisconsin dated June 24, 1993, to Michele Goldstein, then director of HTF states, "I am withholding my contribution until I receive word from you that not one cent will go to some liberal state or federal representative or senator for your political cause." Even in 1993, the public felt the notion of food access was a partisan issue. While the organization is not "political," that is, right/left, but their job is certainly *political.*

During the interview, Mark held some opinions that are not outside the realm of most left/right, democrat/republican circles, especially when it comes to issues of social justice or welfare. Mark noted that when he does do educational outreach, he often receives and perceives the most pushback from more right-wing aligned students. He noted that the rhetoric of people who use pantries as being lazy or lacking work ethic often emerges in these conversations. Mark often responds to these comments in a manner-to-fact way, wherein people who use these services are looking to survive and would probably rather not be using the pantry, but people "use it because it helps." He has hope for the future and told me he was concerned about breaking these generational opinions about people experiencing poverty.

While food security should not be a partisan issue, often the way social inequalities impact different residents of the Milwaukee area make food insecurity to be seen as political. The organization does not shy away from the fact that it is a hunger advocacy organization and received throughout its existence push back from various members of the public, regarding food assistance. The organization was keen on maintaining this positive image of helping those in need, which is something that an advocacy organization should be doing.

At the same time Mark expressed hope for the future, later in our interview, Mark had some interesting things to say about the Northside of Milwaukee. While at some level admonishing right-wing opinions stated that he was north-side averse and would tell others to stay away from the area. Perhaps realizing that what he admitted was explicitly coded, he noted he should not say that, but that is how he felt, even though his job is to help the exact people in the area he feels "uncomfortable" traveling in and through. Hunger Task Force can serve the community due to its locations in the Milwaukee area which include the Hawley Center, the Robles Center, and the farm. These important centers provide connection points to thousands of other affiliates that the HTF works with to provide food to the pantries in the state of Wisconsin.

The Hawley Center

The Hawley Center is located off I-94 in the suburb of West Allis, a low to medium income suburb of Milwaukee that is positioned between the more affluent suburbs of Milwaukee further west and is the main distribution center for the products that come in from local donations and collection points. The distribution center is approximately 15,000 square feet, but all together, the centers are a combination of 50,000 square feet of space. Throughout the year, they also have approximately 15,000 volunteers each year between the farm and distribution centers.

This warehouse contained all the food that was to be distributed at some point to pantries, families, or seniors and people were coming in the building to drop-off deliveries while I was on my tour. The Hawley Center receives upward of approximately nine million pounds of food and two million of that is through direct donations, from Summerfest, Stamp Out Hunger drives where Postal Service workers help gather food items for people as they make their deliveries and other drives throughout the year. For example,

Summerfest is one of the largest music festivals that partners with Hunger Task Force to allow free admission to the festival grounds for anyone that brings non-perishable items for donation. This drive is probably the largest one that they do throughout the year. Mark though was a little hesitant to say that it was a success because many items that do end up being donated are expired goods, which thus may not detail the inherent care of those donating. However, expired food is not wasted but taken to the farm to be used as compost for the items grown there.

While they will take all food, they will only distribute what they consider to be "healthy food" as dictated by the USDA My Plate program, the updated version of the food pyramid that dictated food proportions for so long. The notion of intention and impact become prevalent again. The intention might be one thing, which is often seen as non-harming or with good meanings behind it, but the impact often stings. Therefore, while the intention might be in the best interest, the way that it is carried out might differ from the end result. For example, while the intention is to help people, you may inadvertently impact them in a negative way depending on how that impact is distributed. Therefore, what the Hunger Task Force considers "healthy food" and what people receiving assistance *should* eat is one of those examples of well-intentions with different impacts. Many studies about poverty display that much of the public believes that people receiving food assistance should have their benefits monitored or be barred from purchasing certain items like candy, sweets, or soda. It implies that poor people and recipients are unable to make decisions for themselves which is why they need to be monitored and what led them to be in poverty in the first place.

People in poverty should not be situated as needing to accept everything and anything because it is food, and they happen to be poor. Perceptions of wealth and poverty are key in determining access to free choice. Stating that they only accept and distribute healthy food is still placing some sort of failure on the perceptions of the poor people they are supposedly trying to help. Treating poor people as if they do not know what consists of healthy food erases the larger problem in many of these neighborhoods which is the lack of a sustainable income, grocery stores with fresh foods, and simply the cost of those items. Much of the rest of the populace similarly lacks proper nutrition education, but because they are not actively receiving food share, their poor nutrition habits are of no concern to anyone.

Tariffs Close to Home

In the Hawley Center, they also are the storage point for the USDA's Emergency Food Assistance Program (TEFAP). The TEFAP essentially allocates money for places like Hunger Task Force to buy food from the overstock of the USDA. If there is a significant overstock of items, they can be added as free bonuses and Hunger Task Force can add to their stock of items—which help supply food pantries, families, and senior stock boxes.

One might ask themselves, how can the USDA have an overstock of items and the simple answer is trade wars and increased tariffs where places are no longer purchasing American goods for trade. Instead of US farmers selling their goods to other nations, the USDA will buy the food and then it gets allocated to places like the Hunger Task Force and then they buy it through the allocation program. To account for this, the USDA pays these farmers for their goods. It works like this: if there is an overabundance of food, at present there is about 1.2 billion pounds of commodities—mostly apples, milk, and pork—which is largely excess food that farmers are unable to trade rapidly. The USDA buys that from the commodities market and much of that is purchased by pantries, schools, and food banks. The Hunger Task Force is allocated money from the USDA and purchase items from them. However, there are items that are considered "bonuses" which are food turned down from other places or if there happens just to be a lot of it. Hunger Task Force does not turn down any food, they collect it, separate it by item type—fruit, vegetable, snack foods, and so on—and then those are the items that are available for food pantries/banks and people on request.

Therefore, we might think that larger government operations might not affect groups and organizations like Hunger Task Force, but issues, policies, and decisions trickle down and directly affect those who need assistance. There is a saying in Chicago, "all politics is local" because even though we might imagine federal policies as far off and not readily affecting people directly, these decisions directly impact people's lives. There are also other effects as well that have a negative trickle-down effect, and that comes from decisions about social safety net assistance programs like SNAP, Foodshare, and cash assistance. Just like the USDA governs food pantries, they are also managing these programs as well, so when changes are made at the top, everything below must be juggled and moved around. Therefore, when changes are made, people are kicked off and need to seek other methods of obtaining nutrition, so while statistically it looks like fewer people are on receiving assistance, it does not mean that people are able to provide for themselves—they become invisible. Therefore, the flow between federal policies, to government institutions, to assistance organizations, to the actual consumer/individual creates a large interconnecting web.

Robles Center

The Robles Center is in what many consider the Southside of Milwaukee, in the historic Mitchell Street District. Formerly, this was a highly concentrated

Polish district over time transitioning into a high population of Latinx families. Situated in an old storefront, the center is intended as a self-service station, but with ACCESS service team members available for any questions, issues, or problems. The center is staffed by approximately five people, including a center manager and state representative. They also have signed up detailing that assistance is available in many languages—English, Polish, and Spanish as the primary ones. The center is clean, with computer stations lining the sides of the walls, with the assistance workers present in the center, with the manager and state representative in the back. Robles Center is where much of the advocacy develops and where the ACCESS team is located. This ten-person access team goes out into communities and help people sign up to receive Foodshare benefits—they act as access points to social services because people in need might not know about these benefits, may be afraid to ask for them or feel like they should not ask for them because of the negative perceptions of benefit assistance. I was able to meet with Elaine at the center and she helped answer my questions about the services that the center provides, as well as HTF more generally. How I got in touch with Elaine included working and talking with local community members about HTF, because all my contacts at the organization had been white individuals, but I was interested in interviewing someone with a potential differing outlook and take on how the organization functions for a more well-rounded examination throughout this chapter.

The Farm and Hatchery

The farm is located out in the suburbs in a town called Franklin and is approximately 200 acres and accounts for much of the production of vegetables and fish. The farm itself produces about 500,000 pounds of fruits and vegetables, including 16 apple varieties. The farm also includes a fish hatchery that operates under the condition that 40,000 fish will be redeposited into the lakes and ponds around Milwaukee. The farm and hatchery employ only 9 people that oversee the grounds and 5,000 volunteers annually. Almost all of the farm implements were donated or bought secondhand from local farmers. Food banks usually don't have their own farms. However, this farm seeks to distribute food to a larger distance.

Local Labor Force

The farm was worked by the nine employees and also there was a work-release program from the county jail that sits across the street from the farm. After 2012, former Milwaukee County Sheriff David Clarke stopped the program. Though Clarke "officially" halted the countywide work-release program unexpectedly, the program in Franklin did not shutter, but continued.

The work-release program at the Milwaukee County House of Corrections operates several programs, but the one that is used in connection with Hunger Task Force works to allow for every 24 hours worked, the inmate has 1 day removed from their sentence. These solutions address just part of the problem and as HTF using prison labor while not compensating the people doing it with horticulture, farming, or other certificates or money, seems like an extension of chattel slavery. Education and treatment programs actually have a deeper impact on people in prison and often reduce recidivism.[10]

While this was helpful, Mark still held perceptions about the inmates working on the farm. For example, if there were volunteers on the grounds, there could be no inmates present. However, the county jail that sits across the street enabled men convicted of non-violent crimes to volunteer. What this means is that the perceptions of inmates, regardless of non-violent offence, were still seen as dangerous because of their inmate status. At this jail, non-violent indicates property crime, inability to pay bail, traffic violations, etc. In short, many of the men incarcerated at this prison were poor or working class before entering its gates. Mark even described the inmates as "non-violent but idiots who had just made dumb mistakes." Perceptions of these inmates drifted into the work that they did at the farm and how they "did not" connect with individuals from the outside. The perceptions held by Mark are not any different than any average individual—however, we might think that at a work-release program for non-violent individuals there might be a specter of treating these individuals with a level of respect.

The farm described above also has other programs on its grounds, which include a large kitchen where local chefs from area restaurants come in and hold cooking classes for people in poverty. Recall that Hunger Task Force is well-intentioned but often has problematic impacts because quality nutrition access affects groups across class and race lines. For example, wealthy children might engage in poor nutrition habits that are worse than low-income children, but because they are afforded the veil of wealth, they are hardly a focus. More often, we attribute the lack of nutrition habits to low-income children and their families. For example, the Hunger Task Force states that they "just don't feed kids—we also teach them about healthy eating!" The Force employs an on-staff Dietitian Educator that travels to different Milwaukee Public Schools and teaches low-income children nutrition education. While this is noble, this is perhaps one of those intention/impact approaches that means well in theory but has the appearance of attempting to be a white savior in practice. For example, the assumption is that low-income children do not understand what good nutrition is nor how to cook. The issue with that is that is not solely something experienced by poor people, yet the Force sets its sights on people in poverty, which is important, but also creates and maintains perceptions of those in poverty.

Hunger Focus

In other ways, symbolic annihilation can emerge in a series of ways which help navigate beliefs about people. Websites of organizations are important to examine since they are an extension of their focus and goal; simultaneously, they can reinforce perceptions about people. Many of the children and families pictured on the HTF website are Black children. Just like many of the other perceptions of Black families and children, this becomes an extension of that media focus. For example, positioning Black children as the only ones that need assistance or nutrition assistance erases the fact that other children may benefit from this as well. Using Black children as the figurehead of poverty and then using their images configures in the minds of those who may donate to the Hunger Task Force that are doing a noble task and can avert feelings of negative racial bias. For example, people that donate to the Hunger Task Force might think they are helping alleviate issues of racial inequity with their donations.

While people of color do experience high rates of poverty, by using their images *as* the face of poverty, it creates the continuations of negative perceptions in the mind of the public. Hunger Task Force itself helps service Milwaukee and works with local pantries in other parts of Wisconsin, *but* donations can come from anywhere. For example, when looking at an electoral map of Wisconsin, Milwaukee County is overwhelmingly blue, and its surrounding counties are staunchly red. Wisconsin residents harbor negative and racialized feelings about Milwaukee. However, the Black population in Milwaukee accounts for 6% of the state population (40% in Milwaukee) and the state itself is 88% white. Therefore, the rest of the state and parts of Milwaukee harbor racialized feelings for a very small part of the demographic makeup of the state. Routinely these populations are blamed for the state's problems, instead of looking at structural, systemic, and institutional factors at play, as described above. Therefore, the website could be working to maintain the narrative of poor Black children via this focus, as well as, forgetting that families in these predominately white areas are also disproportionately impacted by poverty.

Symbolic annihilation, regarding the Hunger Task Force, emerges in a multiplicity of fronts because one group can be affected in two ways. Either Black families are always seen a certain way—as poor—even if they are wealthy nor have ever used assistance programs. White families are never seen as poor, even if they are able and have used assistance programs. By making the presence of Black families as needing assistance the focus, it also places white families as somehow persevering in ways that Black families are not able. White families have the luxury of never being seen as needing assistance even though their participation in the SNAP program is half their representative population in the nation.

Where Symbolic Violence and Annihilation Intersect

These perceptions can also materialize in other ways. The lens that people use to gaze onto poverty often sees this issue in a particular manner—one they have personal failings, two things that people in poverty do to supposedly keep themselves in poverty, and three, they just do not know how to care for themselves. Hunger Task Force tends to focus on the final one—that poor people simply don't know how to make good, nutritious food for themselves or their families. For example, if the organization knows better about how people should live their lives.

Thus, again while being well-intentioned, it capitalizes on the idea that Hunger Task Force thinks that it holds the key for people to live better lives. It also shows the significance of the lack of an inclusive and diverse workforce—with the invisibility of voices of color and the echo of white voices, being critically and systemically aware goes unchecked.

This is not solely a problem with Hunger Task Force. Elaine noted that being a Black woman in many social welfare-oriented offices, she noticed some of the same well-meaning or well-intentioned behaviors of her white coworkers that were often out of place or missing the point. For example, she expressed frustration when she would bring up a new idea to solve a problem and people would treat it as a talking point or non-issue, but when a white male meeting attendee said a similar solution, it was met with support. She discussed at length the proper ways to express and *do* allyship. She would confide in a white, male coworker who had her back[3] and he would bring up her ideas, give her credit and bring attention to the double standards within the office culture.

Another social service office, dedicated to homeless and houseless people in the Milwaukee area also struggled with these same issues of race, place, and people that they serve. This organization created a committee staffed with employees seeking greater awareness of how whiteness, privilege, and race play within the workplace. While not always successful, specifically when trying to educate white people on their own whiteness, the intention is important to note.

This last chapter explored how organizations that combat poverty operate, but even within these organizations, they also provide social services. Exploring how these advocacy organizations interplay with social workers, food pantries and people is an important role. Providing a pathway for people to access food is imperative. There is no doubt that Hunger Task Force provides a valuable resource for people in Milwaukee—especially given its historical and current segregation issues. While HTF is noble, they also struggle with many of the issues discussed in previous chapters, where whiteness and privilege often go unchecked. Good intentions are important but there must be attention paid to the impact that these programs may cause.

NOTES

1. Lewis, "Situated voices"; Larson, "Rising Food Insecurity."
2. https://www.hungertaskforce.org/about-hunger/priority-campaigns/school-breakfast/.
3. Heynen, "Monitoring Wisconsin," 3; Witt, "Picking Up the Hammer," 72.
4. Heynen, "Monitoring Wisconsin."
5. Ibid.
6. Ibid.
7. Heynen, "Monitoring Wisconsin," Morabia, "Black Panther Party."
8. Heynen, "Monitoring Wisconsin."
9. Ibid.
10. Gomez, "What 13 States Discovered"; Gritter, *Food Stamps and SNAP*.

Conclusion

An Ode to My Time at Feed the Need

August 7, 2019, was an emotional day as it was my last day at the pantry. The last year and a half were incredibly important to me. Without the assistance and welcoming environment of the GPLC and Feed the Need pantry, this project would not be possible. During the last few months of my volunteering, I was hired as a visiting professor at a university in Oregon, and my research participants would say how much they would miss me or that I, in fact, could not go because they would not let me. Over my time at Feed the Need, I learned much about myself and others—specifically in how people navigate their lives through poverty. The observation at Feed the Need informed much of how I was able to approach recipients met outside the pantry and the social workers that assist in accessing benefits.

The theoretical thread of symbolic annihilation and violence wove through this work to explore the ways in which different people are made present or absent and how that works to highlight (often in negative ways) some groups over others. While white people are the majority population and welfare benefits of all kinds in the United States, nationally they see others as the problem and more importantly, middle-class over all other self-identified class statuses feel the most strongly about the bootstrap mentality. All the while, middle and upper class individuals willfully forgetting all the benefits and assistance received over time and instead replacing it with a romanticized bootstrap version of events. The thread of symbolic annihilation was seen in the ways recipients are consistently configured in media and news discussions, which map onto national survey data regarding welfare spending. It continues weaving through to the daily lives of people, recipients, people locked out from benefits, and those benefit providers. In addition to all these experiences, well-meaning poverty organizations focus their marketing strategies on communities that most definitely are generationally locked out from healthy food access, but also infantilize them at the same time.

Exploring the web of benefit recipientship includes not only the people themselves but also social workers, poverty organizations, and advocacy groups, but also state and federal agencies up through the legislative and executive branches. All these pieces are interconnected and matter to how the process benefit receipt functions. However, receiving welfare assistance need not be so convoluted nor difficult. As other researchers note a concerted effort is made to create processes that place unnecessary barriers in place to disincentivize applying for assistance. The "automation" of inequality is the latest barrier created to disenfranchise people in new ways than geographical barriers, food deserts, and infrastructural barriers that existed previously.

As Milwaukee is one of the most segregated places in the nation, it was imperative to explore the historical formations of urban geography. Through these formations, the unspoken or hidden demarcations of racism, stratification inequality become visible. Exploring the geographical component cements the idea that the creation of the city in this was completed through active decisions from governmental entities, and not on just "natural" tendencies. The appearance of segregation, food insecurity, and deserts are created through systemic, institutional and structural constructions. From white flight in the 1950s through the 1970s, these movements of concerted effort created the northside and segregation that we see presently. Similarly, the lack of food security is a symptom of the movements and infrastructural projects, prompted by the development of I-43 which bifurcated a growing and prosperous neighborhood.

Inextricably linked to the geographical connections are the lives of welfare recipients and how they provide for themselves. The barriers placed by built environments impact how recipients access food and markets cannot be understated. The outcome of this study details a variety of results. Many of the recipients simply just want to provide food for themselves and their families. While they felt this way about themselves, at times they would oscillate between placing themselves in the shoes of people in the similar position or they would repeat opinions held by the public. Often, they would use this common rhetoric about welfare abuse toward their own communities. This implicit bias is not unusual—but also displays how this language is effective.

While I was able to interview and develop rapport with the community I was engaging with, they also cared for their fellow neighbors. During many of the parties that I was invited to attend, Wynette, Harold, Jenny, and Mikayla opened their homes and community rooms to their neighbors around them. While food was a limited commodity, they all described ways where they provided food for their friends and neighbors who they considered an extension of their families—typically for holidays or if there was a particularly nice summer day.

The shutdown bridged the gap between the experiences of the recipients, people unable to receive assistance, and the social workers themselves. All these groups had to endure administrative chaos that was avoidable, and most families are still climbing out of this setback. The media focused its reporting on 800,000 federal workers not receiving paychecks and having no ability to strike led to the ability for everyone to erase the 40 million individuals, families, and children who were unable to access services and food via their SNAP benefits. It also erased the work completed by social workers to quell the anxiety and fear that surrounded this shutdown. Government confusion only increased how recipients were given instructions about their benefits.

For the above to occur, social workers are the link that connects recipients to the benefits to survive. From these interviews, it became clear that many social workers do care about the people in their caseload but can often feel and be overloaded and overworked. The respondents of the interviewees often detailed various self-care activities that they came up with because that was not discussed while achieving their degrees. While social work is not always an easy experience, there were workers who held viewpoints not outside the public—because they work with many recipients on any given day. Consequently, the respondents commented on the organization themselves that they work in that often hides or erases social workers of color.

Therefore, within the respective social worker organizations, there were not just opinions about the recipients themselves (why can they not lift themselves up) but also how their workers interacted with one another as well. This coworker interaction revealed unchecked white privilege and classed connotations exhibited within various interactions. Many of the social workers who identified as white felt as though there were no problems at their workplace or how they themselves worked with their clients. Conversely, the social workers of color noted a variety of issues as well as the often disconnectedness they felt between the white social workers and the clients that they served. The social workers of color consistently felt as though they could connect, build rapport, and keep that rapport over a longer period of time because of the understanding of how intersectional oppression affects different people in different ways.

However, some poverty organizations, like Milwaukee's Hunger Task Force, provide both services—for food access and SNAP/Foodshare access. These social workers often left other state or private social work agencies because of the disagreeable or negative workspace that they encountered. As a multifaceted organization, the HTF provides unquestionable aid to communities and that should be commended and rewarded. At the same time, as HTF does all this great work, they also hide their very important and radical history because any mention or alignment or credit given to a radical Black empowerment group may figure negatively from white donors onto HTF.

WHAT SHOULD WE DO?

At the end of these books, there's always a "what does it all mean" section of the conclusion. What must happen is we need to have an honest and real understanding of how people navigate poverty here in the United States. Much of the rhetoric about poor people or receiving benefits is done by the average person for a person who has access to power. If we keep aiming down or at least making upward mobility impossible for everyone, nothing positive changes and things remain the same for everyone but those with access to wealth. We must address the conditions that marginalize people, not the people.

If we are going to legislate poverty, we need to make sure we have an accurate understanding of what that is for actual people. Economists are forecasting that a variety of expenses will increase in the coming year—but those costs are not matching with wages and standards of living. The costs of groceries, fruits, vegetables, and so on, are going to increase *but* the amount someone receives as a wage or for their food benefits does not increase at the same rate.

The common statement is "if we make wages $15.00 an hour—then the cost of goods will increase." However, to use common slang, this is not the flex people think it is. Unknowingly, people are admitting that capitalism is incapable of paying people living wages—it's the flaw in capitalism. In this pandemic society, across the country, wage workers realizing that their situation as a service worker placed them in a precarious position—in a sense they are not paid enough for health care and the plans that *are* available are still not feasible with hourly wages is motivating this. But if we are basing our understanding on news reports meshed with our, as a nation, lack of understanding of poverty, the dominant narrative seeks to prevail. This is the narrative said by people in chapter 2—people do not want to work, they are lazy and only want to receive money from the government. We know, however, people are just trying to survive.

In the introduction, I mentioned the fact that many nations and many states within the border of the United States already do something like a basic minimum income. Here, people lack the need to worry about basic human needs—like food, shelter, and health care—they are already provided and, therefore, people can focus on work or occupations that are a value add to their lives. The closest thing we have as a national policy is the childcare payments that began being deposited into the accounts of parents in the summer of 2021.

Shutdown and Pandemic Impact

The government shutdown and pandemic highlighted the impact that government issues can have on real people. The miscommunication and mismanagement highlighted eventually for the respondents that they felt neglected by it. It also created general feelings of hopelessness and loss, in terms of what happens when the social safety net disappears. This fear and tension were exacerbated and contributed to how people acted at the pantry among each other, given the increased number and the worry that food might not be available for them throughout these experiences.

Adding to poverty literature, geographical components are important for understanding how Milwaukee came to be the way it is today—through coded language of northern segregation completed through de facto segregation. The unavailability of healthy foods and grocery stores details not just redlining, but nutritional redlining that white residents need not worry about. Additionally, the ways in which the participants and respondents access this food is no different than how any other person would similarly feed themselves and their families.

As for how people "get out" of poverty, what the participants unanimously note is that the amounts they receive for rent, cash, and food assistance are not keeping in time with dollar inflation and increased prices. Depending on the items being purchased, tariffs no doubt will transfer the cost onto the consumer. From their experiences, prices are increasing but they are getting less for their money. Similarly, the respondents also noted that because they fail to go as far as previously, they end up filling the gap with food banks and pantries but can never be sure what they would receive for that week—so there is limited ability to meal plan for themselves or their families. The other goal was to humanize poverty, since the precarity of food is only going to increase because of segregation and speeding toward irreversible effects from climate change—that will affect crops, food access, and so on.

All the participants in the study wanted very similar outcomes. For recipients, they wanted an individual who experienced and understood poverty to be the ones making informed decisions and policy improvements at local, state, and federal government levels. Connected to that, recipients simply wanted their voices to be heard and their concerns taken seriously. Similarly, social workers consistently advocated for better access to self-care and more equitable workplaces. However, the social workers I met with voiced concern as being particularly unhelpful to those in need. Lastly, poverty organizations, such as Hunger Task Force, wanted to simply have their services no longer be needed. In sum, all the respondents in each area noted that they just want to feel secure, safe, and have access to healthy food.

While the original intent of this book was on welfare recipients but during the writing of the book, there were several unexpected impacts experienced by the people across the globe and specifically in the United States. The shutdown was a trial run regarding how unprepared the federal government was in response to their own created problem. The Pandemic of 2020 showed that not only would people in poverty be placed in precarity, but that not much separates those that are not considered in poverty and those that already experiencing poverty. How the nation decided to deal with the pandemic showed how it feels about its largest population—those who are not millionaires or often even "thousandaires," but everyday workers. These are the same workers that at the beginning of this book were treated with disdain but who are now "essential workers." But even during this time, the considerations for workers, across the spectrum, were abysmal at best. But in the end, it shows that we're all in this together and the narratives that seek to separate us bind us together.

Bibliography

Aberson, Christopher L., Carl Shoemaker, and Christina Tomolillo. 2004. "Implicit Bias and Contact: The Role of Interethnic Friendships." *The Journal of Social Psychology* 144 (3): 335–47.

Abrajano, Marisa A., Zoltan Hajnal, and Hans JG Hassell. 2017. "Media Framing and Partisan Identity: The Case of Immigration Coverage and White Macropartisanship." *Journal of Race, Ethnicity and Politics* 2 (1): 5–34.

Ahmed, Sameera T. 2018. *The Cultural Politics of US Immigration: Gender, Race and Media.* Taylor & Francis.

Allen, Ruth, and Janine L. Wiles. 2016. "A Rose by Any Other Name: Participants Choosing Research Pseudonyms." *Qualitative Research in Psychology* 13 (2): 149–65.

Allport, Gordon W. 1954. *The Nature of Prejudice.* New York: Addison.

Anderson, Elijah. 2003. *A Place on the Corner.* University of Chicago Press.

Aschwanden, Christie. 2016. "We asked 8,500 Internet Commenters Why They Do What They Do." *FiveThirtyEight.*

Baldwin, Bridgette. 2010a. "Stratification of the Welfare Poor: Intersections of Gender, Race & Worthiness in Poverty Discourse and Policy." *Modern American* 6 (4): 4–14.

———. 2010b. *'Wisconsin Works'?: Race, Gender and Accountability in the Workfare Era.* Northeastern University.

Batiuk, Mary Ellen, Paul Moke, and Pamela Wilcox Rountree. 1997. "Crime and Rehabilitation: Correctional Education as an Agent of Change—A Research Note." *Justice Quarterly* 14 (1): 167–80.

Bell, Derrick. 1976. "Serving Two Masters: Integration Ideals and Client Interests in School Desegregation Litigation." *Yale Law Journal*, 470–516.

———. 1980. "Brown v. Board of Education and the Interest-Convergence Dilemma." *Harvard Law Review* 93 (3): 518–34.

———. 2004. *Silent Covenants: Brown v. Board of Education and the Unfulfilled Hopes for Racial Reform.* Cambridge: Oxford University Press.

Blauner, Robert. 1969. "Internal Colonialism and Ghetto Revolt." *Social Problems* 16 (4): 393–408.

Bobo, Lawrence. 1983. "Whites' Opposition to Busing: Symbolic Racism or Realistic Group Conflict?" *Journal of Personality and Social Psychology* 45 (6): 1196–210. doi: 10.1037/0022-3514.45.6.1196.

———. 1998. "Race, Interests, and Beliefs About Affirmative Action Unanswered Questions and New Directions." *American Behavioral Scientist* 41 (7): 985–1003.

———. 1999. "Prejudice as Group Position: Microfoundations of a Sociological Approach to Racism and Race Relations." *Journal of Social Issues* 55 (3): 445–72.

Bobo, Lawrence, James R. Kluegel, and Ryan A. Smith. 1997. "Laissez-Faire Racism: The Crystallization of a Kinder, Gentler, Antiblack Ideology." *Racial Attitudes in the 1990s: Continuity and Change* 15: 23–25.

Bobo, Lawrence D., and Ryan A. Smith. 1998. "From Jim Crow Racism to Laissez-Faire Racism: The Transformation of Racial Attitudes." *Beyond Pluralism: The Conception of Groups and Group Identities in America.*

Bonds, Anne. 2013. "Racing Economic Geography: The Place of Race in Economic Geography." *Geography Compass* 7 (6): 398–411.

Bonilla-Silva, Eduardo. 2001. *White Supremacy and Racism in the Post-Civil Rights Era*. Boulder: Lynne Rienner Publishers.

———. 2010. *Racism without Racists: Color-Blind Racism and the Persistence of Racial Inequality in America*. Lanham: Rowman & Littlefield.

Bourdieu, Pierre. 1977. *Outline of a Theory of Practice*. Vol. 16. Cambridge University Press.

Bourdieu, Pierre. 1991. *Language and Symbolic Power*. Cambridge: Harvard University Press.

Bourgois, Philippe. 2009. *Righteous Dopefiend*. Univ of California Press.

Bullock, Heather E. 1999. "Attributions for Poverty: A Comparison of Middle-Class and Welfare Recipient Attitudes." *Journal of Applied Social Psychology* 29 (10): 2059–82.

Chang, A. 2017. "Segregation Didn't Just Go Away. It Evolved." *Vox*. https://www.vox.com/policy-and-politics/2017/7/27/16004084/school-segregation-evolution.

Chappell, Cathryn A. 2004. "Post-Secondary Correctional Education and Recidivism: A Meta-Analysis of Research Conducted 1990–1999." *Journal of Correctional Education*, 55 (2): 148–69.

Cho, Clare Y., and Jill K. Clark. 2019. "Disparities in Access to Supplemental Nutrition Assistance Program Retailers Over Time and Space." *Population Research and Policy Review*, 39 (1): 99–118.

Cole, Nicki Lisa. 2019. "Surprising Facts About Welfare Recipients." *ThoughtCo*. https://www.thoughtco.com/who-really-receives-welfare-4126592.

Collins, Jane, and Martha Gimenez. 1990. *Work without Wages: Domestic Labor and Self-Employment within Capitalism*. Albany: State University of New York Press.

Collins, Jane Lou, Micaela Di Leonardo, and Brett Williams. 2008. *New Landscapes of Inequality: Neoliberalism and the Erosion of Democracy in America*. School for Advanced Research Press.

Collins, Patricia Hill. 1993. "Toward a New Vision: Race, Class, and Gender as Categories of Analysis and Connection." *Race, Sex & Class* 1 (1): 25–45.

———. 2000. *Black Feminist Thought: Knowledge, Consciousness, and the Politics of Empowerment.* East Sussex: Psychology Press.

———. 2003. "Some Group Matters: Intersectionality, Situated Standpoints, and Black Feminist Thought." https://philpapers.org/rec/COLSGM.

———. 2004. *Black Sexual Politics: African Americans, Gender, and the New Racism.* New York: Routledge.

———. 2006. "New Commodities, New Consumers Selling Blackness in a Global Marketplace." *Ethnicities* 6 (3): 297–317.

Collins, Patricia Hill, and Sirma Bilge. 2016. *Intersectionality.* Hoboken: John Wiley & Sons.

Connell, Robert W., and James W. Messerschmidt. 2005. "Hegemonic Masculinity Rethinking the Concept." *Gender & Society* 19 (6): 829–59.

Connell, Robert W., and Raewyn Connell. 2005. *Masculinities.* University of California Press.

Cooley, Charles Horton. 1922. *Human Nature and the Social Order.* Transaction Publishers.

———. 1956. *Social Organization.* Transaction Publishers.

Cooper, Richard A., Matthew A. Cooper, Emily L. McGinley, Xiaolin Fan, and J. Thomas Rosenthal. 2012. "Poverty, Wealth, and Health Care Utilization: A Geographic Assessment." *Journal of Urban Health* 89 (5): 828–47.

Crenshaw, Kimberle. 1991. "Mapping the Margins: Intersectionality, Identity Politics, and Violence against Women of Color." *Stanford Law Review* 43 (6): 1241–99.

Crenshaw, Kimberlé. 1995. *Critical Race Theory: The Key Writings That Formed the Movement.* New York: The New Press.

Davis, Angela. 2003. "Racism, Birth Control and Reproductive Rights." *Feminist Postcolonial Theory–A Reader.* Routledge, 353–67.

Delaney, Arthur, and Alissa Scheller. 2015. "Who Gets Food Stamps? White People, Mostly." *Huffington Post*, February 28, 2015, sec. Politics. https://www.huffingtonpost.com/2015/02/28/food-stamp-demographics_n_6771938.html.

Desmond, Matthew. 2012. "Disposable Ties and the Urban Poor." *American Journal of Sociology* 117 (5): 1295–1335.

Desmond, Matthew. 2012. "Eviction and the Reproduction of Urban Poverty." *American Journal of Sociology* 118 (1): 88–133.

Desmond, Matthew. 2016. *Evicted: Poverty and Profit in the American City.* Broadway Books.

Desmond, Matthew, and Nicol Valdez. 2013. "Unpolicing the Urban Poor: Consequences of Third-Party Policing for Inner-City Women." *American Sociological Review* 78 (1): 117–41.

Diamond, Bernard L. 1966. "The Children of Leviathan: Psychoanalytic Speculations Concerning Welfare Law and Punitive Sanctions." *California Law Review*, 357–69.

Dow, Dawn Marie. 2015. "Negotiating 'the Welfare Queen' and 'the Strong Black Woman' African American Middle-Class Mothers' Work and Family Perspectives." *Sociological Perspectives* 58 (1): 36–55.

Dowler, Kenneth. 2003. "Media Consumption and Public Attitudes toward Crime and Justice: The Relationship between Fear of Crime, Punitive Attitudes, and Perceived Police Effectiveness." *Journal of Criminal Justice and Popular Culture* 10 (2): 109–26.

Ducille, Ann. 1994. "Dyes and Dolls: Multicultural Barbie and the Merchandising of Difference." *Differences: A Journal of Feminist Cultural Studies* 6 (1): 46–69.

Edin, Kathryn J., and H. Luke Shaefer. 2015. "$2.00 a Day: Living on Almost Nothing in America." *Houghton Mifflin Harcourt.* https://books.google.com/books ?hl=en&lr=&id=wLlbCgAAQBAJ&oi=fnd&pg=PP1&dq=%242.00+a+day+&ots =i0EJ-36FYf&sig=pSsyxzuM_AVBEdodgNRtombB4jc.

Ehrenreich, Barbara. 2010. *Nickel and Dimed: On (not) Getting by in America.* Metropolitan Books.

Ehrenreich, Barbara. 2014. "It Is Expensive to Be Poor." *The Atlantic.* January 13, 2014. https://www.theatlantic.com/business/archive/2014/01/it-is-expensive-to-be -poor/282979/.

Eisenhauer, Elizabeth. 2001. "In Poor Health: Supermarket Redlining and Urban Nutrition." *GeoJournal* 53 (2): 125–33.

Elwood, Sarah, Victoria Lawson, and Eric Sheppard. 2016. "Geographical Relational Poverty Studies." *Progress in Human Geography,* 0309132516659706.

Emerson, Rana A. 2002. "African-American Teenage Girls and the Construction of Black Womanhood in Mass Media and Popular Culture." *African American Research Perspectives* 8 (1): 85–102.

Esperian, John H. 2010. "The Effect of Prison Education Programs on Recidivism." *Journal of Correctional Education,* 316–34.

Eubanks, Virginia. 2018. *Automating Inequality: How High-Tech Tools Profile, Police, and Punish the Poor.* St. Martin's Press.

Farris, Emily M., and Heather Silber Mohamed. 2018. "Picturing Immigration: How the Media Criminalizes Immigrants." *Politics, Groups, and Identities,* 6 (4): 1–11.

Fligstein, Neil, and Doug McAdam. 2012. *A Theory of Fields.* Oxford University Press.

Frey, William H. 2018. "Black-White Segregation Edges Downward since 2000, Census Shows." *Brookings* (blog). December 17, 2018. https://www.brookings .edu/blog/the-avenue/2018/12/17/black-white-segregation-edges-downward-since -2000-census-shows/.

Gans, Herbert J. 1962. *The Urban Villagers: Group and Class in the Life of Italian-Americans.* New York: The Frees Press of Glencoe.

———. 1995. *The War against the Poor. The Underclass and Antipoverty Policy.* BasicBooks.

Garand, James C., Ping Xu, and Belinda C. Davis. 2017. "Immigration Attitudes and Support for the Welfare State in the American Mass Public." *American Journal of Political Science* 61 (1): 146–62.

Geib, Paul. 1998. "From Mississippi to Milwaukee: A Case Study of the Southern Black Migration to Milwaukee, 1940-1970." *The Journal of Negro History* 83 (4): 229–48.

Gerbner, G. ed., 1977. *Mass media policies in changing cultures.* New York; Toronto: Wiley.

———. 1978. "The Dynamics of Cultural Resistance." *Hearth and Home: Images of Women in the Mass Media*, 46–50.

Gilens, Martin. 1999. *Why Americans Hate Welfare: Race, Media, and the Politics of Antipoverty Policy*. Chicago: University of Chicago Press.

Gilmore, Ruth Wilson. 2002. "Fatal couplings of power and difference: Notes on racism and geography." *The professional geographer* 54(1): 15–24.

Glauber, Bill, and Kevin Crowe. 2013. "Milwaukee Poverty a Regional Problem, Mayor Tom Barrett Says." *Milwaukee Journal Sentinel.* http://www. Jsonline. Com/News/Milwaukee/Milwaukee-Poverty-a-Regionalproblem-Mayor-Tom-Barrett-Says-B99101258z1-224346311.html.

Goffman, Erving. 1959. *The Presentation of Self in Everyday Life*.

Goldberg, David Theo. 2002. *The Racial State*. Blackwell Publishing.

Golightly, Cornelius L. 1963. "De Facto Segregation in Milwaukee Schools." *Integrated Education* 1 (6): 27–31.

Gomez, Amanda Michelle. 2019. "What 13 States Discovered after Spending Hundreds of Thousands Drug Testing the Poor," April 26, 2019. https://thinkprogress.org/states-cost-drug-screening-testing-tanf-applicants-welfare-2018-results-data-0fe9649fa0f8/.

Gorski, Paul. 2008. "The Myth of the Culture of Poverty". *Educational Leadership* 65 (7): 32.

Gramsci, Antonio. 1992. *Prison Notebooks*. New York: Columbia University Press.

Gritter, Matthew. 2015. *The Policy and Politics of Food Stamps and SNAP*. Palgrave Macmillan US. doi: 10.1057/9781137520920.

Halpern-Meekin, Sarah, Kathryn Edin, Laura Tach, and Jennifer Sykes. 2015. *It's Not like I'm Poor: How Working Families Make Ends Meet in a Post-Welfare World*. University of California Press. https://books.google.com/books?hl=en&lr=&id=3NQkDQAAQBAJ&oi=fnd&pg=PR9&dq=its+not+like+i%27m+poor+&ots=T-bnGIX9SX&sig=95Mu23qKuXBJAs6vpP9oSEshCZo.

Handler, Joel F., and Ellen Jane Hollingsworth. 1969. "Stigma, Privacy, and Other Attitudes of Welfare Recipients." *Stanford Law Review*, 22: 1–19.

Harding, Sandra G. 2004. *The Feminist Standpoint Theory Reader: Intellectual and Political Controversies*. Psychology Press.

Harris, Cheryl I. 1993. "Whiteness as Property." *Harvard Law Review*, 106 (8): 1707–91.

Harrison, Faye V. 1995. The Persistent Power of "Race" in the Cultural and Political Economy of Racism. *Annual Review of Anthropology*, 24 (1): 47–74.

Hellerstein, Judith K., David Neumark, and Melissa McInerney. 2008. "Spatial mismatch or racial mismatch?" *Journal of Urban Economics* 64 (2): 464–79. doi: 10.1016/j.jue.2008.04.003.

Heynen, Nik. 2005. "Monitoring Wisconsin." http://digital.library.wisc.edu/1793/30524.

———. 2009. "Back to Revolutionary Theory Through Racialized Poverty: The McGee Family's Utopian Struggle for Milwaukee." *The Professional Geographer* 61(2):187–199.

Heynen, Nik, Hilda E. Kurtz, and Amy Trauger. 2012. "Food Justice, Hunger and the City." *Geography Compass* 6 (5): 304–11.

Hochschild, Arlie, and Anne Machung. 2012. *The Second Shift: Working Families and the Revolution at Home*. Penguin.

Hoffman, Kelly M., Sophie Trawalter, Jordan R. Axt, and M. Norman Oliver. 2016. "Racial Bias in Pain Assessment and Treatment Recommendations, and False Beliefs about Biological Differences between Blacks and Whites." *Proceedings of the National Academy of Sciences* 113 (16): 4296–4301.

Holley, Peter. 2016. "New York Republican Lawmaker Wants to Ban Welfare Recipients from Buying Steak and Lobster." *Chicago Tribune*, February 23, 2016, sec. National Politics. http://www.chicagotribune.com/news/nationworld/politics/ct-welfare-steak-lobster-ban-new-york-20160223-story.html.

hooks, bell. 1981. *Ain't I a Woman: Black Women and Feminism*. Boston: South End Press.

———. 1995. *Killing Rage: Ending Racism*. New York: Henry Holt and Company.

———. 2000. *Feminist Theory: From Margin to Center*. Pluto Press.

Hopkins, MaryCarol. 1993. "Is Anonymity Possible? Writing about Refugees in the United States." *When They Read What We Write: The Politics of Ethnography*, 121–29.

Hunter, Margaret. 2016. "Colorism in the Classroom: How Skin Tone Stratifies African American and Latina/o Students." *Theory Into Practice* 55 (1): 54–61.

Johnson, Holly, Janelle Mathis, and Kathy G. Short. 2016. *Critical Content Analysis of Children's and Young Adult Literature: Reframing Perspective*. Routledge.

Jones, Patrick D. 2009. *The Selma of the North: Civil Rights Insurgency in Milwaukee*. Harvard University Press.

———. 2013. "March On Milwaukee Civil Rights History Project." *Journal of American History* 99 (4): 1334–1334. doi: 10.1093/jahist/jas645.

Jones, William P. 2007. "Black Milwaukee, Proletarianization, and the Making of Black Working-Class History." *Journal of Urban History* 33 (4): 544–50.

Kain, John F. 1968. "Housing Segregation, Negro Employment, and Metropolitan Decentralization." *The Quarterly Journal of Economics*, 82 (2): 175–97.

Kaiser, Karen. 2009. "Protecting Respondent Confidentiality in Qualitative Research." *Qualitative Health Research* 19 (11): 1632–41.

Kane, Mary Jo. 1994. "The Media's Role in Accommodating and Resisting Stereotyped Images of Women in Sport." *Women, Media and Sport: Challenging Gender Values*. Sage Publication. 28–44.

Kelly, Maura. 2010. "Regulating the Reproduction and Mothering of Poor Women: The Controlling Image of the Welfare Mother in Television News Coverage of Welfare Reform." *Journal of Poverty* 14 (1): 76–96.

King Jr, Martin Luther. 1992. "Letter from Birmingham Jail." *UC Davis Law Review* 26: 835.

Kingfisher, Catherine P. 1999. "Rhetoric of (Female) Savagery: Welfare Reform in the United States and Aotearoa/New Zealand." *NWSA Journal*, 1–20.

Klein, Hugh, and Kenneth S. Shiffman. 2009. "Underrepresentation and Symbolic Annihilation of Socially Disenfranchised Groups ('out Groups') in Animated Cartoons." *The Howard Journal of Communications* 20 (1): 55–72.

Klinenberg, Eric. 2015. *Heat Wave: A Social Autopsy of Disaster in Chicago.* University of Chicago Press.

Knight, Jennifer L., and Traci A. Giuliano. 2001. "He's a Laker; She's a 'Looker': The Consequences of Gender-Stereotypical Portrayals of Male and Female Athletes by the Print Media." *Sex Roles* 45 (3–4): 217–29.

Kost, Kathleen A. 1997. "A Man without a Job Is a Dead Man: The Meaning of Work and Welfare in the Lives of Young Men." *Journal of Sociology and Social Welfare* 24: 91.

Kurtz, Hilda. 2013. "Linking Food Deserts and Racial Segregation: Challenges and Provide Limitations." *Geographies of Race and Food: Fields, Bodies, Markets.* Routledge. 247–64.

Kwate, Naa Oyo A. 2008. "Fried Chicken and Fresh Apples: Racial Segregation as a Fundamental Cause of Fast Food Density in Black Neighborhoods." *Health & Place* 14 (1): 32–44.

Kwate, Naa Oyo A., Ji Meng Loh, Kellee White, and Nelson Saldana. 2013. "Retail Redlining in New York City: Racialized Access to Day-to-Day Retail Resources." *Journal of Urban Health* 90 (4): 632–52.

Lareau, Annette. 2011. *Unequal Childhoods: Class, Race, and Family Life.* University of California Press.

Larson, Tom, Paul M. Ong, and Don Mar. 2021. "Rising Food Insecurity During the Covid-19 Pandemic: The Impact of Institutional Racism." *Business Forum*, 28 (2):52.

Leacock, Eleanor Burke. 1971. "The Culture of Poverty: A Critique." http://eric.ed.gov/?id=ED068606.

Lee, Cynthia. 2012. "Making Race Salient: Trayvon Martin and Implicit Bias in a Not yet Post-Racial Society." *NCL Review* 91: 1555.

Lewis, Gail. 1996. "Situated Voices: 'Black Women's Experience' and Social Work." *Feminist Review* 53(1): 24–56.

Lewis, Oscar. 1961. *The Children of Sanchez: Autobiography of a Mexican Family.* Vintage. https://books.google.com/books?hl=en&lr=&id=IaNraTnDtgwC&oi=fnd&pg=PR13&dq=children+of+sanchez&ots=09aSqUS5ko&sig=EWG-WapPZfHxMQGqT6gn3MP-zYA.

———. 1969. "The Culture of Poverty." https://books.google.com/books?hl=en&lr=&id=ddQwYc_2RGoC&oi=fnd&pg=PA316&dq=culture+of+poverty+&ots=LFZE-7vElf&sig=B1covUqItJdr9kLrFm0MSXXO1Q8.

Lieberman, Robert C. 1998. *Shifting the Color Line: Race and the American Welfare State.* Cambridge, MA: Harvard University Press.

Lind, Rebecca Ann, and Colleen Salo. 2002. "The Framing of Feminists and Feminism in News and Public Affairs Programs in US Electronic Media." *Journal of Communication* 52 (1): 211–28.

Lipsitz, George. 2006. *The Possessive Investment in Whiteness: How White People Profit from Identity Politics.* Philadelphia: Temple University Press.

———. 2011. "In an Avalanche Every Snowflake Pleads Not Guilty: The Collateral Consequences of Mass Incarceration and Impediments to Women's Fair Housing Rights." *UCLA Law Review* 59: 1746.

Loewen, James. 2005. *Sundown Towns: A Hidden Dimension of American Racism.* The New Press.

Loyd, Jenna M., and Anne Bonds. 2018. "Where Do Black Lives Matter? Race, Stigma, and Place in Milwaukee, Wisconsin." *The Sociological Review* 66 (4): 898–918.

Lubiano, Wahneema. 1992. "Black Ladies, Welfare Queens, and State Minstrels: Ideological War by Narrative Means." *Race-Ing Justice, En-Gendering Power: Essays on Anita Hill, Clarence Thomas, and the Construction of Social Reality* 323: 332–33.

Lynch, David, and Damian Paletta. 2019. "Wilbur Ross Says Furloughed Workers Should Take Out a Loan. His Agency's Credit Union Is Charging Nearly 9%." *Washington Post*, January 24, 2019, sec. Business. https://www.washingtonpost .com/business/economy/wilbur-ross-says-furloughed-workers-should-take-out -a-loan-his-agencys-own-credit-union-is-charging-nearly-9-percent/2019/01/24/ be1c9f1e-2020-11e9-8b59-0a28f2191131_story.html.

McBride, Megan. 2007. "Food Insecurity and the Food Environment." PhD Thesis, Citeseer.

McLuhan, Marshall, and Quentin Fiore. 1967. "The Medium Is the Message." *New York* 123: 126–28.

Marshall, Catherine, and Gretchen B. Rossman. 2011. *Designing Qualitative Research.* Sage.

Martin, Katie S., and Ann M. Ferris. 2007. "Food Insecurity and Gender Are Risk Factors for Obesity." *Journal of Nutrition Education and Behavior* 39 (1): 31–36.

Marx, Karl, and Friedrich Engels. 1842. *The Communist Manifesto.* Penguin.

Marx, Karl, Samuel Moore, Edward B. Aveling, Friedrich Engels, and Dona Torr. 1938. *Capital [Vol. 1]: A Critical Analysis of Capitalist Production.* Allen & Unwin.

Massey, Douglas S., and Nancy A. Denton. 1993. *American Apartheid: Segregation and the Making of the Underclass.* Harvard University Press.

Mead, George Herbert. 1934. *Mind, Self and Society.* Vol. 111. Chicago University of Chicago Press.

Merskin, Debra. 1998. "Sending up Signals: A Survey of Native American1 Media Use and Representation in the Mass Media." *Howard Journal of Communication* 9 (4): 333–45.

Mettera, Phillip. 2014. "Subsidizing the Corporate One Percent: Subsidy Tracker 2.0 Reveals Big-Business Dominance of State and Local Development Incentives." Goodjobsfirst.org. https://www.goodjobsfirst.org/sites/default/files/docs/pdf/ subsidizingthecorporateonepercent.pdf.

Meyer, Stephen Grant. 2001. *As Long as They Don't Move Next Door: Segregation and Racial Conflict in American Neighborhoods.* Rowman & Littlefield.

Meyrowitz, Joshua. 1997. "Shifting Worlds of Strangers: Medium Theory and Changes in 'Them' versus 'Us.'" *Sociological Inquiry* 67 (1): 59–71.

Milkie, Melissa A. 1999. "Social Comparisons, Reflected Appraisals, and Mass Media: The Impact of Pervasive Beauty Images on Black and White Girls' Self-Concepts." *Social Psychology Quarterly*, 62 (2): 190–210.

Mills, Charles W. 2003. "White Supremacy as Sociopolitical System: A Philosophical Perspective." *White out: The Continuing Significance of Racism.* Routledge. 35–48.

Mitchell, Bruce, and Juan Franco. 2018. "HOLC 'Redlining' Maps: The Persistent Structure of Segregation and Economic Inequality." https://ncrc.org/holc/.

Mitchell, Don. 1997. "The Annihilation of Space by Law: The Roots and Implications of Anti-Homeless Laws in the United States." *Antipode* 29 (3): 303–35.

Monnat, Shannon M. 2010. "Toward a Critical Understanding of Gendered Color-Blind Racism within the US Welfare Institution." *Journal of Black Studies* 40 (4): 637–52.

Morabia, Alfredo. 2016. "Unveiling the Black Panther Party legacy to public health." *American Journal of Public Health.* 106 (10): 1732–1733.

Morland, Kimberly, Steve Wing, Ana Diez Roux, and Charles Poole. 2002. "Neighborhood Characteristics Associated with the Location of Food Stores and Food Service Places." *American Journal of Preventive Medicine* 22 (1): 23–29.

Morris, Pamela A. 2008. "Welfare Program Implementation and Parents' Depression." *Social Service Review* 82 (4): 579–614.

Moynihan, Daniel P. 1965. "The Negro Family: The Case for National Action (1965)." *African American Male Research.* https://www.utexas.edu/cola/centers/coretexts/_files/resources/texts/1965%20Moynihan%20Report.pdf.

Mulvany, Lydia. 2014. "State to Spend $13.5 Million on Transit to Settle Zoo Interchange Suit." *Milwaukee Journal Sentinel*, May 19, 2014, sec. Milwaukee News. http://archive.jsonline.com/news/milwaukee/state-to-spend-135-million-on-transit-to-settle-zoo-interchange-suit-b99273749z1-259843881.html/.

Newman, Katherine S. 2009. *No Shame in My Game: The Working Poor in the Inner City.* Vintage.

Niemuth, Niles. 2014. "Urban Renewal and the Development of Milwaukee's African American Community: 1960-1980." PhD Thesis, The University of Wisconsin-Milwaukee.

Oliver, Melvin L., and Thomas M. Shapiro. 2006. *Black Wealth, White Wealth: A New Perspective on Racial Inequality.* Taylor & Francis.

Olson, Christine M. 1999. "Nutrition and Health Outcomes Associated with Food Insecurity and Hunger." *The Journal of Nutrition* 129 (2): 521S–524S.

Oppenheim, Maya. 2019. "Number of Young Black Women in US Identifying as Bisexual Has 'Trebled in Past Decade'." *Independent*, June 13, 2019, Women's Correspondent edition. https://www.independent.co.uk/news/world/americas/bisexual-black-women-study-us-sexuality-social-survey-a8955661.html.

Pager, Devah. 2003. "The Mark of a Criminal Record." *American Journal of Sociology* 108 (5): 937–75.

Perry, Leah. 2016. *The Cultural Politics of US Immigration: Gender, Race, and Media.* NYU Press.

Popay, Jennie, Jeff Hearn, and Jeanette Edwards. 1998. *Men, Gender Divisions and Welfare.* Psychology Press.

Prigge, Matthew. 2018. "What Does 'Milwaukee' Mean, Anyway?" Milwaukee Magazine. January 29, 2018. https://www.milwaukeemag.com/what-does-milwaukee-mean/.

Pulido, Laura. 2000. "Rethinking Environmental Racism: White Privilege and Urban Development in Southern California." *Annals of the Association of American Geographers* 90 (1): 12–40.

Quadagno, Jill. 1988. *The Transformation of Old Age Security: Class and Politics in the American Welfare State*. University of Chicago Press.

———. 1994. *The Color of Welfare: How Racism Undermined the War on Poverty: How Racism Undermined the War on Poverty*. New York: Oxford University Press.

Quillian, Lincoln, and Devah Pager. 2001. "Black Neighbors, Higher Crime? The Role of Racial Stereotypes in Evaluations of Neighborhood Crime1." *American Journal of Sociology* 107 (3): 717–67.

Ramasubramanian, Srividya. 2011. "The Impact of Stereotypical versus Counterstereotypical Media Exemplars on Racial Attitudes, Causal Attributions, and Support for Affirmative Action." *Communication Research* 38 (4): 497–516.

Rank, Mark R. 1994. "A View from the inside out: Recipients' Perceptions of Welfare." *Journal of Sociology and Social Welfare* 21: 27.

Roberts, Dorothy. 1993. "Racism and Patriarchy in the Meaning of Motherhood." *American University Journal Gender & Law* 1: 1.

———. 1997. *Killing the Black Body: Race, Reproduction, and the Meaning of Liberty*. New York: Vintage.

———. 2002. "Shattered Bonds: The Color of Child Welfare." *Children and Youth Services Review* 24 (11): 877–80. doi: 10.1016/S0190-7409(02)00238-4.

———. 2011. *Fatal Invention: How Science, Politics, and Big Business Re-Create Race in the Twenty-First Century*. New York: The New Press.

———. 2011. "Prison, Foster Care, and the Systemic Punishment of Black Mothers." *UCLA L. Review* 59: 1474.

Rogers-Dillon, Robin. 1995. "The Dynamics of Welfare Stigma." *Qualitative Sociology* 18 (4): 439.

Rose, Max, and Frank R. Baumgartner. 2013. "Framing the Poor: Media Coverage and US Poverty Policy, 1960–2008." *Policy Studies Journal* 41 (1): 22–53.

Rosenblatt, Peter, and Jennifer E. Cossyleon. 2018. "Pushing the Boundaries: Searching for Housing in the Most Segregated Metropolis in America." *City & Community* 17 (1): 87–108.

Rothstein, Richard. 2017. *The Color of Law: A Forgotten History of How Our Government Segregated America*. Liveright Publishing.

Sandler, Larry. 2012. "Groups Sue to Block Reconstruction of the Zoo Interchange." *Milwaukee Journal Sentinel*, August 9, 2012, sec. Milwaukee News. http://archive.jsonline.com/news/milwaukee/groups-sue-to-block-reconstruction-of-the-zoo-interchange-dj6ehfo-165653316.html/.

Schram, Michelle. 2014. *Supermarket Redlining and Food Deserts: Characterizing Food Insecurity and Urban Decline*. Institute of Urban Studies.

Schneider, Mike.. 2015. "Grocery Chains Leave Food Deserts Barren, AP Analysis Finds." *AP NEWS*. December 7, 2015. https://apnews.com/8bfc99c7c99646008acf25e674e378cf.

Seccombe, Karen. 2007. *"So You Think I Drive a Cadillac?": Welfare Recipients' Perspectives on the System and Its Reform.* Allyn & Bacon.

Sernett, Milton C. 1997. *Bound for the Promised Land: African American Religion and the Great Migration.* Duke University Press.

Shannon, Jerry. 2016. "Beyond the Supermarket Solution: Linking Food Deserts, Neighborhood Context, and Everyday Mobility." *Annals of the American Association of Geographers* 106 (1): 186–202.

Sims, Mario, and Yolanda Rainge. 2002. "Urban Poverty and Infant-Health Disparities among African Americans and Whites in Milwaukee." *Journal of the National Medical Association* 94 (6): 472.

Singer, A. 2004. "Welfare Reform and Immigrants: A Policy Review," in P. Kretsedemas and A. Aparicio, eds., *Immigrants, Welfare Reform, and the Poverty of Policy.* Greenwood Publishing Group, 21–34.

Slocum, Rachel, and Arun Saldanha. 2016. *Geographies of Race and Food: Fields, Bodies, Markets.* Routledge.

Small, Mario Luis. 2009. *Villa victoria.* University of Chicago Press.

Squires, Gregory D. and Sally O'Connor. 1996. *Closing the Racial Gap?: Mortgage Lending and Segregation in Milwaukee Suburbs.* Institute for Wisconsin's Future.

Stevens, Dennis J., and Charles S. Ward. 1997. "College Education and Recidivism: Educating Criminals Is Meritorious." *Journal of Correctional Education,* 48 (3): 106–11.

Sundaram-Stukel, Reka, and Karl Pearson. 2016. "Wisconsin Life Expectancy Report, 2010-2014." Wisconsin Department of Health Services: Division of Public Health, Office of Health Informatics.

Tatum, Beverly Daniel. 2017. *Why Are all the Black Kids Sitting Together in the Cafeteria?: And Other Conversations About Race.* Hachette UK.

Taylor, Keeanga-Yamahtta. 2016. *From #BlackLivesMatter to Black Liberation.* Chicago: Haymarket Books.

Tilly, Charles. 1999. *Durable Inequality.* Univ of California Press.

Trotter Jr, Joe William. 2002. "The Great Migration." *OAH Magazine of History* 17 (1): 31–33.

Tuchman, Gaye. 1978. "The Symbolic Annihilation of Women by the Mass Media." In *Hearth and Home: Imagees of Women in the Mass Media,* 3–38. New York: Oxford University Press.

———. 1979. "Women's Depiction by the Mass Media." *Signs* 4 (3): 528–42.

Valentine, Gill. 2008. "Living with Difference: Reflections on Geographies of Encounter." *Progress in Human Geography* 32 (3): 323–37.

Valentine, Gill, Deborah Sporton, and Katrine Bang Nielsen. 2008. "Language Use on the Move: Sites of Encounter, Identities and Belonging." *Transactions of the Institute of British Geographers* 33 (3): 376–87.

Van Dooran, Bas W. 2015. "Pre-and Post-Welfare Reform Media Portrayals of Poverty in the United States: The Continuing Importance of Race and Ethnicity." *Politics & Policy* 43 (1): 142–62.

Wacquant, Loïc. 2009. *Punishing the Poor.* Duke University Press.

Walker, Renee E., James Butler, Andrea Kriska, Christopher Keane, Craig S. Fryer, and Jessica G. Burke. 2010. "How Does Food Security Impact Residents of a Food Desert and a Food Oasis?" *Journal of Hunger & Environmental Nutrition* 5(4):454–70.

Weese, Karen. 2018. "Why It Costs So Much to Be Poor in America." *Washington Post*, January 25, 2018. https://www.washingtonpost.com/news/posteverything/wp/2018/01/25/why-it-costs-so-much-to-be-poor-in-america/.

Wellington, Darryl Lorenzo. 2016. "Think Being Poor Is Expensive? You've No Idea." *HuffPost*. November 2016. https://www.huffpost.com/entry/think-being-poor-is-expen_b_13574494.

Wilson, David, and Dennis Grammenos. 2005. "Gentrification, Discourse, and the Body: Chicago's Humboldt Park." *Environment and Planning D: Society and Space* 23 (2): 295–312.

Wilson, Helen F. 2016. "On Geography and Encounter: Bodies, Borders, and Difference." *Progress in Human Geography*, 0309132516645958.

Wilson, William Julius. 1978. *The Declining Significance of Race: Blacks and Changing American Institutions*. Chicago: University of Chicago Press.

———. 1987. *The Truly Disadvantaged: The Inner City, the Underclass, and Public Policy*. University of Chicago Press.

———. 1996. *When Work Disappears: The World of the New Urban Poor*. New York: Random House.

———. 2009. *More than Just Race: Being Black and Poor in the Inner City (Issues of Our Time)*. WW Norton & Company.

Witt, Andrew. 2007. "Picking Up the Hammer: The Milwaukee Branch of the Black Panther Party." *Comrades*, 177–213.

Index

About the Author

Stephanie M. Baran, PhD, is an instructor at Nicholls State University, outside New Orleans, Louisiana. She absolutely loves teaching in the bayou and her students bring new elements of culture and excitement to the classroom. She received her doctoral degree in sociology from the University of Wisconsin-Milwaukee in 2019. She received her master of arts in sociology from DePaul University in Chicago. She teaches courses on gender and LGBTQ+ issues, sociocultural history/practices, race, and ethnicity. She desires to use her sociological imagination to ask what is strange in the familiar and the familiar in the strange. She studies inequalities, queer and feminist theory, racism, body and embodiment, and various cultural practices. Her hobbies include antiquing and pursuing social justice and equity. She also enjoys advocating for students and marginalized people so that people can access better services. She currently resides in New Orleans.

www.ingramcontent.com/pod-product-compliance
Lightning Source LLC
Chambersburg PA
CBHW050644280326
41932CB00015B/2776